BERE REGIS & DISTRICT MOTOR SERVICES

BERE REGIS & DISTRICT MOTOR SERVICES

MAP OF OMNIBUS ROUTES

——— SERVICE ON FOUR OR MORE DAYS PER WEEK

- - - - " " THREE OR LESS " " "

SCALE OF MILES

0 1 2 3 4 5 6 7 8

STALBRIDGE

⑤⑰ ④⑦ SHERBORNE

YEOVIL New Town 5·17

18
26

STOURTON CAUNDLE

Ailweston Caundle Marsh 7 17

LONG BURTON

18 26

Lyd-linch

BISHOPS CAUNDLE ⑱

Holwell

Kin

Holnest

Wooton Glanville

PULHAM

Middlemarsh

Lyons Gate Duntish

Brock-hampton

Minterne Magna

BUCKLAND NEWTON Henley

Up Cerne

ALTON PANCRAS

Plus

24

CERNE ABBAS

Nether Cerne

PIDDLE-TRENTH

Godman-stone

PIDDL HIN

Forston

Higher Waterston

FRAMPTON ⑩

Herriston

BRIDPORT ⑧

Compton Valence ⑨

GRIMSTONE

Stratton

BRADFORD PEVERELL

CHAR-MINSTER

1A

BURTON BRADSTOCK

LITTON CHENEY

W'B'N ABBAS

Wireless Station

Burton

Bockh Cros

Berwick

Long Bredy

W'b'n Steepleton

Stinsford

SWYRE

Puncknowle

Little Bredy

W'b'n St Martin

Herring-stone

West Staff

Whito

Bexington

DORCHESTER

①A ③ ④ ⑤
⑥ ⑧ ⑨ ⑩
⑪ ⑫ ⑬ ⑭
⑦ ⑳ ㉔ ㉗

Came Golf Club

⑭ BROADMAYNE

Warmwell Ci

Preston

Osi

21

WEYMOUTH

㉑

For the many men and women who over more than 60 years made Bere Regis & District so special, whether behind the wheel, beneath the bus in the workshop, or in the office.

BERE REGIS & DISTRICT MOTOR SERVICES

The Life and Times of Country Busmen

ANDREW WALLER

First published in the United Kingdom in 2012
by The Hobnob Press, PO Box 1838, East Knoyle, Salisbury, SP3 6FA
www.hobnobpress.co.uk

© Andrew Waller, 2012

British Library Cataloguing in Publication Data
A catalogue record for this book is available from the British Library

ISBN 978-0-946418-85-5

Typeset in Scala 11/15 pt. Typesetting and origination by John Chandler
Printed and bound by CPI Group (UK) Ltd, Croydon, CR0 4YY

CONTENTS

Colour pages I–VIII will be found between pages 102 and 103

Introduction and Acknowledgements

This is the story of how three young men from Dorset villages created a partnership that in its heyday was the biggest privately owned bus concern in the south of England. For a while it ran well over 100 buses and coaches, serving the county's towns and villages, schools, army camps and factories. To meet the needs of soldiers and sailors going home for the weekend, it also reached distant corners of the land.

In the 1920s, as roads and motor vehicles improved, horsedrawn carriers, who had plied between village and market town for a century or more, gave way to country busmen. Indeed many of them sold their horses and bought their own motors. Dorset was too rural to tempt big companies to invest in the kind of transport network that more densely populated counties attracted, so smaller-scale local enterprise thrived.

This book traces how Bere Regis & District's network of rural bus services grew out of the labours of the 19th century carriers and the pioneer busmen of the early 20th century. By the end of World War II it was strong enough to keep expanding for two or three decades. Growing car ownership, the deaths of the three partners and Transport Acts in the 1980s each posed new challenges. Even so the business lasted in one form or another for almost 66 years, longer than any of the big bus companies that surrounded it.

We are well aware that transport enthusiasts would want us to include a complete list of the Bere Regis & District fleet. As we go to press the West Country Historic Omnibus & Transport Trust (WHOTT) *(www.busmuseum.org.uk)* is preparing to publish just such a list. For this reason, and because of its inevitable complexity, we decided not to include one in this work.

As a privately-owned concern Bere Regis & District left no directors' reports or board minutes such as you would find in archives for its big competitors. Unusual and even quirky though the firm was, it has left to this day a palpable sense of loyalty and affection among those who worked for it, whether on the buses, in the workshop or in the office. Members of their families reflect the same loyalty and affection. This has meant that researching its history has been a privilege and a pleasure. So many people have gone out of their way to help that it is very hard adequately to express my gratitude.

John Woodsford and Henry Frier each shared a great deal of their knowledge and experience of Bere Regis & District, as did many others who worked for the firm themselves or whose relatives did so. Jane Johnson and Judith Lafferty gave most valuable assistance, especially with the early years. Many others kindly gave of their time and knowledge, including Ray Applin, Paul Carpenter, Helen Christopher, Kevin Clark, Jeanette Davenport, John Eyers, Malcolm House, Brian Napper, Keith Poyser and Tony White.

Fellow transport historians have been very generous with their memories and information. Norman Aish got me started on the project. I have drawn extensively on the knowledge and wisdom of Roger Grimley and the late Ryan Carpenter, and on the resources of the Omnibus Society Archive, the Kithead Trust and the PSV Circle, which Alan Mills, Alan Oxley, Peter Jaques and Alistair Douglas kindly made available to me.

David Pennels' long professional experience of the bus industry and careful reading of my words kept me on the straight and narrow. He, as well as Les Ronan and John Cumming, have each given most generously of their time and their photograph collections. For valued assistance with photographs I am also most grateful to Chris Aston, John Bennett, Colin Caddy, John Senior and Fred York, and also to Ian Scott of the Salisbury Photo Centre.

Many others have helped greatly with what they know of the transport business generally or of Bere Regis & District specifically. Among them were Roger Atkinson, Alan Bailey, Andrew Bryce, John Chillingworth, Bob Gray, Ian Gray, Peter Impett, Brian Jackson, Alan Lambert, Mike Leatherdale, Bruce Maund, Peter Roberts and Barry Thirlwall. I am also indebted to the Dorset History Centre, Dorchester Museum, and the Poole History Centre, to John Pitfield and Paul Bennett of Bere Regis and to Bill Maunder of the Puddletown History Society.

I am especially grateful to Jacqueline Waller for her constant encouragement and forbearance, also to my trusted and longstanding friend Colin Morris for support over many years and not least for designing the cover of this book.

Andrew Waller
Wildhern, Hampshire
March 2012

I

PREACHERS, PUBLICANS, HIGGLERS AND HURDLEMAKERS

IN NINETEENTH CENTURY Dorset all kinds of men, and sometimes women, plied their trade as country carriers. Their horsedrawn vans bore goods and often people to and from market in Dorchester and other towns. For the most part they travelled along the river valleys, where most villages were to be found. The carriers set the scene upon which the three heroes of our story played out their act once motors ruled the road in the 20th century. They were country lads who formed a partnership that in its heyday ran well over 100 buses and coaches between the towns and villages of Thomas Hardy's Dorset.

Hardy's Tess of the d'Urbervilles had to walk the length and breadth of the county in search of work as a dairy maid in the lean years of the mid-1800s. Carriers' vans bore rural produce to market, and fetched items from town that the village could not supply. Every place of any size had one or two of these enterprising characters, or maybe three. There might be room inside a van for a handful of passengers to share the space with poultry and perhaps a calf, a sheep or a pig. There were trays of eggs and other country produce too, but for many, like Tess, the only way to get about was often to walk.

The railway reached Dorset in the mid-1800s, but it never came to Bere Regis, midway between Poole and Dorchester. Here it was a new turnpike road that opened the way to wider markets. In 1841 the Wimborne and Puddletown

Tolls displayed by a crossroads near Sturminster Newton showed that the wider your wheels the less you paid the Turnpike Trust for using its roads. Narrow wheels churned deeper into what Thomas Hardy called the Blackmore Vale's "narrow, tortuous and miry ways".
© SALISBURY & SOUTH WILTSHIRE MUSEUM

Turnpike Trust spent some £24,000 buying up land upon which to build a new road where there had been no more than a web of narrow lanes. Winding from village to village, these were but rough tracks, muddy in winter and dusty in summer and hardly suited to wheeled traffic.

For those who had a mind to travel farther afield, and could afford the fare, the railway brought London and the wider world much closer. Villages untouched by the railway were still at a disadvantage when it came to long-distance traffic. The population of Bere Regis declined over the latter half of the century. The 1851 census counted 1,494 souls, whilst twenty years later there were 1,366, and in 1891 just 1,144, a fall of almost 25 per cent in 40 years. However, when motors displaced the horse in the 1920s, the lack of a railway probably contributed to the fortunes of the village's own bus company.

It was hard to feed a family on the wage that farm labourers took home, so whilst their menfolk toiled in the fields, village women took in work to eke out the family's resources. At Bere Regis they made buttons, and later on cotton gloves. At Puncknowle, for example, over Bridport way, they made fishing nets. The carrier conveyed these goods to market, along with small livestock and other farm produce.

In the evening the van trundled home with lengths of cloth, needles, thread and other items that kept local crafts going. The carrier also went round town to fetch whatever he or she was asked to purchase from the shops: cooking pots, carpenter's tools, shoes, clothes or bales of twine.

In 1830 Bere Regis had just one carrier, William Taper, who plied the muddy lanes and byways to Dorchester every Saturday and to Poole on Thursdays. Turnpike roads completed in 1842 made the journey easier, so

Charlton Toms drove his van from Bere Regis to Dorchester market twice a week for well over 20 years. Frisby's was a well-known boot seller who sent his wares on sale-or-return by carrier to his country customers.

PAUL BENNETT COLLECTION

he added a Monday trip to Poole, and by 1846 the village had another carrier. Two vans now went to Dorchester on Saturdays and one on Wednesdays, and two went to Poole on both Mondays and Thursdays. By 1851 there were four carriers, one of whom was Reuben Day.

Could it be he that inspired Thomas Hardy, in *Under the Greenwood Tree*, to name the Mellstock tranter Reuben Dewy? A tranter was an irregular carrier, and Mellstock was none other than Hardy's native parish of Stinsford, close to Dorchester on the road from Bere Regis. The novel, published in 1872, tells how Reuben's son Dick fell for the village school mistress, Fancy Day. When an errand took him to Budmouth Regis (Weymouth) to deliver two hives of bees, each 'tied in a cloth to prevent their egress', he chanced upon Fancy near the King's Statue. Was she going to Mellstock that night, he asked. 'Yes, I'm waiting for the carrier' she replied. 'Now I can drive you home nicely, and you save half an hour,' said the eager young tranter.

Bere Regis lay at a crossroads, which gave it access to markets in Blandford and Wareham as well as Dorchester and Poole. In the 1860s, according to *Kelly's Directory*, there was just one village carrier, Mrs Selina Day, Reuben's widow. Her van left at eight o'clock in the morning Monday to Saturday for Dorchester, Poole or Blandford, travelling to each town twice a week. Another carrier was listed in 1871: William Purchase drove to Dorchester on Saturdays but he did not stay in business as long as Mrs Day. In the 1890s Charles Day had succeeded his mother, and a second carrier, Charlton Toms, ran to Dorchester on market days. At the dawn of the 20th century there were three carriers.

In 1911 the directory listed four, including one who went to Wareham, the nearest town with a main line railway station. The census that year counted 1,442 souls in the ecclesiastical parish and 1,059 in the civil parish of Bere Regis. One of them was the four-year-old Reginald William Toop, who was born in 1907, His father

was a jobbing labourer, Albert Edward Toop, who hailed originally from Winfrith and lived as a child in Wareham. Marion Toop, who came from Buckland Newton, was eight years older than her husband. When women won the vote she put herself on the 1922 electoral roll, but her husband apparently failed to so.

Seven years later young Reginald William was to sow the seeds of a business that would one day spread out across Dorset and beyond – Bere Regis & District Motor Services. The Toops lived at number 7, North Street, and all his life Reginald never moved more than a few doors away. Four doors up the road, at number 3, the Roper brothers ran their carrier business, going to Dorchester on Wednesdays and Saturdays, Poole on Mondays and Thursdays and Blandford on Fridays. Twenty years earlier, at the time of the 1891 census, their father William Roper was a carrier at Piddletrenthide, and their mother Sarah was listed as carrier's assistant. In 1915 Frederick Maitland Roper and his brother Ernest John passed their Bere Regis business on to George Vacher, of whom more to follow.

Frank Pitfield's drawing of nos. 3-7 North Street, from *The Book of Bere Regis* which he published in 1978. Frederick Roper conducted his carrier business from no. 3 (on the left) until 1915. As a youngster Reg Toop lived at no. 7 then moved to no. 4, whence he ran Bere Regis & District Motor Services.

Frederick, Ernest and their younger brother Percy Arthur joined the army, presumably in 1915; much of the Dorsetshire Regiment's records were destroyed during World War II so the date cannot be confirmed. According to his son's birth certificate in 1919 Frederick was then

A familiar sight Dorchester market day around 1900: carriers' vans wait beside paved sidewalks, whilst passing vehicles leave tracks in the mud and dust of the High East Street roadway. Channon & Sons were up to date with their "Carriage and Motor Works".   HARRY POUNCY COLLECTION, © DORSET COUNTY MUSEUM

a munition worker and had been a private in the 3rd Dorset Regiment; this was a training unit that spent the whole war at Wyke Regis, where most soldiers only spent a few weeks. Frederick may have been drafted into munition work rather than being sent abroad on active service. Ernest and Percy joined the Queen's Own Dorset Yeomanry, which saw active service in Mesopotamia and Gallipoli. Army records show that Ernest died in January 1919.

Frederick had married Ethel Maud Crocker in 1911; she gave birth to a son on 17 July 1919. Raymond Ernest John Roper, whose middle name evidently commemorated his uncle, was to play his own part in the history of Bere Regis & District Motor Services.

Greater prosperity and better roads meant that Dorset had more and more carriers. By 1903 nearly 40 of them drove from all corners of the county to Dorchester market, crowding the streets on Wednesdays and Saturdays. Others went to Blandford, Bridport or Poole. A

handful went to Shaftesbury, Dorset's only hill town, or Sherborne or over Cranborne Chase to Salisbury. Most only went to town once or twice a week. Typically they were one-man affairs.

Some were also farmers, kept a village shop or doubled up as coalmongers. One or two had other trades; the Toller Porcorum carrier, Mrs J. Cleall, was a hurdlemaker. Steven Crabb from Loders left for Weymouth at one or two o'clock in the morning on Fridays, his horses making the exhausting climb up Portesham Hill. He described himself as a higgler, defined by *The Shorter Oxford English Dictionary* as one who bought up poultry and dairy produce and in return supplied petty commodities from the shops in town. Indeed this was the calling of Tess's father, who told Parson Tringham in *Tess of the d'Urbervilles*: 'I be plain Jack Durbeyfield, the haggler.'

The 1920s offered carriers new challenges and opportunities. The army's wartime needs brought about better designed motor vehicles, which were more economic to operate and cheaper to buy, often from ex-army stock. Many young men had learned to drive and maintain motor vehicles during their military service. Meanwhile road surfaces steadily improved through the decade. A good many of the carriers who took advantage of these developments were later absorbed by Bere Regis & District.

With motors driving upon improved roads it was quicker and more convenient than before for villagers to travel to town themselves. With the advent of moving pictures there was demand for Saturday night buses to take people home from the cinema in towns like Poole or Dorchester. Changes to marketing arrangements meant that carriers no longer carried some of the bulkier items, but the number of passengers kept on growing.

Thirty years later an enterprising transport historian, the late Ryan Carpenter, used the local press to seek people's memories of the horsedrawn vans. Alfred Pitcher, the Litton Cheney carrier, was among those who responded. He used to leave the village at half past eight in the morning and take about two and a half hours to reach Dorchester, a journey of no more than 12 miles. It was left to the traffic to roll the stones into the road, he wrote, and to workmen to rake them over.

The advertisements on Alfred Pitcher's Litton Cheney carrier's van proclaimed the goods he conveyed to villages west of Dorchester in the years before he bought his first motor in about 1911.   © DORSET COUNTY MUSEUM

A number of carriers drove to Bridport, whence factories sent twine for fishing nets out to home-working weavers in the villages. Pitcher said many people worked on fishing nets in Swyre and Puncknowle (pronounced to rhyme with 'tunnel'). He might have only one or two passengers, but there were newly made nets to carry into town and rolls of twine on the homeward run.

In Bridport he left his van on the pavement outside the Cross Keys Hotel. When it was not there local traders could drop off parcels at the hotel for him to deliver. For threepence a day (1.25p) his horses rested in the hotel stable yard until it was time to head home. He charged twopence for parcels, a shilling (5p) for passengers to Bridport and a shilling and threepence (6.25p) to Dorchester.

Pitcher sold most of his horses in 1911 and bought his first motor, a 28/36 hp Daimler, which he kept on the road until 1915. He carried anything, a live pig, a calf, a dog's heart or a swarm of bees. If there was room in the van he would stop anywhere to pick up passengers, mostly labouring people and a few visitors. During World War I many people came out from town to the villages. When he bought the Daimler he put the fare to Dorchester up to a shilling and sixpence (7.5p), and in World War I to two shillings (10p).

By 1915 several of the Dorchester carriers had gone over to motor vans or even buses. Frank Thorne from Cerne Abbas bought his first motor in 1913, and in 1919 began what is believed to have been the first daily bus service to Dorchester. Like Bere Regis. Cerne Abbas was a sizeable village that was some miles from the railway.

One of Ryan Carpenter's correspondents remembered that Thorne's 'heavy motor van was always full of passengers and parcels, and these he dropped off at their destination all the way to Cerne Abbas.... When it was full inside people sat on seats fixed to the roof of the van.' Both Pitcher and Thorne sold out to Bere Regis & District in the 1940s.

South Street, Bridport, on the town's Fair Day in 1911, in front of the Woodman Inn: Alfred Pitcher is at the wheel of Daimler waggonette EL412, with eight passengers in assorted hats. A different body might have been fitted for taking goods to market.
© DORSET COUNTY MUSEUM

Mr S. Lane of Dorchester described to Carpenter the horsedrawn vans that came into town on Wednesdays and Saturdays: 'They could not carry many passengers but managed to bring in fowls, eggs and rabbits, some on the top of the van and on the tailboard at the back. The carrier also brought in villagers, grocery orders etc. Some of the orders he took back and others were delivered by the shop's own horse and van. Some of the big stores used to have a country round as well as a town delivery.'

'It was a common sight to see the carriers' vans parked in the streets and in the yards of some of the hotels,' Mr Lane wrote. 'There was stabling for the horses at the hotels, the carrier usually bringing his own feed for his horse. Most of these hotels kept a hostler, who looked out for the horses. If you wanted the hostler there was a bell that you could pull. At one or two places these bells are still there in the yard [in 1961] with the word 'Ostler' painted nearby...'

'To get into the carrier's van you put your foot on to an iron step at the front, up on to the driver's footboard, step over his box seat and into the van. There was a long seat each side with generally two small oval glass windows in the back... It was often necessary when going up steep hills for the passengers to get out and walk. In winter time, or when the weather was bad, there was a waterproof covering that could be pulled across the front of the van.'

Most people who used the carrier's service rode but rarely on the van themselves. Arthur Upshall, who was born in 1886 and lived as a child at Woolland, wrote: 'One of my earliest recollections is being sent with a note to the old carrier at Ibberton requesting that boots or clothes or other articles on approval be brought back from Blandford, and then the next evening going to collect the parcels on his arrival home, perhaps eight or nine o'clock in the evening.' This was Solomon Elsworth, who put up in town at the Three Choughs Inn, as did Reuben Day from Bere Regis. Upshall described Elsworth as 'an old grey-haired man known to everyone locally as Uncle Solomon, a real old type of local preacher with a religious text or word of warning to everyone, especially if he thought they were not on the right road. He drove a one-horse van and did quite a lot of business as there was no other means of transport for the villagers along the route.

'After him came another man of quite different type named Jimmy Harding. He was a very steady-going sort but not actively religious. His horse was much heavier and slower and I can well remember having to wait till ten o'clock and later for his return with the anxiously awaited parcels.' Later on the publican at nearby Okeford Fitzpaine turned his hand to being that village's carrier. (This was another business that was to pass eventually to Bere Regis & District.)

Upshall continued: 'At the age of ten I was sent to school in a village in the other direction called Hazelbury Bryan. Two of my classmates were brothers named Coombes. Their father, called Johnny Coombes, had a carrier's business, travelling to Dorchester, 16 miles, twice a week with a two-horse van in double harness and much bigger volume of trade, more passengers too as they passed through more villages.'

William (better known as Johnny) Coombes waited until 1926 to buy his first motor bus. He died just two years later and his widow, Betsy Hannah, and their sons carried on the business until 1946, when they in turn sold out to Bere Regis & District.

Carriers came in many guises. The state of the road, the weather, and how many parcels had to be delivered all affected the time he took to reach home. During and after the 1914-1918 War John Elliott plied between Monckton-up-Wimborne and Wimborne market every Tuesday. Locals called him 'Flyer Jack' on account of the speed, or lack of it, of his horse. In a letter to Ryan Carpenter S.R. Cutler recalled that 'As boys we had great fun guessing the time of the appearance of 'Flyer' on his return from Wimborne. This was influenced by the time of his arrival at, or departure from, Horton Inn, the speed of the horse being influenced by whether or not time remained in which to reach the Bull Inn at Wimborne St Giles before 10 pm.'

Quite a few of the carriers, like Solomon Elsworth, were religiously inclined. Another such was James Frederick Ironside, from Winfrith Newburgh. He was a keen preacher who travelled around the district on Sundays. Family lore says the Ironsides originally hailed from County Durham, and were rewarded with lands in Dorset in mediaeval times for service to the crown. When he married Winfrith farmer's daughter Annie Jane Baggs in September 1902, the marriage register said James was a labourer, like his father before him, from Muckleford, which lies up the river Frome on the other side of Dorchester. The newly weds were both 26 years old. By the 1911 census, they were living at Blacknowle (Blacknoll on modern maps), just

to the north of Winfrith, and James's occupation was listed as carrier. Later they moved to Merley, on the road to Lulworth.

Ironside drove his horsedrawn van to Dorchester on Wednesdays and Saturdays, and on Tuesdays and Fridays to Weymouth. He may have succeeded Walter Lillington, who previously worked from Winfrith to Dorchester on the same days. Evidently the local farms provided plenty of business for, like Lillington before him, Ironside was one of three carriers from Winfrith who plied to Dorchester and Weymouth.

In 1911 *Kelly's Directory* said Ironside, Miss Ellen Coleman and James Cornick each

James Ironside's five sons, Walter, William, Charles, Arthur and Leonard, pose before their father's first motor bus, an Albion that he bought in 1920. Already seven years old, FX1553 previously belonged to Cerne Abbas carrier Frank Thorne. Later it bore the legend 'Frisby's for Repairs' above the windscreen.

IRONSIDE FAMILY

drove to Weymouth on the same days of the week. Miss Ellen's van went to Dorchester on Wednesdays and Saturdays too, and to Wareham on Thursdays. James Cornick only drove to Dorchester on Saturdays. In 1914 Thomas Henry Coleman, who had been a groom and gardener, took over Miss Ellen's journeys, but, as far as the local directory was concerned, Cornick had dropped out of the picture by the following year. However, he lived on until 1942, when he died at the age of 90. Coleman became the first Winfrith carrier to use a motor, a 28/36hp Daimler.

James Ironside, who was also a farmer, followed suit in 1920 when he bought Frank Thorne's seven-year-old Albion bus, the 'heavy motor van' described above. Over the windscreen it bore the legend 'Frisby's for repairs': Joseph Frisby was a shoemaker who used to send shoes

A youthful Bill Ironside stands before the roughly painted timetable of his father's Winfrith bus service, to Dorchester, Weymouth and Wareham, which passed to Reg Toop in 1930.   IRONSIDE FAMILY

on approval to villagers who asked their local carrier to fetch them from his premises at 7 South Street, Dorchester.

Ironside also started competing on the Thursday run from Winfrith to Wareham. A rudimentary timetable was painted on the door of the shed where the Albion was kept. It read: 'J. Ironside, carrier etc. A car leaves here for Dorchester Wed Sat, Weymouth Tue Frid, Wareham Thur.' His eldest son, Walter Frederick, emigrated to Canada after World War I. His second son, William James was working on the farm at the age of 15, helping with coal deliveries around the district, and driving the bus.

In 1930 James Ironside, no doubt aware of new regulations that were to affect bus services, decided he would rather concentrate on farming, and passed his bus routes to Reginald Toop. But young William, now aged 22, had more energy for the bus business; in 1936 he teamed up with Toop and Percy Davis in the partnership that took on the name of Bere Regis & District Motor Services.

Percy Davis was born in 1908 at Black Heath Farm, Morden, the fourth son of the farmer, Israel Davis, and his London-born wife Matilda. Since the early years of the 20th century Israel also ran a horsedrawn van to local markets. In August 1925, when Percy was 18, I. Davis & Sons acquired their first motor bus, a 14-seat Ford, which ran between Poole and Dorchester.

Many years later, Percy's daughter Sylvia Gibbs recalled in conversation with transport historian Norman Aish that her father suffered from polio as a child and had a permanent curvature of the spine. He was not very mobile and as a lad even had to travel to school in a donkey cart. She said he found it impossible to get a job so his uncle, Jim Davis, set him up in business with the bus. However, they traded as Israel Davis & Sons.

According to Borough of Poole records Davis was licensed to operate one 'motor

James Ironside bought a new Ford T bus in 1925. It had bench seats along each side. While his older brother posed in front of PR4518, young Leonard took to an unsteady-looking form of four-legged transport.   IRONSIDE FAMILY

omnibus – stage' between Bloxworth and Poole in 1926-1928, and two in 1928-1930. In 1927 he bought a second bus from K. Stroud of Wimborne, who ran via Bere Regis to Poole. It is not clear whether the deal involved Stroud's bus service as well. Davis braved the new regulations that came into force after 1930, and continued his independent business until Percy joined Toop and Ironside in 1936.

The 1914-1918 War left the Dorset countryside much changed. Many young men who might have worked the land had gone to war, sadly never to return. Other folk had moved to town in search of better paid work. At the 1921 census Bere Regis had only 970 inhabitants. But like conflicts before and since, the war spurred technological innovation, in particular the motor car, the lorry, the bus and the motor charabanc, or char-à-bancs as purists still liked to call it.

This heralded the demise of the horsedrawn carrier's van, but a handful still plied the country lanes for a few years yet. Since it lay on the main road between Poole and Dorchester, Bere Regis was a good location for a youthful entrepreneur to launch a motor bus service. Such a man was George Vacher, who took over Frederick and Ernest Roper's carrier business in 1915. He was just 28 years old. Born in Hilton, nestling under the southern slopes of Bulbarrow hill, Vacher was the local carrier there before moving to Bere Regis.

He put his first motor on the road in July 1918. It was a green 28/36hp Daimler-Mercedes van. So began his Bere Regis Motor Service. Reginald Toop was only 11 years old at the time. Local lore has it that the young Toop used to earn pocket money by cleaning boots at one of

A charabanc-style outing from Dorchester's Antelope Hotel in about 1895: it took four horses to pull this brake with some 20 passengers aboard.   © DORSET COUNTY MUSEUM

the big houses nearby, but by the mid-1920s he was driving one of Vacher's buses.

In October 1920 Vacher started a three-days-a-week service between Dorchester and Poole via Bere Regis. That very month Hants & Dorset Motor Services Ltd launched its own service along the same road. It intended to extend this to become a through service to Weymouth. Poole and Dorchester councils agreed, but Bournemouth councillors were wary of a new company that they saw as a potential threat to their tramways. Instead they licensed the Weymouth Motor Company, probably believing it was less likely to take passengers away from its trams. Hants & Dorset drew back from Dorchester, and Bere Regis, for some years yet.

The Weymouth company launched its service on 15 November 1920. Its bus left for Bournemouth at 9 o'clock in the morning six days a week, called at Bere Regis at 10.20 and reached its destination an hour later, returning

to Weymouth at 4 o'clock in the afternoon. Single fares from Bere Regis were one shilling and tenpence (9.2p) to Dorchester, two and tenpence (14.2p) to Weymouth and three shillings and sixpence (17.5p) to Bournemouth.

Vacher replaced his Daimler in 1920 with a chain-driven 30/35hp Commer which carried passengers in the front and up to three tons of coal at the back. Over the next few years he added an American REO and a Crossley. In December 1923 he extended his Dorchester-Poole service to Bournemouth on Fridays, a day on which the Weymouth Motor Company went no farther than Poole. He briefly ran a Bournemouth-Wareham service, but withdrew it after a short while, possibly because Hants & Dorset also reached Wareham in April 1923.

Vacher ran four market services from Bere Regis, one each to Blandford and Wimborne, and two by different roads to Wareham. He became friendly with William Wells Graham,

Motor charabanc outings were a popular diversion after World War I. Few people had their own cars. George Vacher had at least five Chevrolets between 1925 and 1930. The folded hood at the back could be raised to protect passengers from the elements.

JOHN PITFIELD COLLECTION

the founder and general manager of Hants & Dorset, and when his bus went to Bournemouth it was allowed to park in the company's Royal Mews garage.

The Weymouth Motor Company ran into financial difficulties, and was wound up on 8 December 1924. Its assets passed to the National Omnibus & Touring Co Ltd (NO&TC), which was steadily expanding its West Country operations. Vacher took over the Weymouth-Bournemouth licence, but only ran five days a week and reduced the service to Dorchester-Poole, still continuing to Bournemouth on Fridays. Over the next four years he bought four new buses, three Chevrolets and a GMC. One of his drivers, Fred Hann, later the landlord of the Rising Sun at Wimborne, said his buses had no set livery. They might be blue, red, mauve or some other colour.

By 1929, when a new law on licensing bus services was in the air, Hants & Dorset and the Southern National Omnibus Co Ltd, the newly formed offshoot of the NO&TC, each eyed up Vacher's business as a possible acquisition. With the passing of the Road Traffic Act in 1930, the newly appointed Traffic Commissioners, not Bournemouth's councillors, would decide whether to license a through service between Bournemouth and Weymouth, via Poole, Bere Regis and Dorchester.

For each company a link between the two resorts would be a flagship service. Each was talking to Vacher, but in the event it was his friend William Wells Graham's Hants & Dorset that bought him out on 20 August 1930. The

minutes of its board of directors record that Vacher was paid £2,250 for his licences and four vehicles. His garage on North Street, with room for four saloons, became Hants & Dorset's Bere Regis outstation.

The two companies then established a joint service between Bournemouth and Weymouth. Southern National agreed to pay £500 towards the cost of the takeover, plus one third of Vacher's salary as Hants & Dorset's local manager for the rest of his working life. He died at the age of 71 in 1958, whilst helping to round up a runaway pig near his premises in Bere Regis.

You can still see Vacher's name on the Congregational Church on Butt Lane, Bere Regis. Names of those who contributed to an extension in 1930 are inscribed on bricks in the wall. Sunday worship there was a regular informal meeting place for local business folk.

In 1929 local people would surely have got wind of the possible sale of Vacher's service. There must have been some concern that after a century or so the village would no longer have its own carrier. This was much to Reg Toop's advantage when he left Vacher's employ to set up on his own on 29 October of that year.

George Vacher's name still survives on a wall at the Bere Regis Congregational Chapel in Butt Lane, where the local business community gathered of a Sunday

JOHN PITFIELD

2
TOOPY'S BUS

Reg Toop's first bus in 1929 was a little Ford T with 14 seats arranged along either side, with room for packages and parcels in the middle. Under the name 'Pioneer' he ran in competition with both George Vacher and Israel Davis & Sons of Bloxworth, but he followed different routes to Poole, Dorchester, Wimborne and Wareham. On Saturdays and Sundays he ran several journeys each way between Bere Regis and Poole, and one journey each way on Mondays and Fridays. On the other days he ran to market: Wimborne on Tuesday,

Dorchester on Wednesday and Wareham on Thursday.

Two or three prominent local residents lent him money to help buy his first bus. Evidently Toop, who was just 22, had convinced them that he had what we would call today a viable business plan. Two of these backers were Dr George Lys and the local butcher, Thomas Edward Applin.

Raymond Applin, Thomas's grandson, does not know how much his grandfather lent Reg Toop, but believes it must have been to the

Reg Toop was said to be shy of the camera. He it is at the wheel of one of George Vacher's Chevrolets before he broke away in October 1929. His passengers' assorted headgear suggests they wanted to save their hair being ruffled should there be any fast driving, especially if all 28 were travelling in a 14-seater.

G. TOOP

advantage of both doctor and butcher that there should be a local carrier. Very few people had cars and Reg Toop could fetch items from town or drop off packages for customers or patients along the road. Dr Lys and Tom Applin may have foreseen that a big bus company based in Weymouth or Bournemouth would take less interest in providing such a service. Ray Applin believes there was a third backer, Silvester Corbin, then landlord of the Drax Arms, Reg Toop's favourite inn.

It was here, in years to come, that he would drum up business for what villagers called 'Toopy's Bus'. Known until the 1770s as the King's Arms, the pub was named for the Drax family who acquired the Bere Regis estate in 1733 from the surviving Turbervilles, whose ancestors had held land there since the 13th century.

For George Vacher, Hants & Dorset's offer to buy him out must have been persuasive. He was already in his forties, and now faced new regulations that would come in with the impending Road Traffic Act, already mooted by Ramsay MacDonald's Labour government in 1929.

The young Toop was undaunted, although he and his wife suffered a personal tragedy that year, the death of their infant daughter Sylvia. Reg and 19-year-old Evelyn Gladys Legg had married at Bere Regis in August 1927. Tom Applin's wife and Mrs Toop (who was also known as Ethel) were both regular worshippers at the Wesleyan chapel, which in later years found itself in the middle of the Bere Regis & District depot.

Reg was to fall foul of the new regulations more than once, but in 1930 he was ready to expand his business, by taking over James Ironside's carrier service from Winfrith, which ran to Wareham and Dorchester on market days and to Weymouth on Tuesdays and Fridays.

The Ironsides may have retained some kind of interest in Toop's business even at that stage; differing versions of the transaction appeared in later years. Bruce Maund, who interviewed Reg Toop around the end of World War II for *Modern Transport*, put it thus: 'It should be made clear that this was not the commencement of the partnership in which Mr Ironside now participates, these services being a definite acquisition on Mr Toop's part.' In 1956 Ryan Carpenter, who interviewed William Ironside for *Passenger Transport*, wrote that 'In 1930 the two operators merged.' In a subsequent article for *The Omnibus Magazine* he spelled out what seems to be the Bill Ironside gloss on events even more clearly: 'In 1930 the businesses of R.W. Toop of Bere Regis and J. Ironside of Winfrith were amalgamated.'

Less than six months after setting up on his own, Reg Toop had bought a pair of little Chevrolet buses, one of which was kept at Winfrith to run the former Ironside services. One of these 14-seaters was new (TK3897) and the other (MR7761) had seen service in Wiltshire, with Alfred White of Netheravon, also a carrier, who continued as such with an aged Morris van for some ten years yet.

The Road Traffic Act came into force on April 1, 1931, but it was several months before the new Southern Area Traffic Commissioner could get round to licensing every bus service in his bailiwick. It was only in September that Reg Toop's application to continue his nine bus routes was published. He also sought a licence to run tours to the seaside resorts of Weymouth, Sandbanks, Bournemouth, Lyme Regis and Exmouth, as well as to Tidworth and Aldershot, where military tattoos drew big crowds, and to Southampton.

The new licensing arrangement took effect on April Fool's Day but Toop would soon find that they were no jest. Like those of Hants & Dorset and Southern National, his bus services had to be approved by Traffic Commissioner Major-General Sir Reginald Ford.

The 18 September 1931 edition of the *Southern Traffic Area Notices & Proceedings* listed his nine routes:

Bere Regis & District Motor Service.

TIME TABLE

	Mon. & Fri.	Saturdays only				Public Holidays and Sundays only				
	am	am	pm	pm	pm	am	pm	pm	pm	pm
BERE REGIS dep.	10 15	10 15	2 0	4 15	5 45	10 15	2 0	5 30	8 30	9 15
Winterbourne Kingston	10 25	10 20	2 5	4 20	5 55	10 20	2 5	5 35	8 35	9 20
Winterbourne Zelstone ...	10 30	10 30	2 15	4 25	6 5	10 30	2 15	5 45	8 45	9 30
Almer Church ..	10 35	10 35	2 20	4 30	6 10	10 35	2 20	5 50	8 50	9 35
Morden ...	10 40	10 40	2 25	4 35	6 15	10 40	2 25	5 55	8 55	9 40
Organford Cross ...	10 45	10 45	2 30	4 40	6 20	10 45	2 30	6 0	9 0	9 45
Lytchett Minster ...	10 50	10 50	2 35	4 45	6 25					
Lytchett Matravers ...						10 50	2 35	6 5	9 10	9 55
Upton Cross	10 55	10 55	2 40	4 50	6 30	10 55	2 40	6 10	9 15	10 0
Creekmore Lane ...	11 0	11 0	2 45	4 55	6 35	11 0	2 45	6 15	9 20	10 5
POOLE ... arr.	11 5	11 5	2 55	5 0	6 40	11 5	2 55	6 20	9 25	10 10

	Mon. & Fri.	Saturdays only			R	Public Holidays and Sundays only				R
	pm	pm	pm	pm	pm	am	pm	pm	pm	pm
POOLE (George Htl) dep.	4 0	12 30	5 5	9 0	10 45	11 15	3 15	7 0	9 30	10 30
Creekmore Lane ...	4 5	12 35	5 10	9 5	10 50	11 20	3 20	7 5	9 35	10 35
Upton Cross	4 10	12 40	5 15	9 10	10 55	11 25	3 25	7 10	9 40	10 40
Lytchett Minster ...	4 15	12 45	5 20	9 15	11 0					
Lytchett Matravers ...						11 30	3 30	7 15	9 45	10 45
Organford Cross ...	4 20	12 50	5 25	9 20	11 5	11 35	3 35	7 20	9 50	10 50
Morden	4 25	12 55	5 30	9 25	11 10	11 40	3 40	7 25	9 55	10 55
Almer Church ..	4 30	1 0	5 35	9 30	11 15	11 45	3 45	7 30	10 0	11 0
Winterbourne Zelstone ...	4 35	1 5	5 40	9 35	11 20	11 50	3 50	7 35	10 5	11 5
Winterbourne Kingston	4 45	1 10	5 45	9 45	11 25	12 0	4 0	7 45	10 15	11 15
BERE REGIS arr.	4 55	1 15	5 50	9 50	11 30	12 5	4 5	7 55	19 20	11 20

R—Waits for conclusion of Performance of Regent Theatre

R. W. TOOP—Proprietor

Phone – Bere Regis 56

In the early 1930s Reg Toop ran to Poole five times on Sunday, four on Saturday and just once on Monday and Friday. On Sunday he ran via Lytchett Matravers, where Davis & Sons ran the rest of the week. Running time varied between 45 and 55 minutes. Two buses were required in the evenings.

1. Bere Regis – Poole, via Winterbornes Kingston and Zelstone

2. Winfrith Newburgh – Dorchester, via East Knighton and Warmwell Cross

3. Winfrith Newburgh – Weymouth, via East Knighton, Poxwell and Preston

4. Bere Regis – Wareham, via Winterborne Kingston and Lytchett Matravers

5. Bere Regis – Wareham, via Bere Heath, Hyde and Trigon

6. Winterborne Zelstone – Dorchester, via Bere Regis, Tolpuddle and Puddletown

7. Bere Regis – Wimborne, via Bere Heath, Bloxworth and Morden

8. Bere Regis – Wimborne, via Mapperton and Sturminster Marshall

9. Winfrith Newburgh – Wareham, via East Burton, Wool and Stoke

By this time George Vacher's Bere Regis Motor Service was no more, and the licence applications were in the name of 'Reginald William Toop, trading as Bere Regis & District Motor Services'. There was no reference to any Ironside interest in the business.

On the Poole service there was one journey each way on Mondays and Fridays, but four on Saturdays and five on Sundays and public holidays. Toop withdrew the Thursday journey to Wareham via Lytchett Matravers in about 1932, but maintained his other eight routes more or less unchanged.

Meanwhile his two big competitors on the Poole-Dorchester road kept beady eyes on his activities. Each of them laid complaints against him in 1933. Toop was summoned to appear before the Traffic Commissioner at the Burdon Hall in Weymouth. To judge by a local newspaper account the proceedings came as close to theatrical performance as such a hearing was ever likely to. The *Dorset County Chronicle & Somersetshire Gazette* carried a full report. Hants & Dorset, it said, had raised 'strong objections' to Toop's application to renew his bus service licences. His attitude to the whole affair, as recounted by the newspaper, implied that he viewed the terms of the Road Traffic Act as a tiresome inconvenience:

> Mr Toop applied for a continuation of his licence for local services, and the Hants & Dorset Motor Services Ltd, who were represented by Mr A.B. Wells, traffic manager, and Mr V. Lisby, solicitor, of Southampton, objected on the following grounds: That Mr. Toop uses unlicensed vehicles, unlicensed drivers, operates over unlicensed routes, operates at unlicensed times, does not run at scheduled times, cuts fares, does not issue tickets, hires vehicles without notice of them being hired, runs without conductors, takes short cuts, runs coaches without destination marked or with wrong destination marked, uses all his buses for private contract work when they ought to be used on the service, and uses unlicensed motor cars to go round collecting passengers. They submitted he was not a fit and proper person to hold a road service licence.
>
> An objection was also lodged by the Dorchester Carriers' Association, represented by Mr. G Caundle.
>
> Mr. R. Bailey, an inspector of the Southern

National Omnibus Co., stated that he was engaged to keep observation on Mr. Toop's routes. He boarded one of his buses in Bere Regis, which was waiting at one of the Hants & Dorset stands. There were three other passengers, but no one was picked up on the journey to Dorchester. He paid 1s. *[5p]* but received no ticket. The correct fare was 1s. 1d. *[5.25p]*. On the same day he boarded a bus belonging to Mr. Toop at Puddletown and the driver told him he had broken the rules by picking him up. The bus was full of parcels, which he saw being delivered at night after the service runs were finished. The next day he boarded Mr. Toop's bus along the road pointing to Bovington to go to Wareham. Mr. Toop, who was driving, told him he had boarded the bus at the wrong place. It proceeded from the main road along grass tracks and side lanes, a route for which he was not licensed. He picked up passengers and parcels on the way. On one occasion he ran into a farmyard, picked up a farmer, and had to back out. He was charged 1s. for the journey, which he paid on arrival at Wareham.

> Mr. Mitchell (one of the Commissioners): He gave you more for your 1s. than you expected?
>
> Mr Bailey: He gave me a headache. (Laughter).

Questioned by Mr. Toop, Mr. Bailey said he did not force himself on the bus at Puddletown after the driver had told him he could not pick him up.

Mr. G Vacher, sub-manager of the Hants & Dorset station at Bere Regis, said it had been Mr. Toop's policy since he had been running the service to do things which his (the witness's) company considered illegal.

Mr. Caundle said he and other operators in his district were chiefly concerned with Mr. Toop's running of tours.

Cross-examined by Mr. Lisby, applicant said he had been operating since October 1929, and with one exception he was not aware that he had committed any irregularities. The one exception was running a service between Park Corner and Bere Regis on a Saturday afternoon. He had been convicted on one occasion under the Road Traffic Act for overloading.

Further questioned by Mr. Lisby, he said there were continual complaints from the Hants & Dorset people about his running. This was petty spite because he was a small man trying to make a living. The only report of objection he had received was one from Mr. Caundle. He was warned once at Salisbury for an irregularity in running an excursion for a football party. He had never committed any irregularities except two, and the statements made by the other witnesses regarding irregularities were untrue. As far as issuing tickets was concerned, he said that when he became a member of the Dorchester and District Carriers' Association there was no need to issue tickets for a journey which was once a day.

Replying to a suggestion by Mr. Lisby that he drove off the beaten track and stopped at cottages, Mr. Toop said 'I should like to have the pleasure of taking you over that route one day.'

Mr. Lisby: But Mr. Bailey said he had a headache.

Mr. Toop: Well that's his misfortune.

Mr. Lisby: Is it not a fact that you go round collecting people in your taxi and don't charge them anything?

Mr. Toop: No, it's not. Do you think I'm fool enough to take a car out of the garage and carry people for nothing when they can pay or walk to the bus?

Mr. Lisby: What fare do you charge people who use your taxi? -- Mr. Toop: 6d [2.5p] per mile.

In answer to a further question by Mr. Lisby, Mr. Toop said he did not use destination boards on the Wareham and Wimborne buses. He could have brought enough people to fill

the hall to support his statements, but he did not think it was necessary.

Mr. Lisby: I should have had the opportunity of asking them a few questions about you, shouldn't I?

Mr. Toop: Yes, the hearing would only last longer.

Mr. Lisby: I suggest to you that you have not regarded the conditions of your licence.

Mr. Toop: I have run to the schedule.

Mr. Lisby: I am suggesting to you that you have been continually warned about it.

Mr. Toop: Who from?

Mr. Lisby: From the Commissioners.

Mr. Toop: I don't think so. I have been warned on one occasion by the Commissioners.

Mr. Lisby submitted that the enquiry could not have been fairer to Mr. Toop than it had been. The proceedings had been conducted in such a way that everything had really been to his advantage. He had denied almost everything that the objectors had said, and it was very easy to say 'No' to the allegations. 'It is a matter of comment and a matter upon which I should make strong comment that Mr. Toop has appeared here today without a single witness to support him, and I suggest from his evidence that it has not been satisfactory by any means,' said Mr. Lisby. 'He has been committing all sorts of breaches of his licence, and I could have spent a whole day proving other breaches going back over a long period.' It was obvious that he disregarded the complaint that had been made and in these circumstances he (Mr. Lisby) submitted that Mr. Toop's application should be refused. He suggested that Mr. Toop's irregularities were not confined to one, but a list which had been read out earlier in the proceedings. 'You are fully aware of this man's activities, and I submit that it is now time you put a stop to this illegal running and the evil this man is doing,' concluded Mr. Lisby.

Asked by the Commissioners if he had

anything else to say to them, Mr. Toop said that the Hants & Dorset company had a tremendous amount of petty spite against him and were doing all they could to cut him out. He ran to the schedule supplied by the Commissioners. 'If I kept an account of all the irregularities of the Hants & Dorset I should fill a book every day,' he added.

Summing up the case, Sir Reginald Ford said that Reg Toop had kept the court waiting until nearly 11 o'clock, stating that he had other work to do. 'I don't think that you appreciate the seriousness of your position with regard to your licences,' Sir Reginald told him: 'If you put other matters ahead of your livelihood you are making a very great and serious mistake.' Toop had been warned in the past at a hearing in Weymouth. 'On another occasion at Dorchester I can remember quite well giving him a very severe warning that unless his licence was adhered to in every detail we should take very strong action.'

The Commission had received reports from its own officials on the way Toop operated his vehicles, as well as from Hants & Dorset and Mr. Caundle. Sir Reginald said the Commissioners had decided to suspend his licence for the Poole-Bere Regis service for two weeks from Monday 3 October. He concluded: 'If there are further reports of irregularities in any way the only course open to the Commissioners will be revocation and not suspension of licence. I hope you will take steps to have your tickets and indicators in order, and be prepared to abide by the conditions of your licence in every possible detail.'

Reg Toop would surely have chuckled had he known that Bere Regis & District would outlive both the Hants & Dorset and Southern National companies as well as the very licensing regime that they had used to have him summoned before the Traffic Commissioner.

Just a couple of months before the Burdon Hall episode, fire had destroyed one of Toop's buses. He had put 14 gallons (64 litres) of petrol

A publicity shot of the first full-size coach, Dennis Lancet VJ6462 with a 32-seat Willowbrook body. It bears the Bere Regis & District title on the wings motif and "Kingsbere Luxury Coaches" on the roof-top luggage container.   IRONSIDE FAMILY

in its tank before parking it for the night in the yard outside his garage, which stood in a gap between houses off West Street, Bere Regis. There was no room for this bus inside because three other vehicles were already parked there. The alarm was raised at two o'clock in the morning, and the fire brigade was on the scene in about 20 minutes. The *Southern Times* said the bus was completely gutted except for the engine and part of the front. At the height of the blaze people were afraid the flames would reach the thatched roofs of cottages around the yard. 'The Dorchester fire brigade with the aid of villagers poured a large quantity of water from buckets over the bus.'

In January 1934 Reg Toop's fleet consisted of three Chevrolet 14-seaters, and a couple of 26- or 27-seaters, a Star and a Gilford. By mid-1935, when he tendered for contracts to convey children to school, he had added another Star and an American GMC to his fleet. He told the education authorities he could offer two 26-seaters, a GMC and a Star, and another Star with 20 seats. Early in 1936 he bought a Dodge 20-seater (CUL588). It was soon joined by his first full-size coach, a 32-seat Dennis Lancet (VJ6462) that was new to Wye Valley Motors of Hereford in 1934.

Besides the competition from the two big companies that ran between Weymouth and Bournemouth, Toop still had a local rival in I. Davis & Sons, who in 1933 had four bus routes of their own:

- Poole-Bloxworth (daily except Sunday) via Lytchett Matravers and Morden, extended to Bere Regis, Puddletown and Dorchester (Wednesday and Saturday)
- Morden-Wimborne (Tuesday) via Bere Regis, Winterborne Kingston, Lytchett Matravers
- Morden-Blandford (Thursday) via Bere Regis, Winterborne Kingston, Spetisbury
- Bloxworth-Wareham (Thursday) via Morden.

Until about 1933 Davis ran through journeys between Poole and Dorchester six days a week, also competing with George Vacher while he was still on the road. But, faced with heavyweight rivalry from Hants & Dorset and Southern National, he limited the Dorchester journeys to two days a week. The weekly service to Blandford was withdrawn in 1936.

Davis offered to sell the business to Hants & Dorset in 1933, but the company declined the offer. Its board minutes recorded on 24 July that year: 'after consideration of the reports made on the business of Davis & Son of Bere Regis [sic] the General Manager was instructed to advise Davis & Son that the company were not prepared to accept their offer for the purchase of their business.'

Like Toop, Israel Davis had his problems with the law. He was fined 10 shillings (50 pence) in April 1934 for allowing his bus to carry goods in contravention of its insurance conditions. One of his drivers, Kenneth Arthur Hunt, was fined £1 for a similar offence and for carrying too many passengers. According to the *Poole and East Dorset Herald* Police Constable Marsh told the court that as the 14-seat bus passed him Hunt turned round and motioned to the people in the back. At the New Inn a woman carrying a baby alighted, and at the George Hotel 15 adults and 5 children got off, some of them using the emergency door as if trying to avoid being counted. The defence argued the there were only 14 adults and four children. The newspaper added: 'the defendant's statement to this effect was substantiated by two of the passengers, Louisa Pooley and Daisy Fancy.'

In March 1936 Reginald William Toop and Percy William Davis went into partnership under the Bere Regis & District Motor Services banner. William James Ironside, second son of James Frederick, joined them three months later. The partnership only took full legal form the following year, but they lost no time to apply to the Western Area Traffic Commissioner, who had by then assumed responsibility for most of Dorset, for changes in the licensing arrangements for Percy Davis's services. The *Dorset County Chronicle & Somersetshire Gazette* reported on Thursday 28 May 1936:

> Application by Bere Regis & District Motor Services of 4 North Street, Bere Regis, Wareham, Dorset, for licences to run services between Bloxworth and Wareham and between Morden and Wimborne were granted by the Traffic Commissioners for the Western Area sitting at Dorchester this [Wednesday 27 May] morning. An application by the same company for alterations in timetable of the Dorchester-Poole service was granted, on condition that there should be no extension of the service from Bere Regis to Bloxworth.

The deed of partnership between Toop, Davis and Ironside was dated 19 December 1936, with a deed of variation dated 3 March 1937. It stated that the partnership was 'deemed to have commenced on the first day of March 1936.' It stipulated that the three men were equal partners, and the death of one or other of them would not dissolve the partnership.

The deed of variation allowed for a pension of £15 a week to be paid to a partner's widow and made provision for their children should a widow die. It also said that upon a

Reg Toop bought Star Flyer TK2299 from a Weymouth operator in 1934. Sitting pretty on the bonnet beside Bill Ironside is Primrose Whiffen. They married in 1942.
IRONSIDE FAMILY

partner's death his family could not withdraw their share of the business for 10 years. Time was to prove that the way the deed was drafted left room for conflicting legal arguments. The deed of variation also changed the name of the firm's bankers. At first it banked at Lloyds in Poole, but subsequently moved the account to the National Provincial Bank in Wareham, which was nearer to Bere Regis.

Over time Bere Regis & District owned more than a dozen Dodge coaches. Reg Toop bought the first one in 1936, CUL588. Resting on its bows are (left to right) Charlie Bartlett, Arthur Ironside, Bill Ironside, Fred Hann and Jack Toop. Charles Ironside kneels on the bonnet behind his brother.
IRONSIDE FAMILY

Being a legal document, the agreement needed the signature of a witness. This was provided by 18-year-old Raymond Ernest John Roper, son of Frederick, the one-time Bere Regis carrier. The document said he was manager of the Anglo-American Oil Company's outlet in Dorchester, the petrol station on the eastern edge of the town. His father and grandfather had both been carriers but this was Ray Roper's first known relationship with the bus business.

Along with Bill Ironside came two of his four brothers, Charles and Arthur, aged 26 and 23 at the time. Each was to work for the firm for more than 30 years.

The Traffic Commissioner agreed, at a hearing in Dorchester Council Chambers on 3 September 1936 that Toop could surrender eight licences to the partnership:

- Winfrith, Church – Wareham, Red Lion (Thursday),
- Bere Regis, Central Garage – Poole, Red Lion (Monday, Friday, Saturday, Sunday)
- Winfrith, Church – Dorchester, Council Yard (Wednesday and Saturday)
- Winfrith, Church – Weymouth, Royal Yard (Friday and Saturday)
- Winterborne Zelstone, Post Office – Dorchester, Phoenix Inn (Wednesday)
- Bere Regis, Central Garage – Wimborne, Square (Tuesday)
- Bere Regis, Central Garage – Wareham, Red Lion (Thursday and Saturday)
- Excursions from Bere Regis

On a summer's day in the 1930s Bill Ironside attends to a wheel of Star RU9445, with both of its doors open in the yard at Bere Regis. The vehicle on the right is probably another Star. IRONSIDE FAMILY

Israel Davis lived on until 1943. He died at the age of 75 and was buried at Bloxworth. Percy's daughter Sylvia Gibbs told Norman Aish that her father faced a heavy fine after a fatal accident in about 1936. The victim was a Hants & Dorset bus driver, who emerged from the New Inn car park on his bicycle and collided with Percy's bus. This cannot have improved his relationship with the big company and the fine put him under financial pressure. Joining the new partnership no doubt eased the problem. Percy's contribution to its initial capital was £400. Reg Toop and Bill Ironside each put up half the remaining £1,000.

Sylvia Gibbs said her father, like the other two partners, was not particularly well educated, but he was full of charm and very straightforward in business matters, so Toop and Ironside used to have him talk to difficult customers. Percy understood mechanical issues, but his back prevented him from doing much maintenance work, and he concentrated on driving.

Soon after the partnership was formed, it published a new timetable (cost one penny), featuring the Dennis Lancet on the cover as the pride of the fleet. There were now two routes between Bere Regis and Poole, which between them provided daily journeys competing for local traffic with Hants & Dorset and Southern National. However, the partners still only ran to

Dorchester on Wednesdays and Saturdays, from both Bere Regis and Winfrith. There was also a Wednesday-only service from Winterborne Zelstone to Dorchester.

From its very inception the partnership used more than one terminus in Dorchester, the Casterbridge of Thomas Hardy's novels. Percy Davis's old service from Poole stopped at the Phoenix Inn, on High East Street. So did Reg Toop's market day service from Winterborne Zelstone. The twice weekly run from Winfrith, which originated with the Ironsides, used the Council Yard. In later years this became the most popular place for independents to park up in town, but Bere Regis & District used several different locations. Dorchester had no bus station so this was partly a matter of convenience, depending on which road the bus took to leave town, but history played a role too. When the partners took over someone else's service they often went on using the same terminus. Some of their buses started by the statue of William Barnes, the Dorset poet, outside St Peter's Church.

A market-day Bere Regis–Wareham service ran over what was little more than a grass track, calling at isolated farms to pick up people and produce to take to market. Sylvia Gibbs said passengers were loyal to Bere Regis & District rather than Hants & Dorset. They found the big company's timings less convenient and the fares were higher.

WINFRITH TO WEYMOUTH.

Saturdays and Public Holidays only.

			p.m.	p.m.	p.m.
Winfrith Church	...	(dep.)	2.55	5.55	7.40
East Knighton	...	...	3. 0	6. 0	7.45
Galton	...	...	3. 8	6. 8	7.53
Owermoigne	...	...	3.10	6.10	7.55
Warmwell Cross	...	...	3.20	6.20	8. 5
Poxwell	...	...	3.25	6.25	8.10
Osmington	...	...	3.30	6.30	8.15
Weymouth	...	(arr.)	3.40	6.40	8.25

			p.m.	p.m.
Weymouth ...	...	(dep.)	7. 0	r10. 0
Osmington	...	...	7.10	10.10
Poxwell	...	...	7.15	10.15
Warmwell Cross	...	...	7.20	10.20
Owermoigne	...	...	7.30	10.30
Galton	...	...	7.32	10.32
East Knighton	...	...	7.40	10.40
Winfrith Church	...	(arr.)	7.45	10.45

r—Waits for close of Regent Theatre.

WINFRITH TO WAREHAM.

Thursdays only.

		a.m.			p.m.
Winfrith	...	9.30	Wareham	...	3.30
East Knighton	...	9.35	Stoke	...	3.45
East Burton	...	9.50	Wool	...	4. 0
Wool ...	...	10.10	East Burton	...	4.15
Stoke ...	...	10.25	East Knighton	...	4.30
Wareham	...	10.45	Winfrith	...	4.45

8

BERE REGIS TO POOLE SERVICE.

via Bloxworth, Morden, Lytchett Matravers.

Daily except Sundays.

		a.m.	p.m.	p.m.	p.m.
Bere Regis	... (dep.)	8.45	12.45	2.20	6.10
Bloxworth	... ...	8.50	12.50	2.25	6.15
Morden	... ...	8.55	12.55	2.30	6.20
Organford Cross	...	9. 0	1. 0	2.35	6.25
Lytchett Matravers	...	9. 5	1. 5	2.40	6.30
Upton Cross ...	...	9.15	1.15	2.50	6.40
Fleets Corner	...	9.25	1.25	3. 0	6.50
Poole (George Hotel) (arr.)		9.30	1.30	3. 5	6.55

		a.m.	p.m.	p.m.	p.m.
Poole	... (dep.)	11. 0	1.30	3.20	7.15
Fleets Corner	...	11. 5	1.35	3.25	7.20
Upton Cross ...	...	11.10	1.40	3.30	7.25
Lytchett Matravers	...	11.20	1.50	3.40	7.35
Organford Cross	...	11.25	1.55	3.45	7.45
Morden	... ...	11.30	2. 0	3.50	7.50
Bloxworth	... ...	11.35	2.10	4. 0	7.55
Bere Regis	... (arr.)	11.45	2.15	4. 5	8. 0

See page 4 for Sunday Service.

2

BERE REGIS TO POOLE.

via Winterborne Kingston, Winterborne Zelstone, Almer and Morden.

Mondays, Fridays, Saturdays and Sundays.

		Mon. & Fri. a.m.	Saturdays only. a.m.	p.m.	p.m.
Bere Regis	... (dep.)	10.15	10.15	2. 0	5.45
Winterborne Kingston		10.25	10.25	2. 5	5.55
Winterborne Zelstone ...		10.30	10.30	2.15	6. 5
Almer	... ...	10.35	10.35	2.20	6.10
Morden	... ...	10.40	10.40	2.25	6.15
Organford Cross	...	10.45	10.45	2.30	6.20
Lytchett Minster	...	10.50	10.50	2.35	—
Lytchett Matravers	...	—	—	—	6.25
Upton Cross ...	...	10.55	10.55	2.40	6.35
Creekmoor	...	11. 0	11. 0	2.45	6.40
Poole	... (arr.)	11. 5	11. 5	2.55	6.45

		p.m.	p.m.	p.m.	p.m.
Poole	... (dep.)	4. 0	12.30	5. 5	r10. 0
Creekmore	...	4. 5	12.35	5.10	10. 5
Upton Cross ...	...	4.10	12.40	5.15	10.10
Lytchett Minster	...	4.15	12.45	5.20	—
Lytchett Matravers	...	—	—	—	10.20
Organford Cross	...	4.20	12.50	5.25	10.25
Morden	... ...	4.25	12.55	5.30	10.30
Almer Church	...	4.30	1. 0	5.35	10.35
Winterborne Zelstone ...		4.35	1. 5	5.40	10.40
Winterborne Kingston		4.45	1.10	5.45	10.50
Bere Regis	... (arr.)	4.55	1.15	5.50	10.55

r—Waits for close of Regent Theatre.

3

(above and next page) Soon after the partners joined forces Bere Regis & District issued a timetable booklet, price one penny (0.4p). The Dennis Lancet featured on the front. On the back were the ex-Ironside services from Winfrith to Weymouth and Wareham.

However, Hants & Dorset clearly had no intention of letting the grass grow under its wheels. It based a smart Dennis Ace 20-seater at Bere Regis and applied for licences for no less than five stage services from the village. All were approved in 1936: two to Poole (daily via Winterborne Zelstone, and on Mondays to Saturdays via Bloxworth), two to Wareham

BERE REGIS TO POOLE.

via Winterborne Kingston, Winterborne Zelstone, Almer and Mordon.

Sundays only.

		a.m.	p.m.	p.m.	p.m.
Bere Regis	(dep.)	10.15	2. 0	5.30	8.30
Winterborne Kingston		10.20	2. 5	5.35	8.35
Winterborne Zelstone		10.30	2.15	5.45	8.45
Almer		10.35	2.20	5.50	8.50
Morden		10.40	2.25	5.55	8.55
Organford Cross		10.45	2.30	6. 0	9. 0
Lytchett Minster		—	—	—	—
Lytchett Matravers		10.50	2.35	6. 5	9.10
Upton Cross		10.55	2.40	6.10	9.15
Creekmoor		11. 0	2.45	6.15	9.20
Poole	(arr.)	11. 5	2.55	6.20	9.25

		a.m.	p.m.	p.m.	p.m.
Poole	(dep.)	11.15	3.15	7. 0	r10. 0
Creekmoor		11.20	3.20	7. 5	10. 5
Upton Cross		11.25	3.25	7.10	10.10
Lytchett Minster		—	—	—	—
Lytchett Matravers		11.30	3.30	7.15	10.20
Organford Cross		11.35	3.35	7.20	10.25
Morden		11.40	3.40	7.25	10.30
Almer Church		11.45	3.45	7.30	10.40
Winterborne Zelstone		11.50	3.50	7.35	10.45
Winterborne Kingston		12. 0	4. 0	7.45	10.50
Bere Regis	(arr.)	12. 5	4. 5	7.55	10.55

r—Waits for close of Regent Theatre.

4

BERE REGIS TO DORCHESTER.

via Briantspuddle, Affpuddle, Tolpuddle.

Wednesdays and Saturdays only.

		a.m.	a.m.	p.m.	p.m.
		W.S.	W.O.	W.S.	S.O.
Bere Regis	(dep.)	9.20	10.15	2.20	6.15
Briantspuddle Cross		9.30	10.25	2.30	6.25
Affpuddle Cross		9.35	10.30	2.35	6.30
Tolpuddle		9.40	10.40	2.40	6.35
Puddletown		9.45	10.45	2.45	6.40
Dorchester	(arr.)	10. 0	11. 0	3. 0	6.55

		p.m.	p.m.	p.m.	p.m.
		W.S.	W.O.	W.S.	S.O.
Dorchester	(dep.)	12. 0	4. 0	5.30	9. 0
Puddletown		12.15	4.15	5.45	9.15
Tolpuddle		12.20	4.20	5.50	9.20
Affpuddle Church		12.25	4.25	5.55	9.25
Briantspuddle Cross		12.30	4.35	6. 0	9.35
Bere Regis	(arr.)	12.40	4.45	6.10	9.45

W.S.—*Wednesdays and Saturdays only.*
S.O.—*Saturdays only.*
W.O.—*Wednesdays only.*

5

WINTERBORNE ZELSTONE to DORCHESTER

via Winterborne Kingston, Bere Regis, Briantspuddle.

Wednesdays only.

	a.m.		p.m.
Wint'borne Zelstone	9.45	Dorchester	4. 0
Wint'borne Kingston	10. 0	Affpuddle Church	4.25
Bere Regis	10.15	Briantspuddle Cross	4.35
Briantspuddle Cross	10.25	Bere Regis	4.45
Affpuddle Church	10.30	Wint'borne Kingston	5. 0
Dorchester	11. 0	Wint'borne Zelstone	5.15

BERE REGIS TO WIMBORNE.

Tuesdays only

	a.m.		p.m.
Bere Regis	9.15	Wimborne	3.30
Bere Heath	9.25	Lytchett Matravers	3.50
Bloxworth	9.35	Roundhouse	4. 0
Morden	9.50	Morden	4.10
Roundhouse	10. 0	Bloxworth	4.25
Lytchett Matravers	10.10	Bere Heath	4.35
Wimborne	10.30	Bere Regis	4.45

BERE REGIS TO WAREHAM.

	Thurs. only.	Sat. only.		Thurs. only.	Sat. only.
	a.m.	a.m.		p.m.	p.m.
Bere Regis	9.30	9.30	Wareham	3.30	12. 0
Bere Heath	9.35	9.35	Hyde	4. 0	12.30
Hyde	10.15	10.15	Bere Heath	4.15	12.45
Wareham	11. 0	11. 0	Bere Regis	4.45	1. 0

6

WINFRITH TO DORCHESTER.

Wednesdays and Saturdays only.

		W.S.	W.S.	W.O.
		a.m.	a.m.	p.m.
Winfrith Church	(dep.)	9.10	10.55	2.30
East Knighton		9.15	11. 0	2.35
Winfrith, Red Lion		9.25	11.10	2.45
Galton		9.30	11.15	2.50
Owermoigne		9.35	11.20	2.55
Warmwell Cross		9.40	11.25	3. 0
Broadmayne		9.45	11.30	3. 5
Dorchester	(arr.)	10. 0	11.45	3.20

		W.S.	W.S.	W.S.
		a.m.	p.m.	p.m.
Dorchester	(dep.)	10.15	2. 0	4.30
Broadmayne		10.25	2.10	4.50
Warmwell Cross		10.30	2.15	4.55
Owermoigne		10.35	2.20	5. 0
Galton		10.38	2.23	5. 5
Winfrith, Red Lion		10.40	2.25	5.15
East Knighton		10.45	2.28	5.25
Winfrith Church	(arr.)	10.50	2.30	5.30

W.O.—*Wednesdays only.*
W.S.—*Wednesdays and Saturdays only.*

7

(via the Wool road on Thursdays, and via Bere Heath, Morden and Bloxworth on Saturdays), and one to Wimborne via the main road on Thursdays.

In the three short years before Prime Minister Neville Chamberlain reluctantly declared war on 3 September 1939, Bere Regis & District set about expanding the private hire side of its business. In his lengthy article about the firm, published in *Modern Transport* in 1946, Bruce Maund wrote that: 'Private hire and school contract work was largely responsible for the healthy financial position of the undertaking which enabled such considerable expansion later.

Gilford CS105 stands with its nose in the shadow of Bere Regis garage. It was new in 1934 to Western Scottish Motor Traction, which fitted it with a second-hand Leyland engine.   See p.24 for the identity of the six men standing by it.
IRONSIDE FAMILY

The competition: Hants & Dorset's smart Harrington-bodied Dennis Ace 20-seater posed a challenge to Bere Regis & District, whose partners never bought a new bus until 1945.

A.H. WALLER COLLECTION

'It was not uncommon for Kingsbere Luxury Coaches (the fleetname adopted for private hire business) to reach places as far afield as Newcastle-on-Tyne, Manchester and Liverpool, the principal source of these parties being nearby military establishments.' (Kingsbere was the name Hardy gave Bere Regis in his novels, but it is also a modern rendering of the name by which the village was known when the Turbervilles held sway in the middle ages, Kyngesbyre.)

To comply with the Road Traffic Act regular operation of 'private party' work to specific places like Newcastle or Liverpool, London or Bristol would subsequently have to be licensed as express services.

Alan Bailey, whose family had run the bakery in Winterborne Kingston since 1897, said that before World War II there were plenty of people in farming communities like Winterbornes Kingston and Zelstone who never went out of their home villages. Those who wanted to go to Poole or Dorchester took Toopy's bus. On Saturday and Sunday nights

Bill Ironside, leaning on the radiator of Dennis Lancet VJ6462, drove a party of Dorset folk on an outing to Torquay in 1939 or 1940. A second coach was needed, Dodge DTU 516.

IRONSIDE FAMILY

the 10 o'clock bus waited for the show to end at the Regent Theatre before it left Poole.

Toop, Ironside and Davis added no new bus routes in the late 1930s, but the services to Poole and Wimborne via Bloxworth were diverted to run via Lytchett Matravers, and there had been some consolidation of the routes that Toop and Davis had brought into the partnership.

There were special events too, that brought in more passengers, such as the Woodbury Hill Fair. This had been held every September for 700 years on a site overlooking Bere Regis. In

Standing in front of CS105 are (left to right) Johnnie Bowring, Charles Ironside, Fred Hann, Bill Ironside, Percy Davis in his bus driver's cap and Arthur Ironside. This coach worked in London for a while before settling in Dorset.   IRONSIDE FAMILY

olden times it lasted five days, with each one catering for a different public: Wholesale Day, Gentlefolks Day, Allfolks Day, Sheepfair Day, and Pack and Penny Day. By the late 1930s it had shrunk to a two-day amusement fair, but still busy enough to justify Bere Regis & District seeking a short-term licence to serve Woodbury Hill. The fair ceased during World War II, and lasted only a few more years thereafter.

By the end of the 1930s the partners had assembled a handful of larger vehicles to add to a fleet that consisted largely at the outset of 26-, 20-, and 14-seaters. A pair of Gilford Hera coaches joined the Dennis Lancet. A former London Transport Green Line coach (GC6846) was the first of many Leylands; it had a single-deck body on a Titan chassis, normally used for double-deckers. This misled some to conclude that a double-deck was owned before World War II.

Altogether the partners had about 20 vehicles by the time war broke out. They included a clutch of little Dodge coaches, garnered from different parts of England, which made a unique and important contribution. The Bere Regis sign-writer copied the winged badge at the top of the Dodge radiator and it became the company logo, adorning the sides and the boot doors. Bere Regis coaches were painted mid-brown above the waistline and a lighter brown below. Bere Regis people believe these colours were chosen because there was a job-lot to hand. In those days brown was often the sombre colour of choice for wooden panelling on the walls of institutions like schools and village halls.

In 1930 Reg Toop had been one of 36 small busmen who served Dorchester, most of them only on market days. The three big companies, Southern National, Hants & Dorset and Wilts & Dorset, were well entrenched on the main roads to Weymouth, Poole, Bournemouth, Salisbury, Bridport and points west. By 1939, on the eve of war, 28 small operators still ran to Dorchester, but nine years later Bere Regis & District had taken the place of 19 of them, mostly by acquisition.

Bere Regis coaches rarely bore fleet numbers, but Star Flyer RU9445 sported the number 7 as well as an early version of the wings motif. The young Bill Ironside leans on the bonnet. Payne of Bournemouth built the canvas-roofed body.

IRONSIDE FAMILY

Bere Regis had three Wycombe-bodied Gilford coaches before World War II. YG7085 arrived in 1937 after three years in Yorkshire. Bill Ironside leans on the mudguard beside Fred Hann, who like Reg Toop once drove for George Vacher.

IRONSIDE FAMILY

3
WAR ~ BERE REGIS ADVANCES

BY THE TIME Britain declared war on
Germany in September 1939, Toop, Ironside
and Davis had substantially consolidated their
business. For the three young entrepreneurs who
had pooled their resources for the past three years,
wartime presented some golden opportunities,
which were energetically seized. Troops and war
workers had to be moved hither and thither across
Dorset and more widely across England. Several
factories around Poole were engaged on war work.
Indeed, even as Neville Chamberlain had
done his best to achieve 'peace in our
time' the ordnance factories were gearing
up to intensify production.

Bere Regis & District's bus
services only reached as far as Poole,
Dorchester, Weymouth, Wareham and
Wimborne. It still had no more than
20 buses and coaches, and of these
there were generally no more than two
or three of any chassis type. All of them
had seen service with other owners
across the country. Keeping such a
motley collection of vehicles on the road
challenged the skills of mechanics and
fitters, especially in wartime conditions.

Before the war the partners had
built up the private hire side of the
business and offered tours and excursions
from villages to resorts like Bournemouth and
Weymouth. Prewar-style leisure travel inevitably
came to a halt, so such excursions went into
abeyance, not least because of defence activities
along a coastline at serious risk of enemy attack.

A couple of the ordnance factories lay
just to the east of Bere Regis territory: the Royal
Naval Cordite Factory at Holton Heath and the
Royal Ordnance Factory at Creekmoor. Holton
Heath was built during the 1914-18 War, and
during World War II again became an important
source of employment for the Purbeck area.
ROF Creekmoor, where more than 2,000 people
worked at the height of the war, was built in 1940.

There were still children to be taken to

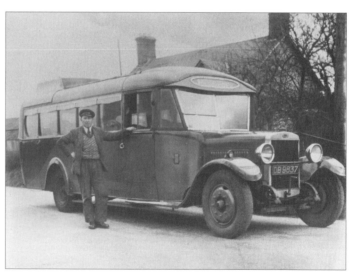

Driver Tom Clark of Briantspuddle stands by Star Flyer DB9837,
acquired in 1940 and kept on the road for five years. After he retired
Tom Clark used to pop into the Dorchester workshops with vegetables
from his garden for an old friend who worked there.

G. TOOP

school, including evacuees to rural Dorset from
towns exposed to enemy air raids. By 1941 there
were nearly 900 evacuees in the Dorchester
Rural District Council area, a high proportion
of them children. Raymond Applin said Mr and

Seven second-hand Dodge coaches were acquired in 1940. ETD141, Percy Davis's "Rosie", came from Charlie's Cars in Bournemouth. For a while Bill Ironside kept FTU149 locked up with no engine so it would be no use for military service: it still wore wartime headlamp masks when it emerged from purdah. The Leyland Tiger beside them, EAL239, was added in 1944.   IRONSIDE FAMILY

Mrs Toop played host to several of these children at their home on North Street. When the British army began to take German prisoners of war, Bere Regis buses were used to convey them from their camp, on the Bridport Road in Dorchester, to work on farms in the countryside around.

Smaller bus concerns, running to market in Dorchester or Blandford once or twice a week, found the inevitable wartime restrictions harder to bear than did Bere Regis & District with its greater resources. Typically their owners were no longer in the flush of youth, so they were ready over the next few years to sell up, or in some cases just to give up their operations.

Most of Bere Regis & District's vehicles remained at work in their home county, but a few, together with their drivers, were busy elsewhere for some of the time. Inevitably from time to time they met with misfortune. In the Arctic winter of January 1940 the *Southern Times* reported: 'Workmen from Swanage and Langton [Matravers] who were travelling by bus belonging to Messrs. Toop, Bere Regis, from Swanage to Shaftesbury...met with an accident in the early morning.'

In fact the workers were Purbeck quarrymen, whose skills were evidently needed somewhere near Shaftesbury. Wartime discretion no doubt prevented the paper going into detail, but it could be that they were excavating bunkers for the Royal Air Force to conceal its bombs at Chilmark, whence, centuries earlier, stone was quarried to build Salisbury Cathedral.

The bus driver had difficulty negotiating the corner of Kingston Hill, near Corfe Castle. A steep sharp bend at the best of times, it has seen many a vehicle come to grief, even in good conditions. 'The driver attempted to drive straight on, but the slippery state of the road caused the bus to skid, forcing the driver to lose control and the bus to crash head-on into a wall near the Eldon Arms', now the Scott Arms Hotel.

'Passengers numbering about thirty received a severe shaking. One or two had some of their teeth knocked out, and others received blows about the head.

'Mr R.G. Keates, licensee of the Eldon Arms, rendered assistance by opening his house, lighting a fire and providing tea. The majority of the seats were stripped from the floor of the coach by the impact. The occupants decided not to proceed to work, and after assistance had been obtained from his [the driver's] firm the men were taken back to their homes.'

Purbeck quarrymen are sturdy folk and evidently all was soon patched up, for 'On the following night all the passengers called at the Eldon Arms on returning from Shaftesbury to express their appreciation of the assistance given by the landlord.' Quarrying is a thirsty business: their appreciation no doubt did wonders for Mr Keates's takings.

For a couple of years during the war Percy Davis lived in Swanage in order to be on the spot to organise transport for workers at military sites. Apart from the ordnance factories, and decoy factories on the Arne peninsula, the Purbeck area included Worth Matravers and the tank ranges at Lulworth. From May 1940 Worth was the nerve centre for the development of radar. At first there were about 200 people working there. By May 1942 there were 2,000, many of them scientists, but one day that month the scientists were evacuated, well away from German bombers, although RAF radar was still active at Worth Matravers until well after the war.

Bere Regis & District must have been one of the firms whose coaches ferried the scientists to their new roost in Worcestershire, a journey graphically described in Reg Batt's *The Radar Army – Winning the War of the Airwaves*, published in 1991.

'Even for Swanage, a holiday resort, it must have been an impressive number of coaches which left the town that morning. It was a motley cavalcade of vehicles old and new,

Leyland Lion BNB228 was one of the mixed bunch of second- and third-hand buses that arrived in 1941. It came from Lancashire, stayed in Dorset six years, and then spent another eight with a Devon coach firm. Even so it still sported Bere Regis two-tone brown when sighted in Salisbury as a showman's bus in 1957.

DAVID PENNELS

supplied by operators large and small from around Dorset and Hampshire.

'It was a perfect day to enjoy the rolling English countryside in its lush green shroud of late spring. The procession was heading due north, and we were soon admiring the broad sweep of the Wiltshire Downs. Spread out ahead were more of our coaches whilst following behind at respectable intervals were yet more. Frequently we would overtake one of the small convoys of large navy-blue Pickford's removal vans.'

The immediate impact of war on Bere Regis & District's bus routes was relatively small, but a couple of market-day services were suspended – Bere Regis-Wimborne via Zelstone and Almer, and Bloxworth-Wareham. However, as the 'Phoney War' turned into hostilities in earnest, the pressure on village bus operators grew ever greater.

Most of them only had one or two vehicles and concentrated largely on market day services, but petrol supply for civilian use was halved, spare parts for ageing buses became hard to come by and, after Japan occupied much of South East Asia, so did rubber for tyres. At the same time the armed forces had greater need of

GPH925 was the only Guy that Bere Regis & District ever owned. A Vixen new to Conway Coaches of Woking in 1938, it came via Edwin Russell of Broadmayne in 1941 and survived long enough to shed its wartime headlamp masks and give another ten years' service.

OMNIBUS SOCIETY COLLECTION

the mechanics with the skills to keep vehicles on the road. Small wonder then that some of the men who had set up in business after World War I were thinking of retirement.

This was Bere Regis & District's opportunity, and Bill Ironside seized it. Between 1940 and 1945 the partnership absorbed a dozen smaller operators. In this way he first tightened the firm's grasp on its existing territory, and then extended its reach to the north and west.

The first to be taken over was William John (Jack) Laws of Briantspuddle, who retired in June 1940. He began with a horsedrawn carrier service to Dorchester, then bought his first motor bus in 1924. No money changed hands but his family were given free passes for travel on Bere Regis & District. There was no problem in absorbing his Wednesday and Saturday service. The market-day bus from Bere Regis was diverted by way of Briantspuddle.

Ten years earlier there had been another bus on part of Laws' route. It belonged to Sam Loveless of Tolpuddle, but he gave up his service in 1931. The village is famed for the six Tolpuddle Martyrs, who were transported to Australia in 1834 for swearing an illegal oath, creating a Friendly Society of Agricultural Labourers. Its leader was George Loveless, and the magistrate found that besides George and his brother

James, the members included no less than seven persons of the name of Loveless.

In December 1941 two more small operators passed to Bere Regis & District, Edwin Russell of Broadmayne and Cyril Edward Jeanes of Dorchester. Russell ran a twice-weekly service from West Knighton to Dorchester via Broadmayne, along the very same road into market as James Ironside's old Winfrith-Dorchester service. Four years earlier Russell had himself absorbed Arthur John Bishop's Broadmayne-Dorchester service, which dated from 1915.

Jeanes had shared the road between Dorchester and Piddletrenthide with Harry Hawker, who was based in that village. Each of them ran into Dorchester five days a week. Jeanes, who ran farther up the valley to Henley, was a

C. E. JEANES, BUS SERVICE		Private Address: 27, Orchard Street, DORCHESTER.
From DORCHESTER.		From HENLEY.
MONDAY.		
9.0 a.m.	Adam's Yard.	9.35 a.m.
12.45 p.m.	Genge's Corner	1.45 p.m.
WEDNESDAY.		
9.0 a.m.	Adams' Yard	9.35 a.m.
12 noon	Genge's Corner	1.0 p.m.
3.30 p.m.	,, ,,	4.15 ,,
6.0 ,,	,, ,,	6.35 ,,
9.0 ,,	,, ,,	9.35 ,,
FRIDAY.		
9.0 a.m.	Adam's Yard	9.35 a.m.
12.45 p.m.	Genge's Corner	1.45 p.m.
5.0 ,,	,, ,,	5.35 p.m.
Saturday same as Wednesday.		
Late Bus every Saturday at 11 p.m. approx. from White Hart Hotel.		
SUNDAY.		
2-30 p.m.	Genge's Corner	3.15 p.m.
6.30 ,,	,, ,,	7.15 ,,
10.30 ,,	,, ,,	11.15 ,,

Bere Regis & District's first bus service along the Piddle Valley came from Cyril Jeanes in 1941. Before the war Jeanes ran five days a week between Dorchester and Henley, calling at Piddlehinton, Piddletrenthide and Alton Pancras.

The only bus taken over from Cyril Jeanes was a Thornycroft A6, seen with original owners Bird Brothers of Yeovil. YC2986 only stayed with Bere Regis a few months.

ALAN LAMBERT COLLECTION

BERE REGIS and DISTRICT MOTOR SERVICES

(*Proprietors*:—R. Toop, W. Ironside, P. Davis)

4, North Street,
Bere Regis,
WAREHAM, Dorset.
'Phone : Bere Regis 56.

7, Bridport Road,
DORCHESTER,
Dorset.
'Phone : Dorchester 79.

ALTERATIONS TO TIME TABLES
Commencing August 1st, 1942.

Dorchester—Piddlehinton—Piddletrenthide Henley

Wednesdays and Saturdays only. Sats only / White Hart

	a.m.	a.m.	p.m.	p.m.	p.m.	p.m
Dorchester (Museum) (*dep.*)	9. 0	12. 0	3.30	6. 0	9. 0	
Waterson Cross	9.13	12.13	3.43	6.13	9.13	
Piddlehinton Camp	9.15	12.15	3.45	6.15	9.15	
Piddlehinton Cross	9.20	12.20	3.50	6.20	9.20	
Piddletrenthide	9.25	12.25	3.55	6.25	9.25	—
Alton Pancras	9.30	12.30	4. 0	6.30	9.30	—
Henley (*arr.*)	9.35	12.35	4. 5	6.35	9.35	—
	a.m.	p.m.	p.m.	p.m.	p.m.	p.m.
Henley (*dep.*)	9.35	1. 0	4.15	6.35	9.35	
Alton Pancras	9.40	1. 5	4.20	6.40	9.40	—
Piddletrenthide	9.45	1.10	4.25	6.45	9.45	—
Piddlehinton Cross	9.50	1.15	4.30	6.50	9.50	
Piddlehinton Camp	9.55	1.20	4.35	6.55	9.55	
Waterson Cross	9.57	1.22	4.37	6.57	9.57	
Dorchester (*arr.*)	10.10	1.35	4.50	7.10	10.10	

Sundays only. White Hart

	p.m.	p.m.	p.m.	
Dorchester (*dep.*)	2. 0	5. 0	9. 0	
Waterson Cross	2.13	5.13	9.13	
Piddlehinton Camp	2.15	5.15	9.15	
Piddlehinton Cross	2.20	5.20	9.20	—
Piddletrenthide ...	2.25	5.25	9.25	—
Alton Pancras ...	2.30	5.30	9.30	—
Henley (*arr.*)	2.35	5.35	9.35	—
	p.m.	p.m.	p.m.	p.m.
Henley (*dep.*)	2.35	5.35	9.35	—
Alton Pancras ...	2.40	5.40	9.40	—
Piddletrenthide ...	2.45	5.45	9.45	—
Piddlehinton Cross	2.50	5.50	9.50	
Piddlehinton Camp	2.55	5.55	9.55	
Waterson Cross ...	2.57	5.57	9.57	
Dorchester (*arr.*)	3.10	6.10	10.10	

Fridays only. White Hart

	p.m.	p.m.
Dorchester (*dep.*)	5.30	10.30
Waterson Cross	5.43	10.43
Piddlehinton Camp (*arr.*)	5.45	10.45
	p.m.	p.m.
Piddlehinton Camp ...	6. 0	10.50
Waterson Cross ...	6. 2	11. 2
Dorchester (*arr.*)	6.15	11.15

Piddletrenthide—Piddlehinton—Dorchester

	M.T.F.	W.S.	W.S.	S.O.	S.O.
	a.m.	a.m.	p.m.	p.m.	p.m.
Piddletrenthide (*dep.*)		11. 0	1.40	4.15	6. 0
Piddlehinton	9.40	11.10	1.50	4.25	6.10
Waterson ...	9.45	11.15	1.55	4.30	6.15
Dorchester (*arr.*)	10. 0	11.30	2.10	4.45	6.30

	M.T.F.	W.S.	S.O.	W.O.	S.O.	S.O.
	p.m.	p.m.	p.m.	p.m.	p.m.	p.m.
Dorchester (*dep.*)	3.30	12.15	3.15	4.30	5.15	9. 0
Waterson ...	3.45	12.30	3.30	4.45	5.30	9.15
Piddlehinton	3.50	12.35	3.35	4.50	5.35	9.20
Piddletrenthide (*arr.*)	4. 0	12.45	3.45	5. 0	5.40	9.30

M.T.F.—Mondays, Tuesdays and Fridays only.
W.S.—Wednesdays and Saturdays only.
W.O.—Wednesdays only.
S.O.—Saturdays only.

Hy. Ling Ltd., Printers, Dorchester.

relative newcomer, for he had only appeared on that road in 1924. Hawker began in the days of the horse in 1902, bought a Daimler carrier's van in 1916, and stayed the course until he died on 19 March 1942. His widow took over for a short while before selling out to 'Ironsides', as the Hawker family put it. Evidently not everyone in that part of Dorset saw it as 'Toopy's bus'. Taking over Jeanes and Hawker gave the partners, or perhaps we should say Bill Ironside, a foothold along the upper reaches of the Piddle Valley.

Just two months after taking over Jeanes and Russell, Bere Regis & District made the first two of what would be five acquisitions in 1942, including Hawker. In February the businesses of Frank Whitty & Son of Dorchester and Frank Thorne of Cerne Abbas each brought significant benefits. Their bus routes went where Bere Regis & District had never reached before, upstream from Dorchester along the Cerne and Frome valleys. Whitty had only one stage service, but his garage at 7 Bridport Road, Dorchester, became Bere Regis & District's main focus of operations. Within a very short time this moved the firm's centre of gravity away from Bere Regis, the village where Reg Toop continued to hold sway for the rest of his life.

Bill Ironside, who used to live in a wooden bungalow on the Winfrith-Lulworth road, married Marjorie Louise Primrose Whiffen in 1942. They were able to move into the bungalow on Whitty's old premises, and it

Timetables were drawn up in August 1942 for newly acquired bus routes serving the Piddle valley. Maybe the army asked for the weekend evening workings to Piddlehinton Camp to be cancelled to keep the troops in camp as D-Day approached in 1944.

BERE REGIS and DISTRICT MOTOR SERVICES

(*Proprietors* :—R. Toop, W. Ironside, P. Davis)

4, North Street, Bere Regis, WAREHAM, Dorset.	7, Bridport Road, DORCHESTER, Dorset.
'Phone : Bere Regis 56.	'Phone : Dorchester 79.

ALTERATIONS TO TIME TABLES
Commencing August 1st, 1942.

Dorchester—Charminster—Stratton—Frampton

Wednesdays only.

		a.m.	p.m.	p.m.	p.m.
Dorchester	(dep.)	9.40	12.45	3. 0	5. 0
Charminster	...	—	12.53	3. 8	5. 8
Bradford	...	—	12.57	3.12	5.12
Stratton	...	9.50	1. 0	3.15	5.15
Grimstone	...	9.55	1. 5	3.20	5.20
Frampton	(arr.)	10. 0	1.15	3.30	5.30
		a.m.	p.m.	p.m.	p.m.
Frampton	(dep.)	10. 0	1.15	3.30	5.50
Grimstone	...	10. 5	1.20	3.35	5.55
Stratton	...	10.10	1.25	3.40	6. 0
Bradford	...	10.15	1.30	3.45	6. 5
Charminster	...	10.20	1.35	3.50	6.10
Dorchester	(arr.)	10.30	1.45	4. 0	6.20

Fridays only.

		p.m.	p.m.
Dorchester	(dep.)	12.45	3.30
Burton	...		
Charminster	...	12.50	3.35
Bradford	...	12.55	3.40
Stratton	...	1. 0	3.45
Grimstone	...	1. 5	3.50
Frampton	(arr.)	1.15	4. 0
		a.m.	p.m.
Frampton	(dep.)	10. 0	1.15
Grimstone	...	10. 5	1.20
Stratton	...	10.10	1.25
Bradford	...	10.20	1.35
Charminster	...	10.25	1.40
Burton	...		
Dorchester	(arr.)	10.30	1.45

Saturdays only.

		a.m.	p.m.	p.m.	p.m.	p.m.	p.m.
Dorchester	(dep.)	9.40	12.45	3. 0	4. 0	5. 0	8. 0
Charminster	...	—	12.55	3.10	4.10	5.10	8.10
Bradford	...	—	1. 0	3.15	4.15	5.15	8.15
Stratton	...	9.50	1. 5	3.20	4.20	5.20	8.20
Grimstone	...	9.55	1.10	3.25	4.25	5.25	8.25
Frampton	(arr.)	10. 0	1.15	3.30	4.30	5.30	8.30
		a.m.	p.m.	p.m.	p.m.	p.m.	p.m.
Frampton	(dep.)	10. 0	1.15	3.30	4.30	5.50	8.30
Grimstone	...	10. 5	1.20	4.35	4.35	5.55	8.35
Stratton	...	10.15	1.25	3.40	4.40	6. 0	8.40
Bradford	...	10.20	1.30	3.45	4.45	6. 5	8.45
Charminster	...	10.25	1.40	3.55	4.55	6.15	8.55
Dorchester	(arr.)	10.30	1.45	4. 0	5. 0	6.20	9. 0

H. Ling Ltd., Printers, Dorchester.

Taking over Frank Whitty's business in 1942 provided Bere Regis & District with its Top o' Town premises in Dorchester as well as a bus service up the river Frome to Frampton.

was from there that he took charge of further acquisitions. Primrose helped out in the office and on occasions she would drive a 20-seat bus.

Whitty had only gained his Monday-Saturday Dorchester-Frampton route in 1939, from Mrs R.L. Platt. She had taken it over in 1937 from Bertie Cox, who had plied the road and called in at the villages either side of it since 1925. It was still called Cox's Motor Bus Service until Bere Regis & District acquired it.

Frank Thorne had run a motor bus between Dorchester and Cerne Abbas for nigh on 30 years. He was so well entrenched on the route that he persuaded the Traffic Commissioner in 1937 to have Southern National withdraw a competing service. In the 1930s Wilfred Yearsley's Abbot's Cernel Bus Service covered the same road, continuing northwards to Minterne Magna on Wednesdays. His wife took over the licence in 1938, but ceased operation when war broke out, so Thorne ran his bus to Minterne Magna in her stead. Before the war he also ran through to Weymouth on summer Thursdays. This facility was suspended during the war, but Bere Regis & District revived it in 1949.

A matter of months after expanding northwards from Dorchester the firm reached out to the southwest of the county town, and then to the northeast. In June 1942 it took over Edgar Markey's Winterbourne Abbas to Dorchester service, which dated from 1925. It ran four days a week, via Winterbourne Steepleton and Martinstown. This was not a heavily populated area, but once more it was new territory, and it was Bere Regis & District's first thrust out towards Bridport. Back in the 1920s there had been another bus on this road, run by Charles H. Ralph, of the Brewer's Arms in Martinstown, but he pulled out soon after a hearing with the Traffic Commissioner in 1931.

In September 1942, just three months after Markey's service was absorbed, there was a much more substantial purchase, in the opposite direction, Lewis Sprackling's Ivory Coaches, based at Winterborne Stickland. This gave the firm a foothold in Blandford Forum, to which Percy Davis had run a weekly market bus until 1936. Sprackling, who also used the catchy title 'Milton Abbas and Stickland Motor Services' for his stage bus operations, had started out with a lorry-bus in 1916. He took over the two bus services of T.K. Bower's Milton Abbas Motors in about 1930. These ran to Blandford and Dorchester, each of them three days a week.

Lewis Sprackling's Ivory Coaches, of Winterborne Stickland, was the biggest concern that Bere Regis & District took over in the 1940s. Four vehicles came with the business, including Harrington-bodied Leyland Cub ATB772.
OMNIBUS SOCIETY, RYAN CARPENTER

over this operation in about March 1942. He was then ready to sell the rest of his passenger business to Bere Regis & District, but he held on to his freight activities until after the war, when they passed to South West United Haulage Ltd. Sprackling retained his haulage depot at Winterborne Stickland, so Bere Regis & District initially used separate premises from which to run the Milton Abbas services.

After the war Blandford Camp held a large number of National Service conscripts, so there was heavy demand for express services to convey them on weekend leave to many parts of the country. This was work that Bere Regis & District took on eagerly, and was vigorously protective of it when Wilts & Dorset competed for the business.

R. Lovell started the two routes in 1915, and they passed to Bower around 1927.

Between 1931 and 1939 Sprackling also ran a bus from Winterborne Stickland and Milton Abbas to Bere Regis, timed so his passengers could catch one of the big companies' buses to Weymouth or Bournemouth. Besides Bower's Milton Abbas Motors he also absorbed the Winterborne Stickland-Blandford service of E.H. Lyne; though based in Tarrant Rushton, Lyne had acquired this from R.J. Vacher (not thought to be directly related to George), but he must have found such a route tiresome and uneconomic to run from his base the opposite side of Blandford.

As it happened Reginald was not the first Toop to run a motor bus (of sorts) along part of the road from Milton Abbas to Dorchester. In 1911 Miss Ada Toop's Daimler carrier's van ran between Milborne St Andrew and the county town. Local memory has it that the Daimler was piloted by a retired steam-roller driver.

The vast complex of Blandford Camp, which lay on the downland to the east of the town, offered lucrative opportunities to a bus operator. Wilts & Dorset Motor Services Ltd notwithstanding, Sprackling conveyed workmen between the town and the camp in the early part of the war. However, the Salisbury company took

Even by the standards of the time Lewis Sprackling had a very mixed fleet. TK1024 was a Dennis to which he fitted a Garner radiator. It was new to T.K. Bower of Milton Abbas, whose business passed to Sprackling in about 1930, but he only kept it until 1934.　IRONSIDE FAMILY

With expansion into new territory, at the top end of the Winterborne valley, it was decided to have a new range of tickets. Printed by the Bell Punch Company, they were titled 'Bere Regis & District Motor Services' and listed three telephone numbers: Bere Regis 56, Dorchester 79, and Milton Abbas 224, the last being the exchange for Winterborne Stickland.

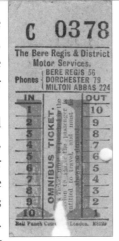

The tickets were all printed on the same block, but in different colours for each value, with the fare and the letter R for returns overprinted in red or green. On issuing a ticket the driver or conductor would punch a hole against a number that represented the stage at which the passenger boarded. Each ticket bore a serial number to keep a tally of how many were issued to passengers. It was said that Primrose Ironside sometimes extracted one ticket from the middle of a pack before passing it to the conductor at the start of his shift, so she could check whether he noticed the gap between serial numbers.

By the end of 1942 Bere Regis & District had come by around 36 more buses and coaches from different parts of England and Scotland. A dozen or so of these had come from the small concerns that had been absorbed. Now the partners could dispose of some of their most work-weary vehicles.

Besides Blandford Camp another major source of traffic during the war, and indeed for the rest of the firm's life, was Bovington Camp on the south Dorset heathland, part of Thomas Hardy's Egdon Heath. It was here that T.E. Lawrence enlisted in the tank corps in 1925 to put behind him his role in World War I as Lawrence of Arabia.

Alan Bailey, whose home in Winterborne Kingston lay midway between the two camps,

George Caundle gave up his Puddletown – Dorchester service in about 1943. Thirty years earlier he stood proudly by his first motor bus in the yard of the White Hart Hotel in Dorchester. FX1636 was a 28/36hp Daimler with a grey body, probably built locally.

NORMAN WYATT

TIME TABLE. Revised July, 1937.

TIME TABLE

Leaves PUDDLETOWN	a.m.	p.m.				Leaves DORCHESTER		p.m.		
Mondays	10.0					Mondays	12.30			
Tuesdays	10.0					Tuesdays	12.30			
Wednesdays	10.0	2.0	5.30			Wednesdays	12.30	3.30	6.15	
Thursdays	10.0					Thursdays	12.30			
Fridays	10.0	2.0				Fridays	12.30	3.30		
Saturdays	10.0	2.0	4.50	6.0	8.0	Saturdays	12.30	3.30	5.20	7.30
							9.0			

FARE CHART

PUDDLETOWN to
- 2d. Troytown
- 3d. 1d. Bockhampton-Kingston
- 4d. 2d. 1d. Stinsford
- 6d. 4d. 3d. 2d. Dorchester

Return Fare 1/-

DORCHESTER to
- 2d. Stinsford
- 3d. 1d. Kingston, Bockhampton
- 4d. 2d. 1d. Troytown
- 6d. 4d. 3d. 2d. Puddletown

Children 3 to 12 years Half-price.

Later Service on " Special Occasions " by arrangement.

OPEN & CLOSED PRIVATE HIRE CARS

G. CAUNDLE
Weatherbury Garage
Puddletown
PHONE 11.

EXCURSION & PRIVATE COACH
PARTIES CATERED FOR.

PASSENGER & GOODS STAGE
SERVICE TO DORCHESTER.

The Fare chart on George Caundle's 1937 timetable shows that he passed through the heart of Hardy country on his way into Dorchester.

believes they were Reg Toop's best money-spinner. 'He got contracts from both of them for taking troops on leave to London, Birmingham and I think other destinations, or embarkation. I am pretty sure that is how afterwards he could start buying new vehicles.'

In about 1943 George James Caundle withdrew his Puddletown-Dorchester bus. He had inherited the carrier service along this road from his father in 1907, and bought his first motor in 1913. One of his coaches was known as The Puddle Queen, and he ran extra journeys to Tolpuddle when required, for example for the centenary of the Tolpuddle Martyrs in 1934.

Caundle's withdrawal left Bere Regis & District as the main independent on his old route. Puddletown folk could also choose to travel into Dorchester with one of three big companies; Hants & Dorset, Southern National and Wilts & Dorset all passed that way on long distance services between Weymouth and Bournemouth or Salisbury. Bere Regis took over a couple of Caundle's vehicles, but did not absorb the business itself. However, it did start running to a similar timetable and also applied

after the war to renew Caundle's former tours licences. One of his drivers joined the firm, and later on manned the petrol pumps at 7 Bridport Road.

There were no more takeovers in 1943, but it was time to consolidate the gains of the past three years, and there was an urgent need for more buses to fulfil all the wartime contracts the firm had won. By the end of the year it had assembled a collection of around 40 vehicles of no less than 14 different chassis makes. Leyland, Bedford, Gilford, Dodge, Commer, Star, Guy, Dennis, AEC, Albion, Thornycroft, Morris, Chevrolet and Ford were all represented.

Bere Regis & District does not seem to have suffered too heavily from war damage. However Ray Applin, who was a lad in Bere Regis at the time, said some of its vehicles were used by the Royal Air Force at Warmwell airfield. 'I remember ... these buses coming back from Warmwell that were painted green, like camouflage, and I assume the windows were blanked out with tin or metal or something, and they had bullet holes in them, and they used to come back to be repaired.' He added: 'They were

The wartime bus fleet included a couple of Albions that came from Scottish Motor Traction in 1941. Before it was scrapped in 1954 Albion Victor VD6298, the younger of the two, was dumped at the back of Bere Regis depot.
PSV CIRCLE, ROBERT GRIEVES

on a coach on its way to pick up the evening load, and, despite the care with which our driver picked his course, expected at any minute to find that we had been shot through the roof.'

He said that despite the variety of vehicles in the fleet 'a very high standard has been maintained in rolling stock.' Following the acquisitions of 1942 there were now three principal garages, Bere Regis, Dorchester and Winterborne Stickland, and a number of buses were kept overnight in outlying dormy sheds. In fact many spent the night outside their drivers' homes.

Reg's buses. I assume they were commandeered or he used to rent them out.'

Two Spitfire squadrons, 152 and 609, were based at RAF Warmwell at the time of the Battle of Britain. On 25 August 1940 the Luftwaffe attacked the airfield, as well as Portland Dockyard and Weymouth. Warmwell suffered only minor damage, but this might have included any Bere Regis buses on site.

Bill Ironside was more reserved about letting the military have their way with his buses. John Woodsford, who joined Bere Regis as a youthful conductor in 1944, said one of its best vehicles at the time was a 1939 Dodge – FTU149, which came from a firm in Runcorn in 1940. It was kept for part of the war behind the closed doors of a garage on Charles Street, Dorchester, minus its engine, 'so that it would not be commandeered'. At the time the company had nearly a dozen of these little brown Dodge coaches.

The state of the roads evidently took its toll on the buses. In *Modern Transport* Bruce Maund observed that: 'The buses have had to stand up to very hard work, a number of the contract jobs involving passage through areas used by the army for tank training, with the result that roads are sometimes barely discernible. We travelled

Just before the war Bob Bailey, who ran the bakery in Winterborne Kingston with his brother Eddie, had built a chalet beside the Bere Regis road to serve as a teahouse for passing motorists. In wartime it became home to a Mr and Mrs Joliffe, who had been obliged to move out of London. Reginald Joliffe drove a bus for Bere Regis & District, a 20-seat Dodge whose first owner was an Isle of Man concern. Alan Bailey said JPK518 spent its nights in his family's paddock: 'I think it was used mainly for school runs. Starting up its noisy but reliable engine was probably what helped me and my sister to wake up.'

Like bus concerns across the country, Bere Regis & District felt the pinch of vehicle shortages. Reg Toop told Bob Bailey, whose bakery van he often saw doing the rounds of the villages, how his own buses had once nearly mown him down as he tried to hail them on the highway. Four coaches had gone to London one weekend with a full complement of soldiers, returning empty to Dorset. Alan Bailey takes up the story: 'After they had gone some problem meant he needed to reuse one of them as soon as possible. There was no way of directly contacting the drivers, so he went some way

A couple of Gilford 168OTs from Lincolnshire Road Car Company found their way to Bere Regis during the war. Strachan-bodied VO3963, new to a Lincolnshire independent in 1930, only lasted a few months with the Dorset firm and ended its days as a caravan.   ALAN DUKE

towards London to waylay them.' (There were no mobile phones in those days, nor tachographs or restrictions on hours at the wheel). So Reg Toop 'stood by the side of the road and waved the first two down, but the drivers either did not see him or ignored him. So for the following two he stood in the middle of the road. They did not stop either and he just managed to jump into the hedge in time.'

When he spoke to the drivers later on 'they were able to plead that they had rigorously obeyed the black-out rules.'

Wartime production of new buses was controlled by the Ministry of Supply, and vehicles were allotted to operators by the Ministry of War Transport. Given Bere Regis & District's contribution to the transport of troops and workers at military construction projects, it might have been in order for the concern to receive a handful of utility Bedford OWB 32-seaters. However, the partnership never took delivery of a new vehicle until November 1945, when four of the peacetime version of these little buses joined the fleet. By then wartime restrictions had eased and their bodies had a more curvaceous profile than the box-like

version which was all that was available whilst hostilities lasted.

In August 1944 two of these utility buses, with their wooden-slatted seats and 'lobster-back' roof profile, did come Bere Regis & District's way (ATK857 and BFX32). They were little more than a year old when they were passed on by Sheasby's of Corfe Castle (South Dorset Coaches). The transfer of this pair of Bedfords, together with a prewar Leyland Tiger that had been new to a Nottingham coach firm (EAL239), may have had something to do with the contracts that Percy Davis was managing on the Isle of Purbeck. In postwar years Bere Regis & District bought quite a few of the utility Bedford OWBs that had seen service elsewhere in England or in Northern Ireland.

Meanwhile in the run-up to D-Day the military needed so many extra buses that on top of every vehicle Bere Regis could lay its hands on it still needed more. There was a Leyland TS4 coach (WM7930), lurking in the yard at Winterborne Stickland with no cab, glass missing from its windows and so derelict that Bere Regis & District had ignored it when it took over Ivory Coaches in 1942. However, its engine

Wartime restrictions only permitted one type of single-deck to be built, the Bedford OWB. DHR 201 was a typical example. It was new in 1943 to Lampard's Garage of Pewsey, Wiltshire, but came to Bere Regis & District in 1947 via Wakes of Sparkford, Somerset, and kept going another seven years.   A.M. WRIGHT

Vale. It took over Mrs Emma Lugg's market services from Hazelbury Bryan on 1 June 1944. Her late husband Gilbert bought the business in 1919 from Edwin Drake. Lugg's bus, named 'Girl Pat' in memory of a trawler of that name that foundered off the Dorset coast, went to Dorchester two days a week, passing through Pulham, Duntish, Mappowder and Buckland Newton before heading down the Piddle Valley to market.

Girl Pat also made fortnightly market trips to Yeovil, to Sherborne and to Sturminster Newton, which had a busy cattle market every other week. There was a Saturday afternoon journey to Yeovil too, so villagers could go to the cinema there. Reaching out to Yeovil meant that for the first time a regular Bere Regis bus service crossed into Somerset. Lugg contributed

started first time, and Jimmy Musselwhite, from the Bere Regis workshop, hastily constructed a cab and glazed the windows. It was pressed into service to convey the kit of American servicemen encamped at Guy's Marsh, near Shaftesbury.

British, American and Canadian troops took ship, or flat-bottomed landing craft, from the south coast to the Normandy beaches. There had been some 80,000 American troops in Dorset. The U.S. 1st Division, known as the Big Red One, embarked from Weymouth and Portland Harbours. Hundreds of Americans spent the days running up to 6 June in wooded troop concentration areas near the coast. No doubt with such deployment in mind, the Wilts & Dorset timetable carried the warning that its Weymouth service 'is liable to alteration during June, 1944.'

Just before D-Day Bere Regis & District made its own modest foray into new territory, northwards into the Blackmore

Leyland TS8 Tiger EAL239, with stylish Harrington coachwork, lasted longer than most of the wartime acquisitions. New in 1938 to Robin Hood Coaches of Nottingham, the War Department requisitioned it in 1940. Later it passed to Sheasby's of Corfe Castle, thence to Bere Regis. It was still working with a metal destination plate thrust into the radiator grille in 1956.   DAVID PENNELS

Three of Alfred Pitcher's early buses carried the same body one after the other. In 1920 it was fitted to American-built Federal FX5203. When Pitcher sold out to Bere Regis & District, an elderly Morris was the only bus involved in the deal.
© DORSET COUNTY MUSEUM

school contracts and excursion licences as well, and from then on Bere Regis & District always kept a handful of its buses at Hazelbury Bryan, parked in the entrance to a field. By 1946 there was a bus on the Hazelbury Bryan-Dorchester service every weekday.

On New Year's Day 1945, six months after it secured a base at Hazelbury Bryan, the firm reached across to the eastern fringe of the Blackmore Vale when it took over Charles Fripp's bus service at Okeford Fitzpaine. Fripp, who once kept the village pub and also had a garage business, ran a market bus to Blandford and to Sturminster Newton. He too held excursion licences, which would be revived once the war was over.

Two more small independents were absorbed in 1944-45, George Churchill of Puncknowle, and Alfred Pitcher of Litton Cheney. This strengthened the firm's hold on

the area southwest of Dorchester. Churchill had run to Bridport six days a week, and Pitcher to Dorchester on Wednesdays and Saturdays. Both also contributed excursion licences.

Churchill and Pitcher had each spent a lifetime as carriers, taking people and their produce to market from the villages on the hills that lie between the Dorchester-Bridport road and the English Channel. Churchill's family had been in the carrier business since at least the 1870s. He took over in 1907 and bought his first motor bus in 1920. Pitcher, whose own early memories are described in Chapter 1, bought his first motor in about 1911.

Absorbing these two concerns gave Bere Regis & District the opportunity to combine vehicle economy with the provision of a new through service between Dorchester and Bridport. It ran on Wednesdays and Saturdays, calling at Long Bredy, Litton

Cheney, Puncknowle and Swyre. Bruce Maund wrote in *Modern Transport*: 'The new facility was greatly welcomed and much difficulty was experienced on the first day of operation in handling the traffic offering, which was far beyond expectations.'

John Woodsford, who learned to drive soon after he joined the firm, remembers going with Bill Ironside to fetch Pitcher's elderly Morris 14-seater (TK4857) and bring it back to Dorchester. 'You had to swing the starter handle to get the engine to turn. It started all right, but once I was a little way up the road it stalled. I didn't know where he was or how to start it.' Bere Regis & District did not use it as a bus, but John used to drive it to pick up spare parts that came by rail to Wareham. It had a calf box at the rear, a tailboard and wide doors for loading goods. On one occasion, driving through Tolpuddle, the doors flew open and a load of tyres rolled out on to the road.

Woodsford, who came from Alton Pancras, at the head of the Piddle valley, said Bill Ironside took him on as a conductor after he recovered from serious illness in 1944. He earned £2 a week, out of which he had to pay for his lodging in Dorchester. Of this two shillings and sixpence (12.5 pence) went to his mother for her to do his washing. His father was a strict trade unionist (Alton Pancras is not 10 miles upriver from Tolpuddle), so he joined a union at first, but when he tried to claim sickness benefit, the union refused because he had not paid his dues. In any case Bere Regis & District did not recognise any trade union, so there were no restrictions about hours. Asked about overtime, he laughed as though the very idea was a good joke. The legal minimum age for driving a bus was 21, but John said he was already behind the wheel at 18, mostly driving buses but also delivering parcels by van.

By the time Germany surrendered in May 1945, Bere Regis & District had earned enough from wartime contracts to fund expansion of its services and the purchase of new vehicles over the next few years. The little fleet of 20 vehicles had more than doubled to around 45. All those acquisitions meant there were fewer potential competitors, and the ongoing presence of the military in substantial camps dotted about the Dorset countryside would continue to contribute substantially to revenue for years to come.

Once people could put their wartime worries behind them a party from Dorset paid a visit to the Houses of Parliament. Glen Willcox drove them there in a Bere Regis coach, Duple-bodied Leyland TS7 Tiger CKO224, which was acquired from a London firm in 1946.

4
REG TOOP'S AMBITION

BERE REGIS & DISTRICT had risen so well to wartime challenges that it emerged with substantial gains. Its buses now covered a much more extensive network of routes across a large part of Dorset and it had more than doubled the size of its fleet. It had gained considerable experience of contract operations, and built up a useful portfolio of properties. It kept up the momentum over the rest of the 1940s while Britain was emerging from wartime austerity. The big challenge to the bus industry of growing car ownership still lay in the future.

Between 1946 and 1948 five more local bus concerns were taken over. This reinforced the Bere Regis hold on the Blackmore Vale, whence Tess of the d'Urbervilles began her tragic adventures in Thomas Hardy's novel. The first big peacetime move to consolidate the territorial gains came in 1946 when the partners applied successfully to extend Frank Thorne's old Dorchester-Cerne Abbas route northwards to Sherborne, despite opposition from Southern National. Though it lost out this time, the big company was allowed later on to reintroduce its summer service between Yeovil and Weymouth.

Bere Regis & District joined up routes that it had absorbed so that many villagers gained a more frequent bus service that gave them a choice of town in which to do their shopping. Within a short time there were through services from Dorchester to Yeovil via the Piddle Valley, to Sturminster Newton via Hazelbury Bryan and to Bridport via Puncknowle. There was also a direct link between Sturminster Newton and Yeovil, using various routes to allow more villages to be served at different times.

For more than a year after Charles Fripp sold out, his three market services from Okeford Fitzpaine carried on unchanged: to Blandford on Thursdays, Sturminster Newton on alternate Mondays, and Shaftesbury on Thursdays. The

Bill Ironside was listed first among the partners when the Sherborne service was announced in January 1947. He was in charge at Dorchester, by then steadily gaining ground over rural Bere Regis as the centre of operations.

Bere Regis church tower dates from about 1500, the two garage sheds in front of it from 1948. They boosted the capacity of Reg Toop's pre-war bus depot, and sandwiched the Methodist chapel between old and new sheds. The exit to West Street is just off to the left of this 1963 aerial view. Houses and a car park now occupy the site.

WESTERN GAZETTE

locals wanted better facilities, especially in the villages of East and West Orchard, which were on the roundabout Shaftesbury route. Hants & Dorset and Southern National both objected to Bere Regis & District's original proposals, but two regular daily services were introduced on 1 April 1946: Blandford-Okeford Fitzpaine-Woolland and Woolland-Shaftesbury via Sturminster Newton and the two Orchards. In Shaftesbury, known to many for the picturesque image of Gold Hill, the brown buses now reached within a mile of the Wiltshire border.

The main garage was still at Bere Regis, where all repairs could be dealt with except major engine overhauls. There were similar facilities at Frank Whitty's old premises in Dorchester, and running repairs and general maintenance could also be carried out at Winterborne Stickland.

Bruce Maund wrote in *Modern Transport* that the fleet had grown so much that the

Bere Regis premises, with their narrow access between nos. 32 and 33 West Street, no longer filled the bill. It was intended to erect new buildings as soon as conditions allowed. A new garage with pits was built in 1948 behind the Methodist Church, which stood beside the old sheds. The office was farther down the street.

The most important new site was at 7 Bridport Road, Dorchester, where Bill Ironside held sway. There Bere Regis fitters carried out maintenance and repair work for both the firm's own vehicles and those of other local concerns, a sideline that added neatly to the earnings. When Norman House, who ran Mid-Dorset Coaches of Hilton, fell ill in the very busy days towards the end of the war, they helped to keep his buses on the road, a favour that his family remembered many years later.

Outside contractors painted the Bere Regis wings that had been copied from the

Dodge radiator. The job took three hours and cost £7.10s (£7.50). The price also included the legal lettering that every bus had to display on the lower nearside panelling. At one time all the moulding was removed when vehicles were being repainted. If painters were pushed for time a bus would be given a quick rub down when it came off the road, then painted up until two o'clock at night so it was back on the road in the morning. Often it was the drivers who painted the buses when they were not needed behind the wheel. It was said that you could always tell where a Bere Regis driver lived because he had a brown front door.

In November 1945 the firm's first ever batch of brand new buses was delivered, a quartet of Bedford OB saloons (BJT168-171). They had 32-seat bodies by Duple of Hendon, which was to become one of the principal coachbuilders used by Bere Regis & District. Up until the early 1950s the OB became the chosen workhorse of small bus and coach concerns across Britain, usually in its 29-seat coach version. Altogether the Luton factory turned out 12,693 OB chassis, which cost just over £500 apiece. Over the next few years Bere Regis & District built up a substantial fleet of this type, together with a sprinkling of the box-like wartime OWBs. In 1949/50 three of these were completely refurbished more or less to OB standard and rebodied by Lee Motor Bodies of Bournemouth.

In 1946 the first double-decks joined the fleet, a pair of 10-year-old Leyland Titans which came from Chester Corporation (AFM518/9), via a dealer in the Midlands. They were the first Bere Regis buses to have diesel engines. Alan Bailey remembers that some of the villagers at Winterborne Kingston had never seen a double-deck before and these buses, towering above the hedges along narrow country lanes, caused quite a stir.

They proved invaluable on busy journeys to Poole. Ten years later AFM519 could still carry a full load the 16 miles from Poole to Bere Regis at an average speed of more than 23 miles an hour. The double decks also ran between Dorchester and Piddlehinton Camp on Saturday evenings, when 1,100 soldiers had a break from square-bashing and headed for the bright lights in town.

Quite a few buses were needed for this job even though, so long as the police were not

Bedford OWB GXD642 was new in 1943. It came to Dorset three years later after government service at Bletchley Park in Buckinghamshire, where the German Enigma code was deciphered. In the 1950s this bus was rebuilt to full front layout by Vaile of Hazelbury Bryan.
BRIAN JACKSON COLLECTION

Four Bedford OBs with Duple saloon bodies were the partnership's first ever new buses, delivered in November 1945. BJT168, parked at the back of Bere Regis depot, was the first of them.   DAVID PENNELS

looking, 50 soldiers could be packed into a 32-seat single-decker. John Woodsford used to act as conductor, boarding each bus as it began its circuit round the camp, issuing a pink one shilling and threepenny (6.25p) return ticket to each soldier, then jumping off as the bus left the camp and leaping on to the next one to repeat the process. Some more savvy and agile young squaddies walked from camp up Waterston Hill, where they waited for the elderly double-decker to change down to second gear. There they hopped on to the open rear platform without paying; in those days police in rural Dorset had better things to do of a Saturday evening than check

The first double-decks, a pair of Leyland TD5 Titans from Chester Corporation, arrived early in 1946. Their highbridge bodies by Massey of Wigan were a foot taller than three deckers that followed in 1948, hence more prone to argue with overhanging branches. AFM519 rests at Bere Regis on 10 March 1956 after returning from Poole.

DAVID PENNELS

Lee Motors of Bournemouth rebodied and reregistered more than a dozen Bedford chassis for West Country operators between 1948 and 1950. DJT806, an OWB from Staffordshire, was the first of three for Bere Regis & District. It still frequented Fire Station Yard in Dorchester after it passed to W.J. Willcox of Litton Cheney in 1956.

DAVID PENNELS

whether an overcrowded 52-seater was carrying the regulation conductor.

On the more urban route to Poole, where double-decks were used at busy times, it was quite another story. On weekend nights the driver of the 10.30 bus back to Bere Regis always waited for the show to finish at the Regent cinema so he would not leave homeward-bound filmgoers stranded in town. Sometimes there were as many as 90 of them squeezed into one of the hard-worked Leyland Titans. The rear

platform scraped the road as the bus swung round the corner over Fleets Bridge, and the conductress clung on tight to stop unsteady passengers tumbling off.

What Bere Regis & District did not know, at first, was that a Hants & Dorset inspector would hide in the George Hotel to watch for overloading. Passengers sat on the floor to avoid being spotted, but if he saw that too many were aboard he tipped off his brother, who was a motorcycle policeman.

Local people were loyal to the firm and generally preferred to travel with Bere Regis & District, whose timings were more convenient and fares lower than Hants & Dorset's. Gordon Day, who used to catch the bus at Lytchett Matravers, said there were no bus stops. Riding on a single-deck, 'if you wanted to get off you'd get up and walk down the coach. The driver would ask if this was OK, and you said 'yes' and got off.' Of an evening he would walk out with a hurricane lamp to see someone off on Toopy's bus: 'Waiting at Hall's Corner in Lytchett you'd hear the Bedford coming round the corner in second gear.'

A few months after the two double-decks a dozen brand new Bedford OB-Duple Vista coaches arrived. They emitted a characteristic wail when driving in low gear. The firm also bought a mixed bag of 10 second- or third-hand buses from Valliant Direct Coaches Ltd, of Ealing, whose directors were G.R. and W.D. Valli. These vehicles were

(above) Five coaches and four buses came from Valliant Direct Coaches of Ealing in 1946, including Plaxton-bodied Leyland TS8 Tiger LMG734, which gave Bere Regis & District another 14 years' service.
DAVID PENNELS

(left) BPR401 was one of the dozen Bedford OB-Duple Vista coaches that arrived new in 1946. All of them lasted at least 12 years, and this one survived in service until 1959, a year after it was photographed in the yard at Dorchester.
DAVID PENNELS

no longer needed for contract operations in the London area. They included a pair of Leyland Lion saloons, new to Eastbourne Corporation in 1939 and requisitioned on the outbreak of war. While with Valliant they were given Middlesex registrations, LME131 and LME394.

In March 1946 the one-bus operation of Ernest John Bale of Owermoigne was taken over. His little red Morris 14-seater (TK7048) had been criss-crossing the river Frome since 1931, taking villagers from either side of Hardy's 'Vale of the Great Dairies' to market in Dorchester twice a week. On Thursdays it went to Wareham instead. Bale bought his first bus in 1925 after taking over his parents-in-law's carrier service between Hurst and Dorchester. He moved to Owermoigne in 1938.

In December 1946 a second Hazelbury Bryan concern was absorbed. Betsy Hannah Coombes & Son. The Coombes family, of whom Arthur Upshall reminisced (see chapter 1), had been in

the carrier business since 1890. After William Coombes died in 1928 his widow and their son Teddy continued the business, running to Dorchester, Sturminster Newton, Sherborne and Yeovil, on the same days as Gilbert Lugg's Girl Pat had done, but by different routes. Their Dorchester route took them over the hills to

Together with Betsy Hannah Coombes' Hazelbury Bryan services came a 1933 Bedford WLB 20-seater, AGH961. Lined up beside a 1945 OB and a wartime OWB, it shows how Duple body design evolved over the years.
IRONSIDE FAMILY

Taking over Vic Little's market day services from Marnhull in 1947 consolidated the partners' hold on the Blackmore Vale. The only vehicle involved was JT4745, a Heaver-bodied Commer PN4. It stayed in Dorset just a few months more. By the time it was photographed it belonged to Elms of Kenton, Middlesex.

J.C. GILLHAM

the east of the Piddle Valley, serving Melcombe Bingham and Cheselbourne. Bere Regis & District kept the Coombes' 1933 Bedford 20-seater (AGH961) on the road for another couple of years.

Four months later, in March 1947, the firm took over the licences of James E. Pickett of Buckland Newton. He had been running his bus service since about 1922, down the Piddle Valley to Dorchester most days of the week, to

Sherborne on Thursdays, and Weymouth on summer Fridays.

Yet another acquisition gave Bere Regis & District a base in the very heart of the Blackmore Vale, at Marnhull, in August 1947. Vic Little, who ran market services thence to Dorchester on Wednesdays and to Sturminster Newton on alternate Mondays, had taken over the business in 1945 from his old employer, Albert Trim. Trim started a taxi service in 1915 and bought his first bus in 1920, a Ford known as the Whiz-Bang. In the 1930s he also ran to Yeovil, Weymouth and Bournemouth. Little's bus was an unusual Commer with a 25-seat body built by the Wiltshire firm of Heaver (JT4745). It remained with Bere Regis & District for a year or so.

One more local concern came the partners' way in June 1948, that of Sidney Harmer of Milton Abbas, whose bus ran to Dorchester and Blandford. In the 1930s Harmer competed with Sprackling's Ivory Coaches. It seems there was little love lost between the two, who shared the road between Milborne St Andrew and Dorchester with Wilts & Dorset's Salisbury-Weymouth bus. Sprackling wrote to Wilts & Dorset in 1936 complaining that Harmer had 'omitted to operate the Tuesday service from April 30th to Oct 8th last year,' and he was bringing back passengers from Dorchester late on Saturdays. 'How does this stand, certainly he has no [licence for a] late service on Saturdays, therefore he has no business to be operating one, what are you doing about it, I should like to know, so far he has

YG710 was 16 years old when Bere Regis bought it in February 1948. For a few months it ran to Poole; it stands at the stop on Kingland Road in June that year. This Leyland TD2 was new to Ripponden & District in Yorkshire, and spent 10 years with Western Scottish Motor Traction before coming south.

ALAN CROSS

Once newer double-decks arrived YG710 shed its old guise and reappeared with a second-hand Eastern Counties coach body and a more up-to-date CovRad radiator. It probably only ran a short while in this form.
OMNIBUS SOCIETY, ROY MARSHALL

Transport, said Reg Toop believed there was great scope for new bus services in Dorset. 'He envisages ultimately the establishment of daily services to practically every village in the area and the linking up of existing services to provide new facilities with connections to and from all parts of the county.' It was appreciated that some routes might never be very remunerative, but Toop believed in keeping the firm in the public eye and saw the bus services as important for establishing goodwill around the villages, especially given that private hire and contract work played so important a part in the business.

not applied for one.' Whether Wilts & Dorset responded or no, its reply would no doubt have been more circumspect.

Coombes, Pickett, Little and Harmer each ran excursions from their home villages, so now Bere Regis & District could combine this traffic from different places. As they brought together all the services they had inherited, the partners faced the challenge of balancing the provision of better facilities for passengers with the need to sustain the operation economically.

Bruce Maund, writing in *Modern*

Eight Maudslay Marathons delivered in 1947-48 were the first full-size coaches that Bere Regis bought new. CJT534 waits at Dorchester for the local run to Little Bredy, but these Whitson-bodied 33-seaters often ranged much farther afield.
DAVID PENNELS

The firm got its first new Leyland coach in February 1948. Santus of Wigan built the 33-seat coachwork on PS1/1 Tiger CJT 820. It is parked up at Chatham between weekend express journeys, next to an old Salford Corporation bus of Kent Oil Refinery.
PM PHOTOGRAPHY

Whether Bill Ironside fully shared these views at the time does not appear to have been recorded.

Describing the firm's timetables and other publicity Maund said the aim was to keep it simple for 'it has been found that the agricultural community is not, as a rule, well versed in the reading of timetables.' If farming folk do indeed suffer from this lamentable disability, they surely share it with many in other walks of life.

New vehicles were still hard to come by in 1947 and 1948, but in each of these years around 20 buses and coaches joined the fleet, many of them older machines which had seen some years' service in other parts of the country. However, between November 1947 and February 1948 Bere Regis & District took delivery of its first nine brand new 33-seat coaches. All but one of these were Coventry-built Maudslay Marathons with bodies by the Middlesex firm of James Whitson (CJT533-540). The other was a Leyland Tiger bodied by Santus of Wigan (CJT820).

In 1945 Reg Toop planned to order a dozen diesel-engined AEC Regal coaches, but this was not to be. There was huge post-war demand for new buses, many of them for export. Just one Regal materialised, and not until 1950. DTK747 had Duple-style coachwork by Lee Motors of Bournemouth.

PM PHOTOGRAPHY

Whilst these coaches gave good service, they fell short of what Reg Toop hoped for. After interviewing him for *Modern Transport* in 1945, Bruce Maund wrote: 'The future programme envisages a fleet of some 72 vehicles, of which 36 will be buses with diesel engines and the remainder coaches. It is intended to replace buses after three years. As a first stage, an order has been placed for 12 oil-engined AEC Regals.'

Over the years the fleet included a number of this type, but in the event only one was ever delivered new, and that not until 1950 (DTK747). Like all vehicle builders in the early post-war years the AEC works at Southall in Middlesex struggled to meet all the needs of bus operators desperate to modernise their war-weary fleets. In addition a high proportion of Regals built in the early post-war years went for export.

The intense pressure on coachbuilders to meet the huge postwar demand for new vehicles meant that some used unseasoned timber ; metal-framed bodies were not yet the norm. When the timber started to dry out this led to problems. Over the next few years several second-hand Leyland Tigers were acquired from Lancashire operators. The ones with Santus

bodies had large detachable rear mudguards which were reputed to be tiresome to repair.

In the late 1940s Glen Willcox was driving a Leyland Tiger that was in collision at Organford Cross with another coach. He had been made garage foreman at Bere Regis when he returned from war service, and also acted as driver and courier on long-distance private hire journeys. The compensation he received as a result of the accident enabled him to join the small coach business of Cyril Darch, of Martock in Somerset. Some 30 years later Darch & Willcox was merged with A Pearce & Co Ltd, of Cattistock, to become Pearce, Darch and Willcox Ltd, also known as Comfy-Lux.

The Maudslays gave Bere Regis 10 years' service or more, appearing from time to time on the Poole route. Some were modified to carry extra passengers – one eventually had 41 seats. They were also used on the important contract with the U.S. military to ferry American soldiers between Southampton Docks and Guy's Marsh, and thence to other camps around the country. The busiest time of year for this was June, and John Woodsford said there were sometimes fights between black and white soldiers. The demand was so great at times that coaches had

The big luggage container on the roof of EUJ57 proved useful for ferrying American troops and their baggage between Guy's Marsh and other camps. Other coaches had to be fitted with box-like containers for this work. This Mulliner-bodied Leyland PS1/1 Tiger was acquired in 1949 from J. Whittle & Son, of Shropshire.
OMNIBUS SOCIETY COLLECTION

to be hired from whatever other operator could make them available. On one occasion a 33-seat coach was so laden, with 50 troops and all their gear, that it had to be pushed up the steep hill into Shaftesbury.

Because the soldiers had so much kit, Cyril Vaile of Hazelbury Bryan was called upon to fit roof racks to some of the Maudslays. The load was so heavy that stanchions were needed inside the coaches to support the roof. Just one coach that was originally built with a sturdy luggage container on the roof joined the fleet in 1949, a year-old Leyland Tiger ex-J. Whittle & Son, of Highley, Shropshire (EUJ57).

Besides passengers the buses carried parcels too. Agents were appointed in the larger villages to handle this business. In the mid-1940s, while most packages were conveyed on the buses, a pair of Dodge vans were entirely devoted to the parcels service. Bruce Maund described this activity as being on a limited scale, but said it was intended to expand it when conditions were more favourable. His description perhaps did less than justice to the

variety of 'packages' that came John Woodsford's way, and no doubt that of other drivers.

They went to the station yard in Dorchester to pick up parcels to be delivered 'all over the place'. They might contain anything from Lipton's tea to car radiators being sent for repair. One man worked full time in the parcels department. One of the Dodge vans was used to deliver Red Ring flour in packs of half a dozen three-pound bags to shops around West Dorset, in Bridport and Sydling, as well as Lyme Regis and Charmouth, which were well beyond the reach of the firm's bus services. The bags of flour were kept in a shed at 7 Bridport Road to await delivery. On one occasion this led to considerable embarrassment. Bill Ironside had a black spaniel called Sam, who tore the bags to shreds whilst hunting rats.

Bedford was for many years the partners' chassis of choice, but they had very few pre-war models. ETX167, a Willmott-bodied WTB2, new in 1940 to R.S. Davies of Port Talbot, came to Bere Regis nine years later via Excelsior of Bournemouth.

K.A. JENKINSON

One day John Woodsford was asked to take 'a box' to Damers House in Dorchester, described as a Public Assistance Institution. The box turned out to be a coffin, and when John arrived at Damers he was asked to help lift a corpse into it. The undertaker gave him half a crown (12.5 pence) for the job. Another time he picked up a coffin and its accompanying mourners at Bere Heath to drive them to a funeral at Affpuddle Church. The 'hearse' was a brown van bearing the invitation 'Try our luxury tours'.

elderly rear-entrance bus. As he swung round a corner its malodorous load slithered down the steps and had to be recovered from the road.

Ray Applin has happier memories of the parcels service: 'As a kid I used to pick mushrooms on my grandfather's farm up at Milborne, and I could bring them home and go down to Mr Toop and say 'Can they take them into market?' The driver would say 'Yes, that's all right', and they'd take them in and get maybe seven and sixpence (37.5p) for them, which obviously came to me. I don't know what they

(left) Bere Regis drivers in the big city: John Woodsford and Bob Sprules take time off at London's Petticoat Lane before driving back to Dorset.
JOHN WOODSFORD

(above) Guy Vixen GPH925 waits outside the depot at 7 Bridport Road to work the Piddle Valley service to Hazelbury Bryan. The dark brown streamline panel over the rear wheel was earlier painted in the paler shade.
OMNIBUS SOCIETY, C.F. KLAPPER

One load he did refuse to carry. He was driving a Bere Regis bus from Sydling St Nicholas to Dorchester to help out a local man whose regular vehicle had broken down. Sydling was one place to which the firm never ran its own bus service. The villagers there were used to their bus taking a calf to market along with its human passengers, and saw no reason why Bere Regis should not do likewise. John said they became quite indignant when he refused.

The worst kind of package he had to handle was dog's meat wrapped in sacking. Once he was driving a load of this cargo on the floor of an

used to charge, sixpence or something.'

Eventually Bill Ironside decided to limit the parcels service. He told John Woodsford: 'I want people on the buses, not parcels.' However, packages could still be handed in for carriage on the bus at agents around the villages in the mid-1950s, and also at the firm's own booking and parcels offices at Dorchester, Poole, Wimborne, Bere Regis, Sherborne, Weymouth, Sturminster Newton and Blandford.

The firm's own business sometimes occasioned lengthy journeys in what seemed unlikely vehicles. John once towed a Bedford bus all the way from Manchester behind a little Dennis Ace. When the firm's one and only Guy bus 'dropped an engine' he was despatched to Wolverhampton in an Austin 7 van to pick up a new unit from the Guy Motors factory. Later he had to collect a new axle shaft for the same bus in a Morris van. As it happened he had been celebrating his brother's return from the army the night before, so his brother drove the van. The Guy (GPH925), inherited from Russell of Broadmayne in 1941, seems to have been prone to requiring special attention: it once collided with a US army truck at Grimstone, but the damage was repaired and it kept on working until 1950.

Working for Bill Ironside, besides driving, conducting, delivering parcels, cleaning and painting buses, you could also find yourself collecting gravel or parts of old army huts to be used for expanding the premises at 7 Bridport Road, where a builder's yard adjacent to Whitty's old site had been acquired. For this work Ironside bought an ex-U.S. Army GMC petrol tanker. He had its tank removed to store diesel, which was delivered from the Upton Oil Company in Poole. An ordinary lorry body was mounted on the chassis, and Jack Stacey and John Woodsford were despatched to Warmwell gravel pits to load up. While they were there the GMC did yeoman work hauling out other firms' trucks stuck at the bottom of the pit.

This lorry was no tipper, so not only did they have to load the gravel by hand

but they had to shovel it off when they returned to Dorchester. Another task was to collect parts of disused Nissen huts from a wood at Church Stanton, near Taunton. These were intended for building shelters on the Bridport Road site. The two men had great difficulty piloting the old American truck round the trees on the steep slope in the wood, especially with a full load of asbestos flooring.

Other ex-army lorries were bought to provide spare parts for the buses. When all the useful bits had been removed the remains were cut up and loaded on to a lorry and sold to a scrap merchant in Gloucestershire. Ironside gave strict instructions to the driver to collect the cheque in person: he concluded at first that the scrap merchant might be in financial difficulties, but then he saw that the cheque was made out to Mr Ironside himself, not to Bere Regis & District.

Lunch break at Bridport Road was a time to keep a low profile if Percy Davis was in town. If he could nab one of the drivers he would ask them to 'give Rosie a wash'. This was his favourite Dodge coach (ETD141), which came from Charlie's Cars of Bournemouth in 1941. It

Bere Regis parked its Bedford OBs on Sheep Market Hill in Blandford. BJT171 was one of four delivered in November 1945 with bus bodies by Duple. FAA243, with the more common 29-seat Duple Vista coach body, came from Hants & Sussex in 1949.

PSV CIRCLE, ROY MARSHALL

painted its coaches in a smart plum and cream livery, and for a while Percy refused to have it painted brown.

In the early post-war years, if word came that the Ministry of Transport was about to conduct an inspection, any vehicles in poor condition were driven out into the countryside. One year a Bedford OWB plunged over a hedge near the Sunray Inn at Osmington. For fear of bad publicity in the local press over the Easter break, and with the busy holiday weekend coming up, the bus was disguised beneath a hastily dismantled hayrick. At Martinstown a yet more bizarre fate is said to have consumed another Bere Regis bus, presumably a scrapped one: it was the bonfire on Guy Fawkes night.

By 1949 the network of bus routes reached its greatest extent. The timetable numbered them up to 35. Except on the double-decks the numbers hardly ever featured on the buses. Usually they showed no more than the final destination, often on a paper sticker in the windscreen or on a panel thrust into the radiator grille. As routes were withdrawn their numbers were assigned to those that remained, so that by 1971 the series only ran up to 20.

Bere Regis & District challenged Hants & Dorset by applying in October 1949 to run single- and double-decks between Blandford

In the summer of 1946 three Bere Regis drivers relax while their passengers enjoy the seaside at Weston-super-Mare: "Dapper" Hall with cigarette, Jack Toop, and Charles Ironside perched on the mudguard of Leyland Tiger LMG734.

IRONSIDE FAMILY

and Poole six days a week. The Bournemouth company objected and promptly put in its own rival application. In the event both were refused, probably with the intention of avoiding competition with the newly nationalised railway which still ran between the two towns.

Many of Bere Regis & District's regular passengers have fond memories. Doug Chant, who has spent most of his life at Winfrith, said: 'The drivers on Bere Regis were always without exception very courteous and helpful to their passengers. One thing you could be sure of was if the timetable gave a time the bus would turn up at that time. You never heard excuses about traffic etc holding them up. The only exception to this was when a new driver was on the run from Dorchester to Winfrith and East Knighton they sometimes got the order of serving the two places in the wrong order.'

A trip to the races was always well patronised. Originally a London bus (LGOC's T192), GH622 gained its Duple coach body while with the Valli family's Valliant Direct Coaches of Ealing in 1940. Dodge JPK518 started life on the Isle of Man, but came to Bere Regis in 1944 via a Surrey operator.

ALAN CROSS

ENT242 pulls away from the bus stop on High East Street, Dorchester. This Maudslay Marathon, with coachwork by Burlingham, came to Bere Regis from J. Whittle & Son of Shropshire in 1949. Later it was a mobile Bible school in Bournemouth. DAVID PENNELS

'The late bus from Weymouth to Winfrith never left anyone behind even though it was usually very full. I've counted 72 passengers on a 28-seat bus. It didn't do the springs much good. It was four to a wooden-slatted seat. Sometimes those at the back were so squashed the bus would stop to allow them out of the [rear] emergency door to come round to the front for some relief. Passengers at the front would sometimes have to hang on to the driver's visor over his head. Passengers for Osmington would have to get out at the bottom of the hill. They didn't care too much for that but the bus would never have restarted if it stopped on the hill. The bus didn't half make a racket climbing the hills. The engine would get so hot you couldn't go near the engine cover inside the vehicle, you would get burnt if you touched it.'

Buses that turned round at Winfrith church laid over there for about 20 minutes. Doug Chant said 'one of the regular drivers, not sure of his real name but he was always known as 'Tosh', used to stop at our house for a cup of tea. By parking on the grass verge he could step straight from the emergency door over our wall and through the garden.'

When he was courting Doug often went into Dorchester for the evening with his future wife. 'On the journey home there would be enough passengers to put on a relief, the intention being that the relief would go as far as West Knighton and the main bus could go direct to Winfrith. The trouble was she lived at West Knighton and I of course lived at Winfrith. Naturally we wanted to ride on the same bus, the result being the relief bus had to continue to Winfrith from West Knighton with just me on board. I don't think the drivers were too happy about that but I got to know a lot of them in time. One driver, Ted Wilkes, was going out with a receptionist who lived at West Knighton so he always liked to do that particular run.

As wartime restrictions gradually eased, express coach services – suspended during hostilities – came back into their own. The big player in this part of the world was Royal Blue, jointly owned by the Western and Southern National Omnibus Companies. At peak times they were short of coaches to meet demand, so they hired them in from other operators, including independents. These tended to charge less than neighbouring big companies, which were not so happy with Royal Blue's preference for this cheaper option.

For Bere Regis & District this was an opportunity to generate new revenue, but it did depend on the quality of the vehicles on offer. Unknown perhaps to Toop and Ironside, Royal Blue had strictures on hiring their coaches. Each Bere Regis vehicle had to be inspected to ascertain that it was clean and roadworthy, and passengers were not to board until this had been done. Royal Blue staff were not faced with such strictures on any other proprietor's vehicles at Bournemouth.

Even so, the firm ran a steady flow of relief journeys for Royal Blue, between London and Cornwall via Yeovil. The drivers had no rest days while doing these runs for a week or two at a time. They carried on until they were tired out. Alan Bailey was highly impressed when he was a passenger on such a journey: 'I remember an exhilarating all-day service trip Exeter-London in one of his [Toop's] Maudslays on hire to Royal Blue in 1948 or 1949. From refreshment stops at Exeter, Yeovil and Hartley Wintney we were the last of the nine on that run to leave, and the first to reach the next one.'

In peacetime, like the express services, regular private hire contracts resumed as well. One of these involved meeting a ferry in Southampton to convey French girls on exchange visits to various destinations. On one occasion John Woodsford had to set off in such a hurry for Southampton that he drove there in his pyjamas. What the French girls thought of this is not recorded.

The hours on private hire work could be highly demanding and there were often quick turnarounds. John once left Piddlehinton at five o'clock in the evening to drive a Maudslay full of soldiers to London, returned to Dorchester around two o'clock in the morning for a quick

sleep. Then he had to clean another Maudslay in time to leave Wyke Regis at 7.45 the next morning to take a coachload of sailors to Portsmouth. 'That would have been a pleasure trip for the passengers and I would have slept on the back seat until they came back,' John told the *Blackmore Vale Magazine*. 'When you picked up at Portland, you knew you were in for a full day because Portlanders never came back until the pubs closed.'

On Mondays there was a regular run from Dorchester to Minterne House, which at that time was still being used as a Royal Navy Hospital. The bus waited at the railway station in Dorchester for sailors returning from a weekend away. One bus that did this run was a prewar Leyland Lion (BNB228); its engine could only be fired by using the starting handle that projected through the radiator, but it had a vicious kickback. This hurt driver Len Hayward's hand so badly that young Woodsford, still not licensed to drive a bus, had to take over the wheel.

Drivers' cabs were not heated, so in winter they took to wearing RAF flying boots to keep their feet warm.

Year by year Bere Regis & District could now offer a bigger choice of tours to other parts

John Woodsford's work tickets for 30 and 31 July 1948 show how long working hours could be. He picked up troops at Piddlehinton at 5 pm on Friday, drove them to London and came back empty that night. He was up again early next morning in time to clean out another coach to take sailors on a day's outing from Wyke Regis to Portsmouth.

of the country. Many rural folk had still rarely travelled beyond their local market towns, and a coach excursion was something of a trip into the unknown. The *Blackmore Vale Magazine* retold the adventure of Charlie Wills, a farm worker from Winterborne Kingston known to his mates as 'Goldflake'. They all went on a Bere Regis mystery tour, which gave them a couple of hours to wander around their destination.

This turned out to be London. 'Poor old Goldflake got lost. First he needed a toilet and was directed down some steps. But he went down the wrong steps and ended up in the Underground instead.' Finding himself lost, he asked a couple of policemen in his broadest Dorset: 'Yer, Oi don't z'pose arny o' you fellers 'ave zin arny o' Toopy's buses roun' yer, 'ave 'ee.' The big city

DTP417, one of the dozen Bedford OBs that came from the Hants & Sussex group, rests beside the Methodist Chapel at Bere Regis depot in the late 1950s. Lurking behind it is Bere Regis & District's first "minibus", Trojan Personnel Carrier OOW912.

PHOTOBUS

law was not that familiar with Toopy's buses, nor possibly with Goldflake's turn of phrase, so it couldn't help much. His mates sent out search parties and eventually rescued him.

In 1949 Bere Regis & District bought a large number of second-hand coaches, many of them nearly new, from other independents. The biggest purchase was of a dozen Bedford-Duple Vista 29-seaters, four Leyland Tiger coaches, and two Leyland Titan double-decks from Basil Williams' Hants & Sussex Motor Services and its subsidiaries. Three Tigers had already arrived at the end of 1948. None of these vehicles was more than three years old. Williams had perhaps over-invested in his fleet. The two Titans, FCG526/7, became regulars on the Poole and Sherborne services.

This deal caused a stir on each side of the transaction. The Chief Engineer at Hants & Sussex, Paddy O'Sullivan, negotiated the sale but soon found himself in a tight spot. Newly established at the firm's office in Cosham, he told his boss that the vehicles had fetched £100 apiece. An appropriate receipt was duly issued. A privately published account of what followed said: 'by some mischance the receipt came back to Hants & Sussex through the post and it was

A pair of two-year-old Leyland Titans, with lowbridge bodies by Northern Coachbuilders of Newcastle, came from Hants & Sussex in 1949. FCG526 pulls out on to West Street, Bere Regis, to work the 1420 to Poole on 10 March 1956, watched by the late John Santer.

DAVID PENNELS

Hants & Sussex sold no fewer than seven Leyland PS1/1 Tigers to Bere Regis & District in 1948/49, including GAA252. All had 35-seat Duple coachwork, so they added useful extra capacity at a time of expanding opportunities.
DAVID PENNELS

According to one version of the story these approaches included a suggestion that Hants & Sussex might be able to take over the Guy's Marsh contract with the U.S. military.

Williams met O'Sullivan in Southampton on 30 July 1952 and they had a long talk. An eyewitness account said: 'Paddy was the typical silver-tongued Irishman, most persuasive, and insisting he had learned his lesson and would be wholly trustworthy in future... Paddy was very capable if he wished to be; he knew the business inside out... Also he was a man of extreme energy, quick-witted, resourceful.' In the end he got the job with Hants & Sussex, but that company and Basil Williams were soon in serious financial straits, not of O'Sullivan's making, as chronicled by transport historian Alan Lambert.

The arrival of all these coaches from Hants & Sussex coincided with a fall-off in the intense volume of work that Bere Regis & District had enjoyed during and immediately after World War II, so it came under financial pressure.

discovered that the amount had been altered to £150.'

So Basil Williams, the owner of Hants & Sussex, interviewed O'Sullivan in the presence of the company's solicitor. O'Sullivan 'admitted having altered the receipt and failing to pay in the correct amount to the company, so he was asked for his resignation.'

O'Sullivan followed the coaches westwards and became Bere Regis & District's Chief Engineer. John Woodsford recalled that he was a stickler for proper titles like 'Mister' or 'the boss'. But Toop, Davis and Ironside all used to drive buses themselves so there was more of a family atmosphere, and they were always known by their first names or nicknames. O'Sullivan tried to put a stop to this, which caused much ill feeling.

He stayed no more than three years, for by 1952 he was making tentative approaches to Basil Williams for his return to Hants & Sussex, which was looking for a general manager.

DTP416, one the dozen Bedford OBs that came from the Hants & Sussex group in 1949, waits at the roadside where the cows have just passed. It was registered in Portsmouth because it had belonged to the group's Southsea Royal Blue Coaches.
PSV CIRCLE, ROY MARSHALL

The Social Club held its 1947 annual dinner in the gymnasium at Poundbury Barracks, hard by 7 Bridport Road. Bill Ironside sat in the centre for the group photograph, with his wife on his right and Percy Davis next to her. Reg Toop was not there. In the top row John Woodsford is sixth from the left and Ray Roper on the extreme right. Maurice Crocker, wearing glasses, stands in front of him, and Jack Toop is seated on the floor in front of Percy Davis.

JOHN WOODSFORD

Bill Ironside (standing third from right) and Percy Davis (centre) at a black-tie event with the licensed victuallers of Dorset: Primrose Ironside is seated second from left.

IRONSIDE FAMILY

However, having a big stock of coaches boosted its competitive edge when it launched a large number of express services in the 1950s to convey naval and army personnel home on weekend leave. Bluebird Coaches of Chickerell, which in the past had done good business carrying Royal Naval personnel from Portland Dockyard, might logically have bid for the express services, but at the time it only had about 10 coaches.

Reg Toop, whose ambitious plans seemed at the time to have put Bere Regis & District under financial strain, thereafter increasingly left the management of the business to Bill Ironside in Dorchester and preferred to remain in the village where he was born. Ray Applin remembers how he would stand opposite the Drax Arms 'waiting for buses to come back, with his little cigar in his mouth.' Being a driver himself, he was fond of his drivers and he might say: 'I'm just waiting for Ted. He's coming back from London.' When Ted Steele arrived he would park his coach in the depot and walk back up the road, and Reg would say 'Come on, I'll take you for a drink'.

Applin, who never worked for Reg Toop himself but knew him well, said: 'You couldn't have got a better boss than Reg. He was a very friendly man. He had this kind of faith in his drivers. They were normally lads that lived in the village.'

By the late 1940s Bere Regis had enough coaches to see off rival bids for big private hire contracts. With three Leylands, an AEC and five Maudslays lined up on Weymouth Esplanade, it could carry nearly 300 people on a Marks & Spencer's outing for staff and their families.

IRONSIDE FAMILY

5
THE SOUTH'S BIGGEST INDEPENDENT

BY THE END of the 1940s Bere Regis & District had come as close as it ever would to achieving Reg Toop's ambition to run a bus service to every village in the area. The addition in 1949 of some 40 'new' buses and coaches to the fleet was the biggest intake of vehicles that the firm ever received in a single year. Nearly all of them were second-hand, but some elderly machines could now be withdrawn.

We can only guess at Bill Ironside's view of these developments, but the years ahead would demonstrate that his way of doing business and his style of management both differed from Reg Toop's. Through the 1950s he steadily increased his grip on the firm. He used Frank Whitty's old

premises in Dorchester to shift the heart of the business to the county town, having taken up residence in the bungalow on site at 7 Bridport Road. Later on he moved to Sundown, Rothesay Road, Dorchester. From Dorchester the man from Winfrith developed other business activities, some of them closer than others to the original terms of the partnership agreement.

Reg Toop and Percy Davis each frequented the Drax Arms in Bere Regis, where they drummed up private hire business among the regulars. Percy Davis had returned from Swanage to Bloxworth and later moved to Glenair, Wareham Road, Lytchett Matravers. Raymond Applin, who witnessed the goings-on in Bere Regis as a young man, described Bill Ironside's more rigorous approach to time-keeping than those of Toop or Davis. 'If something happened in the morning and a bloke didn't turn up or there was something wrong with him, either of them would take the bus. They'd do the job. Not so Mr Ironside. He'd stand outside, and I've seen him do it... One or two of the drivers were habitually kind of late comers in... He would

1950 was unique in Bere Regis history: of the 22 coaches acquired that year all but two were brand new. There were two batches of six Leyland PS1/1 Tigers with Gurney Nutting bodies. DTK344, picking up passengers on Sheep Market Hill in Blandford, came with the first batch. PSV CIRCLE, JOHN BENNETT

When he was a student the late Reverend David Green was a conductor with Bere Regis & District. He stands by ex-Chester Corporation AFM518 at Godmanstone, hefting his Bellgraphic ticket machine. A Weymouth clergyman in later life, David Green doubled as a dealer in second-hand buses.   DAVID GREEN

For the first few years after the war economic austerity still afflicted a heavily-indebted nation. There was a ready market for day trips by motor coach to the seaside and other attractions, for few families had their own cars. Such days out were often privately organised by clubs or local associations, whose members might well frequent the Drax Arms. Like bus companies across the country, Bere Regis & District also offered its own tours and excursions. Unlike private hire journeys these had to be licensed by the Traffic Commissioner.

Starting in 1947 the firm put in a stream of applications for such E&T licences, as they are known in the trade (excursions and tours). Among these were its own prewar licences, which had fallen out of use during the war, and those of all the smaller firms that had been taken over. For example, in January 1948 Bere Regis & District was licensed to run excursions to 27 different destinations from Marnhull, formerly run by Vic Little. On these journeys it was allowed to pick up trippers at Fifehead Magdalen, Todber, Stour Provost, Manston, and Hinton St Mary.

Doug Chant of Winfrith remembers: 'We often went on their afternoon mystery tours ending up at places like Bulbarrow. Whilst the

stop them and apparently what he used to say was: 'what time do you call this then? You're supposed to be here at eight o'clock. It's ten past eight. You obviously must be tired. Go on home and have the day off.' He would send them home... Reg, he was a different type of person; he'd jump up in the bus and do the job, and worry about the problem afterwards.'

A seasoned observer of the business described the partners as running it 'on a relaxed basis.' He said the finances were 'vexed' but as a private partnership they did not have to publish accounts. Valuation of the coaches was subjective. There was a case of fraud, but this did not involve the partners.

Dorchester shopping obviously exhausted a small passenger waiting for NRF174 to leave the Fire Station Yard on the ex-Whitty service to Frampton. The Santus-bodied Leyland PS1/1 Tiger spent a few months with Happy Days of Woodseaves, Staffordshire, before joining Bere Regis in March 1948.   OMNIBUS SOCIETY COLLECTION

Bedford OWB LMG461, new in 1943 to Valliant Direct of Ealing, passed to Bere Regis in 1946. In August 1952 it was in Yeovil, leaving Somerset to return to Dorchester. ALAN CROSS

trips were scheduled for a couple of hours you often got three and a half hours. The drivers knew the country like the back of their hand, all the little side roads to Sherborne for instance.'

In 1949 the firm ambitiously sought consent to run as many as 20 coaches on any one day on excursions from Bere Regis itself, with a list of 56 different destinations. The licensing process could take months if objections were raised. Not surprisingly Hants & Dorset and Wilts & Dorset both had things to say about the Bere Regis proposal, as did Ernest Toomer, who ran a local bus in the Wimborne area and wanted to protect his own business. At the end

Two stalwarts who worked out of Bere Regis depot: Tommy Clark and Len Cox wore drivers' badges issued by different Traffic Areas: HH24577 by the Western TA and KK32347 by the South Eastern TA.

FRANK PITFIELD

of the year Bere Regis revised its application, proposing a choice of only 33 destinations. This time Hants & Dorset, Southern National and the nationalised Railway Executive all made submissions. However, all 33 were granted, so long as no more than four coaches went to any one destination on a particular day. This still allowed for well over 100 trippers at a time.

Even though the partners did not formally take over George Caundle's Puddletown business in 1943, they applied in 1950 to renew his E&T licences, along with those of Frank Thorne of Cerne Abbas, Frank Whitty of Dorchester, and Gilbert Lugg of Hazelbury Bryan. The last was quickly approved, but the other three took the best part of a year for licences to be granted.

As Reg Toop had foreseen, when Bruce Maund interviewed him for *Modern Transport*, private hire was also a useful source of revenue. The firm gained a reputation for very competitive pricing. One of its customers ran a pub at Mere in Wiltshire. Jim Newton used to hire a coach for parties of his regulars to go on an outing or travel to a darts match. Newton was also a part-time driver for Leather's Coaches, from nearby Maiden Bradley. Leather's charged seven shillings and sixpence a seat (37.5p) for the hire of a coach. Bere Regis & District quoted only four shillings a seat (20p), even if its coach had to drive empty half way across Dorset.

Because they had absorbed so many small bus concerns in the 1940s, the partners now had E&T licences that let them pick up day trippers all over the area served by their stage buses. The big bus companies that surrounded them limited the firm's scope to expand stage operations, but this did not apply to E&Ts, so it extended its reach by taking over other coaching firms.

The first of these was H.V. Fear's Wimborne Queen, acquired in October 1949.

When the firm expanded to the east by taking over Wimborne Queen in October 1949 Charles Ironside took charge of the garage on Leigh Road. EKP512 was one of three pre-war Duple-bodied Bedford WTBs included in the deal.
IRONSIDE FAMILY

Six Wimborne Queen coaches joined the Bere Regis fleet in 1949, including a 1948 Austin CXB, the only one the firm ever owned. Plaxton-bodied CPR797 sets down its passengers on the front at Swanage.   VENTURE PUBLICATIONS

activities, tours and excursions as well as private hire and contract work.

Eight coaches came with the Rambler business, including three 35-seat Dennis Lancets and a pair of smaller Commer Commandos. Fred Hann, who like Reg Toop had been a driver for George Vacher, was put in charge of the Rambler Garage. The firm now had a presence on the northern outskirts of Bournemouth. This would be a useful base a few years later when it ran express services to convey civilian workers from different parts of Bournemouth to military workshops in Dorset.

Bill Ironside and Reg Toop also obtained a garage in Seldown Lane, near Poole town centre. It was a concrete building with room for eight or nine buses, with a yard at the rear that could hold another 15 or so. Buses based in Bere Regis were used on the stage service to Poole, and the premises in town were used for coaches working on regular contracts.

The 1950s proved to be boom-time for weekend leave express journeys for servicemen from Portland Dockyard and army and Royal Air Force camps around Dorset. The post-war Labour government's policy had been to ensure that as far as possible servicemen on

William Fear founded the business in 1920, and it passed to his son on his death. Apart from half a dozen coaches, this gave Bere Regis & District a garage at Leigh Road, Wimborne, with petrol pumps on the forecourt. The six coaches included three prewar Bedfords. There was also an Austin 29-seater and a Dodge, as well as a more modern Bedford.

Three years later the partners bought out G. Robertson (Longham) Ltd, who traded as Rambler Coaches. He had been in the business since 1918. Although he sold his bus service to Hants & Dorset in 1925, he had held on to his coaching

DRT800 was one of the last Dodges that Bere Regis & District operated. This Duple-bodied 30-seat SBF came with the Wimborne Queen business. It was withdrawn in 1954.

OMNIBUS SOCIETY, RYAN CARPENTER

BERE REGIS AND DISTRICT MOTOR SERVICES
SOCIAL CLUB
(Kiddies Xmas Party Fund)

Grand Carnival

DANCE

Following the Kiddies Xmas Party at the

VILLAGE HALL, FERNDOWN

on

TUESDAY, DECEMBER 30

MUSIC BY FRANK STONE AND HIS ORCHESTRA

M.C. HARRY CLARK
Dancing 8.30 p.m. till 1 a.m.
Cabaret, Competitions, Refreshments, Prizes

GUESTS - HANK & HIS HAREM
Admission by Ticket 2/6
Limited Number obtainable from all staff

This is a real Bumper Party Show !

The Bere Regis & District Social Club was evidently a lively affair in the 1950s.

weekend leave travelled on the railways that it had nationalised. After the Conservatives won the 1951 election, the licensing authorities changed their approach. Coach travel was cheaper, and usually more convenient for young National Service conscripts who wanted to make

the most of their time away from camp. Some were even prepared to sleep on the narrow luggage racks above the seats in the coach.

In May 1951 Bere Regis & District sought 13 weekend express licences from Portland, five from Dorchester and Piddlehinton and two from Lulworth and Bovington Camps. They were to run on condition that there were at least 10 passengers, and ranged as far afield as Liverpool, Manchester and Leeds, as well as linking up with other naval towns on the south coast. The railway station at Portland Dockyard closed down in 1952, so for sailors based there the coach became virtually the only option.

On a Sunday evening as many as ten Bere Regis coaches might head back to Dorset from the London terminus in Waterloo. Most of the licence applications were approved but some ran into objections from big companies with their own express services. One such was Portland-Brighton. From the Brighton end Gerald Duckworth, Traffic Manager at Southdown Motor Services, complained that 'the essential distinction between this application and the acknowledged type of leave service is that Bere Regis obviously intend to run around the countryside dispersing the servicemen themselves rather than allow them to take advantage of existing facilities.' Bere Regis & District was granted its licence but its coaches were barred from setting down and picking up passengers at several places around Portsmouth and Worthing.

At Blandford Camp the challenge came from Wilts & Dorset. Maurice Crocker, Traffic Supervisor at Bere Regis, wrote to its Salisbury headquarters in September 1950 to say his firm objected to its application for weekend expresses from Blandford to London and Birmingham. In the event Bere Regis & District got the Birmingham licence and

Bedford 29-seaters as well as full-size coaches ran to London on hire to Royal Blue when it needed extra capacity. EFX290 was the last OB delivered new to Bere Regis, in July 1950.

PSV CIRCLE, ROY MARSHALL

CJT345 was the first of three Dennis Lancets taken over from Rambler Coaches of Longham. New in 1947, it lasted with Bere Regis for eight years, ending its days in derelict state at Winterborne Stickland garage.   DAVID PENNELS

Wilts & Dorset the London one. However, given that Blandford Camp was remote from Salisbury Plain, the main focus of its military express operation, Wilts & Dorset may initially have been quite content with its well patronised road/rail feeder service between the camp and Salisbury railway station. This was supplemented in due course with express services from Blandford to London and Bristol.

Different operators' drivers on the weekend expresses helped one another out if there were problems, but they also vied with each other to pick up servicemen who turned up at the big city terminus with no return ticket to camp. The independents picked up at Bayliss Road, Waterloo, and Wilts & Dorset at Victoria Coach Station. However, one of the big company's drivers recalls that they used to turn up early at Bayliss Road to pick up potential Bere Regis passengers. Wilts & Dorset staff knew well that Bere Regis & District followed an equally flexible approach to the rules by picking up and setting down passengers in Salisbury.

In 1954 there was a new express from the RASC (Royal Army Service Corps) Camp at West Moors to London. With the end of National

Service nine years later the demand for weekend leave coaches inevitably diminished. However, some continued for many years yet.

The licensing authorities sought to smooth out rivalries among smaller local competitors. Bere Regis & District was only allowed to run its Lulworth Camp-London service after Percy Webb of East Chaldon and Sheasby's Coaches of Corfe Castle had each filled one of their coaches on the same run. Sheasby's later dropped out of this arrangement.

Doug Chant, who was a civilian worker at Bovington, said the Bere Regis

DJT313, the newest Dennis Lancet that came from Rambler Coaches. Like the first it had a Whitson 35-seat body, but with slightly sleeker lines. The other Dennis, CJT655, had Duple coachwork.
                OMNIBUS SOCIETY

drivers used to race the Webbs' coach. 'Mad they were,' he said. Although the weekend leave operators competed vigorously, there was strong camaraderie between their drivers. It was not unknown for a Salisbury Plain operator's coach to stop and pick up passengers from a stranded Bere Regis vehicle.

Bere Regis representatives went to the camps to sell tickets for the express services. John Woodsford – by now promoted to inspector, was surprised on one occasion when an officer at Blandford told one of the drivers 'don't use Bere Regis tickets, use mine.' One version of

BERE REGIS & DISTRICT MOTOR SERVICES

PROPRIETORS   R.W.TOOP, W.J.IRONSIDE & P.W.DAVIS

4 NORTH STREET
BERE REGIS, WAREHAM
DORSET
TELEPHONE BERE REGIS 256 (TWO LINES)

TELEPHONES
DORCHESTER 79
BLANDFORD 457

RAMBLER COACHES
NORTHBOURNE 16

TELEPHONES
MILTON ABBAS 224
STURMINSTER NEWTON 173
WIMBORNE QUEEN
WIMBORNE 32

By September 1950 the letterhead already listed Rambler Coaches and Wimborne Queen as part of the business, even though it was some time before the Rambler concern would be completely absorbed.

this story has it that this was at the time of Paddy O'Sullivan's tenure.

The leave services kept coaches busy on two nights a week. Having reached their destination late on Friday or in the wee small hours of Saturday, they could be hired out to local coach operators coping with heavy weekend demand. There was no tachograph in those days to clock drivers' hours and typically the journey back to Dorset started quite late on Sunday.

During the week there were school runs for Dorset County Council, which brought in substantial revenue. When Percy Davis was a lad in Morden he travelled to school in a donkey cart. Come rain or shine his fellow pupils mostly had to walk to be in time for their lessons, some

of them for several miles. When school finished for the day they would wend their way back home on foot too.

All that changed under the 1944 Education Act. Winston Churchill's wartime government was concerned to legislate for a better peacetime Britain even while war still raged. The Act dealt with the quality of schooling and raised the leaving age to 15, but it also looked at children's travel to and from school. It stipulated that children under eight years old should not have to walk more than two miles to school, and those over eight no more than three miles. In a thinly populated county like Dorset there were many whose schools lay beyond these limits. This created new opportunities for bus companies

Lancashire Motor Traders supplied two 14-year-old ex-Glasgow Corporation AEC Regent chassis in 1954, DGB415 and 418. LMT replaced their double-deck bodies with 33-seat Duple coachwork that also dated from 1940. DGB415's body came off another Bere Regis coach, AEC Regal GH622.   DAVID PENNELS

Baskerville Place has long since disappeared from the centre of Birmingham, but it was once the regular weekend haunt of Bere Regis coaches. Harrington-bodied MTF988, parked there in March 1959, had been with the firm three years. It was new to Silver-Grey of Morecambe in 1951.

F.W. YORK

and it became an important source of revenue for Bere Regis & District in years to come.

Works express services and contracts also helped to keep the growing fleet of coaches and their drivers busy through the working week: taking people to their jobs in the morning and back home in the evening, or at the end of their shifts. Military establishments dotted around Dorset employed a large number of civilians, and factory workers often had to travel a fair distance too.

Express services conveyed civilians to REME (Royal Electrical and Mechanical Engineers) workshops at Bovington and just north of Dorchester, at Charminster. Some of these started in Bournemouth. On occasions the firm had to alter its proposed routes to overcome objections raised by Hants & Dorset, ever ready to defend its home territory against competition. In the early 1950s there were seven services to Bovington REME, from Dorchester, Weymouth, Wareham, East Knighton, Briantspuddle, West Lulworth and Lytchett Matravers.

Over the years the pattern changed. Some services were withdrawn and new ones were added, from different places. In the mid-1950s typically the army paid £4 day for the hire of the coach and deducted four shillings (20p) a week from each employee's pay under what was known as the Assisted Travel Scheme. At that time fourteen coaches a day were used on the Bovington contract.

Bere Regis & District was less successful when it wanted to run express services from Bournemouth and Poole for workers at the RASC depot at Blandford Camp. Both Hants & Dorset and Shamrock & Rambler Motor Coaches Ltd put in strong objections and the firm withdrew all five of its licence applications.

Works journeys to civilian factories tended to be covered by contracts with the firms concerned, so there was no need to go through the often lengthy licensing procedure. However, Bere Regis & District came unstuck in 1959 when it tendered to convey workers from Portland to the UK Atomic Energy Authority site at Winfrith. The Southern National company also tendered, but because of the way payment for the service was structured this one

Two Bere Regis Leyland Tigers neatly parked at Baskerville Place: DTK342, with Gurney Nutting coachwork, was one of the first PS1s delivered in 1950. Ten years later Lancashire Motor Traders supplied second-hand PS2 LTE919, bodied by Trans-United Coachcraft of Rochdale.

F.W. YORK

Weymouth manager John Woodsford and a fitter pose with one of their charges outside the depot at Radipole. MTJ444, a Leyland PSI Tiger with King & Taylor coachwork, was ex-Silver-Grey of Morecambe.   JOHN WOODSFORD

did need a licence, and Southern National won it.

Its lawyer took the opportunity, at the Traffic Commissioners' hearing in Weymouth, to point out that Bere Regis & District had admitted 'that they have not complied with the award of the National Council for the Omnibus Industry [on wage rates] made in February 1958 and that they have been in default in that respect for a period of over 12 months.' The contract with the UKAEA contained the Fair Wages Clause, he added, and this made it a condition that the operator must be paying fair wages at the time of the contract. In fact Southern National won the case on the ground that it was the more established operator along the route.

Early in 1958 the Industrial Disputes Tribunal had ordered Bere Regis & District to observe the rates of pay laid down by the National Council. Their buses passed the homes of the Tolpuddle Martyrs on a daily basis, but the Bere Regis partners would not countenance

their employees being unionised. Pay levels may have fluctuated up and down depending on the state of the business at any particular time. It was customary for local authority contracts to contain a clause stating that drivers' wages and conditions must be on a par with the average for the area, but Bere Regis & District did not always fulfil such terms.

In May 1953 Bill Ironside turned his attention to Weymouth. The Spa Garage, at 148 Dorchester Road, Radipole, was purchased from Ellis & Betts, motor engineers. John Woodsford, one of the firm's two inspectors, was put in charge there. At first he lived with his family in a caravan placed in a lock-up garage on the site, but later a Woolaway bungalow was built for them.

As in Wimborne, the sale of petrol, batteries and Pirelli tyres to motorists continued at the garage. The Cleveland petrol pump hose was suspended on a long arm that swung across the forecourt. A small shop at the site

For a couple of years in the mid-1950s Bere Regis & District's choice for new coaches was the Commer Avenger III. There were seven, all with Duple 41-seat bodies. For a year or two they were the pride of the fleet. JJT214 posed for a publicity shot in front of The Keep in Dorchester.

IRONSIDE FAMILY

road those based at Weymouth were parked outside the depot by day to draw attention to the company's excursions and tours. This was a prime site for such advertising, right beside the main road in and out of Weymouth. By night the Commers took shelter inside the garage and older coaches lined up outside.

One of Bill Ironside's sidelines at the Spa Garage was to accommodate cars belonging to holidaymakers who took the ferry from Weymouth to the Channel Islands. Besides their publicity role the coaches parked on the forecourt kept the cars hidden from passers-by. Another lucrative sideline was the purchase and resale of cars that had been used for a season for self-drive hire on the Channel Islands, but were no longer needed there in winter.

The depot in Radipole also covered regular contracts to convey workers from Weymouth

entrance, which had been a dry cleaner's, was used as a booking office.

Up to 23 coaches were based at Weymouth. Two pits were dug in the garage for routine maintenance. They came in handy one winter when Reg Toop's Rover was brought in. It had seized up because there was no anti-freeze in the radiator. Altogether Bere Regis & District had ten fitters working at Dorchester, Bere Regis and Weymouth in the mid-1950s. Their workshops could carry out any repairs that were needed except for crankshaft grinding. Every diesel-engined bus or coach was thoroughly overhauled after it completed 100,000 miles.

Seven Commer Avenger IIIs delivered in 1955/56 with 41-seat Duple bodies were the pride of the fleet for several years. When they were not out on the

Former Hants & Sussex Leyland Titan FCG527 waits at Dorchester to work the Cerne valley route in September 1956. The advertisement on the side gives telephone numbers for Bere Regis & District in Poole, Bere Regis, Dorchester and Weymouth.

J.H. ASTON

Leyland TS7 Tiger KG5641, new in 1935 to Western Welsh, has an oil check before working the 1420 Dorchester service on 21 January 1956. The slate-roofed building behind it is Bere Regis Methodist Chapel, which lay between two of the depot's sheds.

DAVID PENNELS

JRU60 was one of the more bizarre acquisitions. New in 1936 to the Ebor Bus Co. in Mansfield, it came to Bere Regis in 1954 from a Somerset firm. Lee Motors had rebodied it four years earlier and reregistered in Bournemouth.

OMNIBUS SOCIETY

In the mid-1950s five former Devon General AEC Regals were added to the fleet. New in the 1930s, they worked for a spell in South Wales before returning to the south coast. The type was familiar in Dorchester for Devon General ran such buses from Exeter to Weymouth. DOD474, parked at Bere Regis, had a 35-seat Weymann body.

J.D. JONES

The Bournemouth ex-Prisoners of War Club hired AEC Regal JP8149 to take them to Westminster. It was one of five coaches acquired from J. Smith of Wigan in 1955, three AECs and a pair of Leyland Tigers, all with distinctive full-front bodies by Beccols of Chequerbent, Bolton.

PSV CIRCLE

and Portland to other towns. Up to three coaches took women workers to Joseph Gundry & Co Ltd's rope factory in Bridport, and two more ferried workers to Millers' pie factory in Poole. The depot also handled contracts for Portland Dockyard and the army camps at Piddlehinton, Lulworth and Bovington.

There was the holiday camp business too, with excursions on weekdays and transfers between railway station and camp on Saturdays, as well as transport for the camp cleaning staff. A couple of years before it bought the Spa Garage Bere Regis & District had tried to start a half-hourly bus service between Bowleaze Cove and Weymouth. Not surprisingly Southern National took exception to the idea of the independent muscling in on its territory in this fashion and the idea was dropped.

Bere Regis asked in 1953 that coaches running tours from Dorchester be allowed to pick up passengers at Spa Garage. This was refused at first, but the firm was more successful a couple of years later when it sought

licences for tours starting at Radipole. Once again Southern National and Bluebird Coaches of Chickerell raised objections. Bere Regis & District was told it could only run three coaches a day on these tours and no more than two to any one destination. Even though it was not allowed to pick up passengers in the centre of Weymouth, the fares it charged and the choice of 36 destinations still tempted people to make their way out of town to join a coach at 148 Dorchester Road.

With the Weymouth base secured, the partners turned their attention to the coaching business in Sherborne, close to the border with Somerset. The first of two concerns taken over, in 1954, was E.A. Seager's Enterprise Garage. When A.J. Macklin's Antelope Tours followed the next year, the firm gained a monopoly on E&Ts from the historic abbey town.

Seagers had been in business since the early 1920s. Before World War II, besides running their own coaches, they had been agents for the Gilford Motor Company Ltd of High

LUP13 starts back to Dorset at the end of a Tuesday market-day excursion to Salisbury. It was one of a pair of Burlingham-bodied Leyland Tigers that came from the Lanarkshire firm of Baxter's Bus Service in 1958. On the right Silver Star Leyland Titan GWV360 pulls away from the Blue Boar Row stop.   DAVID PENNELS

Bere Regis & District bought its first underfloor-engined coaches in 1958, a pair of Harrington-bodied AEC Regal IVs which had three previous owners. New in 1951, LAD518 is in Liverpool on a weekend express for servicemen based in Dorset. PSV CIRCLE, ROY MARSHALL

Wycombe, which built bus and coach chassis. In its early years the Bere Regis partnership had several examples of this marque, all of them bought second-hand from elsewhere. Three elderly Gilfords came with the Enterprise Garage, but the Bere Regis fleet had no need of them. One of them (CS105) was new to Western Scottish Motor Traction in 1934 and had spent time with Bere Regis before Seager took it off the partners' hands in 1945. A pair of Bedfords also came from Enterprise. One was pre-war and did not last long, but the other served on for another dozen years or more.

The Macklin family kept the Antelope Hotel, and had a couple of coaches to run excursions from there. Before World War II they also ran a hearse. Mrs A.M. Macklin had been running the business since the mid-1930s. Bere Regis & District took over and ran her two coaches. One of them was the first forward-control Bedford SB type to join the fleet, a 33-seater (ETK235). Over the next ten years this

type, which succeeded the OB, was to become the mainstay of Bere Regis operations.

Not one lightly to surrender its E&Ts, the firm continued to apply separately every three years to renew the licences acquired from each of the two Sherborne operators. It now had its own base in the north Dorset town, where Gilbert Lugg's son was put in charge. This was convenient for running school contracts in this part of the county, and in 1959 a local service between Lillington and Sherborne was initiated. It only ran on Thursdays at first, but proved popular enough for Saturday journeys to be added a few months later. Lillington had been served before by an extension of the service from Dorchester.

By the mid-1950s the fleet had grown to some 140 vehicles. This made it one of the half-dozen biggest independent bus operators in England, although it had a lower profile than the others. The only bigger privately-owned concerns all hailed from north of the river Trent:

Lancashire United Transport, West Riding Automobile Services and Barton Transport in the Nottingham area.

With passenger numbers growing the partners had to buy more and bigger vehicles. In 1950 they took delivery of a dozen brand new Leyland Tiger 33- and 35- seat coaches, as well as their AEC Regal and a handful of Bedfords. The Surrey firm of Gurney Nutting, better known for its work on luxury motor cars, built the bodies on the Leylands. Local lore has it that Bill Ironside, irritated by the propensity of their roofs to leak, approached the Gurney Nutting stand at a motor show and asked if they could thatch the roofs more effectively.

Most of the coaches added in the next few years came with the Robertson and Seager businesses, but a handful of elderly vehicles were acquired for spare parts, including a clutch of London Transport STL double-decks.

Plaxton Venturer-bodied AEC Reliance NDG951 joined Bere Regis & District from Marchant of Cheltenham in 1959. On weekdays it ran local services, but went all over the country on forces leave work at weekends, hence the London destination blind.   DAVID PENNELS

The AEC radiators, bonnets and diesel engines from two of these were fitted to the two 1939 ex-Eastbourne Corporation Leyland Lions. Like Bournemouth, the town had wanted to protect the tranquillity of its streets from the noise of diesel units, which were already standard by that time.

With 41 seats the Commers that arrived in 1955/56 could (legally) carry more people than any coach the firm had ever run before. (John Woodsford remembers once driving a 26-seat Bedford with 40 aboard). The Commers' three-cylinder TS3 engines gave a slightly better than average performance, in terms of miles per gallon (mpg), than the other diesels, but they were not always popular with drivers; John commented: 'Put 'em in first gear and you didn't know whether you were going forwards or backwards.'

On the eve of World War II LME394 was new to Eastbourne Corporation as an all-Leyland petrol-driven LT8 Lion registered JK8420. Within months it was called up for war service. It later went to Valliant Direct coaches of Ealing, who reregistered it in Middlesex, and came to Bere Regis in 1946. Nine years later it was given the diesel engine, radiator and bonnet from a retired London Transport STL-type double-deck.

DAVID PENNELS

Writing in *Passenger Transport* in October 1956 Ryan Carpenter said Bere Regis vehicles had run a total of 2,500,000 miles in the

The miniature coach on display outside the Smiths Arms at Godmanstone, claimed in its day to be the smallest public house in England and said to be Bill Ironside's favourite. He and Ray Roper stand on the left of the picture.

IRONSIDE FAMILY

Morecambe or Manchester joined the fleet. Three years later the first underfloor-engined coaches arrived. AEC Regal IVs that had been new to Gloucestershire operators were soon put to work on weekend leave services to Liverpool and other cities well north of Dorset.

John Woodsford accompanied Ironside on one of his northern coach-buying forays in March 1956, so he could drive one of the purchases back to Dorset. Always one to spot an opportunity, Bill Ironside's eye lighted on a miniature coach when they were at Lancashire Motor Traders' premises in Oldham. Built by Ernest Johnstone of Brighton in the shape of a Commer Avenger with Harrington body, it had a two-stroke 125cc Villiers motorcycle engine to turn its wheelbarrow wheels.

This little vehicle, now preserved at Walsall, had belonged to Hardings of Birkenhead. John removed a front seat from the full-size Leyland Tiger coach he was to drive home, and slipped the single-person machine in through MTF988's emergency door. It was soon painted in Bere Regis two-tone brown and pottered around Dorset publicising the firm. In its first year it went to no less than 23 village fêtes, where it was a great success.

past year. On stage and express services diesels averaged 15 miles to the gallon, compared with only 10 for petrol-engined vehicles on similar work.

By this time Ray Roper had become General Manager and was responsible for the day-to-day running of the business. This left Bill Ironside time to play a more strategic role in determining policy. He managed the purchase of other operators and was the architect of vehicle policy.

Ironside began travelling to Lancashire to buy second-hand coaches. From 1955 batches of Leyland Tigers and AEC Regals which had spent a few years working from Wigan,

Three 10-year-old AEC Regal 33-seaters came from well-known Manchester independent A. Mayne & Son in 1958. Their bodies, by Bellhouse Hartwell of Westhoughton, Lancashire, were an unusual sight in southern England. JNC3 awaits its next working at 7 Bridport Road.

DAVID PENNELS COLLECTION

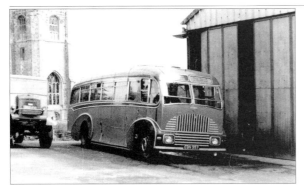

With St Peters church in the background Leyland PS2 Tiger EBN957 awaits its next duty at Bere Regis depot, alongside the firm's Bedford QL recovery vehicle. In the 1950s some Lancashire operators preferred to keep radiators hidden, a requirement amply met by Blackpool coachbuilder H.V. Burlingham.   P. TREVASKIS

Generous chrome beading was a feature of Riviera style bodies by Yeates of Loughborough. Bere Regis & District bought a couple of 36-seat Bedford SBOs with this coachwork via Lancashire Motor Traders in 1958. TTC10 had previously had four years' service in Rochdale.
                           PSV CIRCLE, R.H.G. SIMPSON

'I remember driving it to Yeovil,' John told the *Blackmore Vale Magazine* many years later. 'It used to jump all over the place and you had to hang on for grim death. The brakes weren't too healthy either! The maximum speed was 20-25 mph.' It was used to promote tours until it was retired in 1972. Later on it appeared on a specially constructed shelf above the office door at 7 Bridport Road, where it stayed until 1994.

A trio of chassisless Beadle Rochester coaches, also with Commer TS3 engines, were

delivered in 1957 shortly before the company that built them, John C Beadle Ltd of Dartford, ceased production. One of them had a different entrance layout from the others, and they arrived in off-white livery, with brown roofs and flashes. They ran for a season or so in these colours before appearing in the standard two-tone brown. They often appeared on weekend expresses along the south coast to Gosport or Brighton or on the London and Chatham service.

Altogether a collection of 40 coaches was

Nobby Clark drives KPR517 home from Wembley Stadium. This Commer-Beadle Rochester had already been repainted in Bere Regis colours, but KPR688 behind it was still in the off-white livery in which both were delivered.
                                                          OMNIBUS SOCIETY, R.H.G. SIMPSON

acquired between 1955 and 1958. Thirty of these were second- or third-hand, including a couple of oil-engined Bedford SBs from Lancashire with elaborately styled bodies by Yeates of Loughborough. It was not until 1959 that the first half-dozen new SBs arrived. By then the type was already the mainstay of many independent coach operations, as it was now to become for Bere Regis & District right up until the 1980s.

The boxy war-time body of a Bedford OWB was care-worn by the 1950s, so some were rebodied to give them a new lease of life. BUX788 was one of three with Whitson coachwork that came from a Somerset operator as late as 1959. It survived another three years.

PSV CIRCLE, T.W.W. KNOWLES

Second-hand coaches remained a popular option. If they had an unpopular body make and were painted in a dark livery, so much the cheaper. Bere Regis's two-tone brown could hide dark colours far more easily than the paler liveries favoured by many coach concerns. By 1959 the fleet had shrunk a little from the peak of four years earlier. By the firm's own account it was down to 80 coaches, 42 saloons and two double-deckers, still used on the Poole and Sherborne routes. Many of the 'saloons' were no doubt more elderly coaches used on school contracts.

Branches hanging low over the road had to be cut to keep them clear of the two 55-seat Leyland Titans with well-proportioned Northern Coachbuilders bodies, which had come from Hants & Sussex in 1949. The firm used a cut-down Bedford OWB bus to carry out its own tree-lopping, but when this had not been done for a while the bus driver simply had to dodge the branches. Faced with a cattle truck coming the other way this was no longer an option and on one occasion the roof of the bus was badly damaged.

In 1956, when Dorchester's population stood at 11,750, Bere Regis had 17 bus services between there and other towns and villages around Dorset. Nine of these were daily, and the others ran three or four days a week, or only on market days. Poole, with a population of 84,540, remained by far the biggest town to which there

was a daily service. There were two daily services to just one town beyond the county boundary, Yeovil (23,850). In Weymouth (37,760) local services were the preserve of Southern National, but Bere Regis & District ran there from villages farther afield, like Winfrith, on Saturdays.

The other market towns served at that time were Sherborne (7,230), Bridport (6,700), Blandford (3,620), Shaftesbury (3,740), Wareham (2,770), and Sturminster Newton (1,710). Sherborne and Blandford each had two daily services, and Sturminster Newton four, plus others on one or more days a week. With the exception of Sturminster Newton all these towns also had regular daily services run by at least one of the three nationalised bus companies operating in the area. Poole was the only place where Bere Regis buses carried a number of passengers on purely town journeys, hence the close watch that Hants & Dorset kept on them.

There had been a limited reduction, or what would nowadays be called rationalisation, of Bere Regis & District's bus services in the early 1950s. Typically this meant that journeys were withdrawn on certain days of the week, but some services ceased altogether. These included a pair of market journeys that dated from Reg

Toop and Percy Davis's early days: Winterborne Kingston – Bere Regis – Wimborne, and Bere Regis – Bloxworth – Wareham. In 1952 the firm gave up a market service from Briantspuddle to Wareham that had only run for a couple of years. George Caundle's old Puddletown – Dorchester service was withdrawn, although the bus from Bere Regis still ran along the same road.

Fewer people were heading into town by bus for an evening at the movies, so the Wednesday and Saturday evening journeys

A pair of Leyland Royal Tigers came to Bere Regis in 1959 after eight years with Samuelson New Transport, part of London Coastal Coaches. Their 41-seat central-entrance Duple Ambassador bodies were no use for one-man bus operation, but well-suited to express work. MLF426 is parked up in Leeds ready to return to Dorset on Sunday night.

PM PHOTO

on Dorchester–Cerne Abbas–Sherborne were withdrawn. The Dorchester–Frampton service was reduced from five days a week to four, but in 1957 a special service from Dorchester to Saturday evening dances at Frampton village hall was introduced. Fares were charged in the normal way, but the dance organisers agreed to make up the difference if the takings fell short of two pounds ten shillings (£2.50).

Bere Regis & District saw an opportunity to extend the reach of James Pickett's old summer Fridays-only express from Buckland Newton to Weymouth. In 1955 it was replaced by two new Weymouth services that ran on both

Fridays and Saturdays. One started from Bagber and the other from Fifehead Magdalen. They wended their way through different villages in the Blackmore Vale, then headed down the Piddle Valley along Pickett's old route to Dorchester and Weymouth. Southern National insisted that they must not pick up passengers travelling between Dorchester and Weymouth.

Operating costs had risen substantially, especially because of wage increases, fuel price rises and falling passenger numbers. More and more people were buying their own cars. Writing in *Passenger Transport* in October 1956, Ryan Carpenter commented that 'the stage services have become less and less remunerative so that today the point has been reached when it is doubtful whether the actual cost of operation will be met from receipts on the stage services.'

As car ownership increased oil companies were keen to expand their presence on the forecourt. This was an opportunity for Bill Ironside to reach a deal with one of the petrol suppliers. By 1956 Cleveland had only 6.7 per cent of the retail petrol sales market, compared to Regent's 13.7 percent. In return for some helpful business support, Regent became Bere Regis & District's chosen partner. A full page advertisement in the 1956 timetable proclaimed: 'Regent packs punch. It's best. It's British. All Bere Regis vehicles now run on Regent petrol and Regent derv.' Later on the last sentence may no longer have applied.

That autumn Britain and France invaded Egypt, which had incurred their governments' wrath by nationalising the Suez Canal. Middle East oil shipments were diverted around the Cape of Good Hope. Restrictions to domestic supply followed, leading to further service cuts early in 1957.

The Thursdays-only Dorchester–Piddle Valley–Holwell–Sherborne service was withdrawn. So was the twice-weekly Hazelbury Bryan–Cheselbourne–Dorchester run, which left Violet House's Hilton Bus Service alone on the road down the Devil's Brook valley. To the west of Dorchester the little village of Compton Valence lost its Wednesdays-only service to market. The following year Bere Regis & District decided not to renew the licence for its three-days-a-week Sturminster Newton–Bishop's Caundle route.

Bill Ironside was eager to promote a pair of minibuses that he bought in 1959, still an unusual move in the bus industry at that time. Publicity for services offered adorned these Bedford CAV 11-seaters. MPR177 posed for the camera before The Keep at Dorchester Barracks.   IRONSIDE FAMILY

As passenger numbers fell and the average bus had more seats, the number of relief journeys could be reduced. However, in so rural an operation the time that buses had to stand idle between journeys was still a problem. After children had gone to school and workers to their jobs, there were shoppers to convey, but most had reached town by 1030 and were not ready to return home until 1230 or so. The pattern was similar in reverse in the afternoon, and the demand for evening travel had steadily fallen off.

Buses from five different depots worked the stage services: Dorchester, Bere Regis, Blandford, Marnhull and Winterborne Stickland. But, as the owner of a Wiltshire coach business commented, wherever you went in Dorset you could see Bere Regis coaches parked in gateways and at the side of the road, near where drivers lived. This was easier for an early morning start. Driver Bill House kept his bus overnight near Upton Cross, just outside Poole.

Lightweight petrol-driven buses, generally Bedford OBs, were still used on the most rural routes, but bigger diesel units worked the more heavily-trafficked ones, and double-deckers the Poole and Dorchester-Sherborne services. One consequence of the Suez crisis was to accelerate the change to more economic diesel engines among independent bus operators.

The nature of Bere Regis & District's bus services meant that the type of bus it used on a particular route could vary. Whilst a double-decker would be used on the Sherborne run at peak hours and on market days, at other times a Bedford 29-seater was all that was needed. Bigger single-decks generally worked the Yeovil, Sturminster Newton and Little Bredy services, but a Bedford could handle the Bridport journeys.

Norman Aish recalls that travel with Bere Regis could be 'interesting'. Heading out of Dorchester one day on a fully loaded Leyland Tiger bound for Sherborne, he noticed movement above his head. The fixings of the internal luggage rack had come loose and it was swaying about. On another journey, he noticed rivets fixed across the roof of a Bedford SB going to Hazelbury Bryan. The driver explained that it had been bought second-hand for spares after it accidentally rolled over, but on second thoughts it was decided to put it to work instead.

Bere Regis & District's timetables were not like those of other bus companies. There were pocket guide book descriptions of places served by its buses or tour coaches, and a mid-1950s edition contained advertisements by three breweries listing between them some 260 hostelries around Dorset and neighbouring counties. Naturally the Drax Arms at Bere Regis was included, and the Smiths Arms at Godmanstone, Bill Ironside's favourite and a contender for the title of England's smallest pub. One of the breweries helpfully described each of its houses: the Smiths Arms was 'the gem of Dorset', and the Half Moon in Dorchester was 'a comfortable little pub which was the hangman's home.'

Writing in 1956 Ryan Carpenter said there had until recently been no uniform fares structure for the whole network of bus services; the partners were reluctant to alter the different ways that former proprietors had fixed their fares. 'An example of the many anomalies which existed was that the same distance could be covered by one route for 4½d as against 7d on another route' (1.9p & 2.9p). On some weekly market services receipts were as low as 8d (3.3p) a mile, rising on a few occasions to one shilling and eight pence (8.3p).

There had been two fare increases, but rates were generally still below those of the nationalised companies that served Dorset. Carpenter said a third fares revision ironed out anomalies and provided a unified fare system for all routes. However a County Council survey 20 years later found there were still anomalies.

In about 1950 Bere Regis & District replaced the Bell Punch system of different-coloured tickets for each value, which implied that a stock of new values had to be ordered each time fares were revised. The new system used pre-printed tickets, on which the driver or conductor simply wrote the fare through an

The three Commer-Beadle Rochester coaches came in non-standard off-white livery. On 3 March 1958 KPR688 called at Dorchester on a forces leave express after picking up sailors at Portland Dockyard. Two of these coaches had the door in the centre. The third had a front entrance.   DAVID PENNELS

The 1957 notepaper for the Dorchester office listed W.J. Ironside first of the three proprietors. Telephone numbers at Poole, Weymouth and Sherborne have been added, but Milton Abbas and Northbourne no longer feature as they did in 1950.

aperture at the top of the Bellgraphic machine. This held the tear-off tickets in a concertina-like pad with carbon copies. Checking that conductors kept a proper tally of the takings was always an issue for bus companies: hence Primrose Ironside's ruse with the missing serial number.

Two inspectors, John Woodsford when he was still based in Dorchester, and Geoff House, who covered Hazelbury Bryan, Sturminster Newton and Blandford, carried out spot checks on whether fares were being charged correctly. Woodsford said he once caught a conductor who had reissued used tickets so he could pocket passengers' fares.

After 30 years and more, the partners' bus services between Poole, Bere Regis and Dorchester came to an end in July 1959. Takings were down and Hants & Dorset took over the three licences: two Bere Regis-Poole services, via Bloxworth seven days a week and via Winterborne Kingston at weekends, and the Monday-Saturday Bere Regis-Dorchester service. Hants & Dorset combined the three routes with its own existing services. The weekly market service from Winterborne Zelstone to Dorchester also ceased, effectively replaced by Hants & Dorset, but with a change of bus at Bere Regis.

In the same year Bere Regis & District gave up the Saturday evening cinema service between Winfrith and Weymouth, which James Ironside had started. Percy Webb's Dorset Queen Coaches took it over. Since his garage was at East Chaldon, the journey demanded less 'dead mileage' of him than an empty coach coming from Bere Regis.

The Tuesday and Friday Dorchester–Bridport journeys were also withdrawn, leaving just the Wednesday and Saturday workings. Bere Regis–Wareham was reduced from two days a week to one on Thursday.

For Bere Regis & District the loss of the Poole services marked the end of an era, taking away the routes that from the 1920s had been at the heart of Reg Toop's and Percy Davis's activities. It did not take the heart out of the business but there could no longer be any shadow of doubt that it was at Dorchester that it throbbed.

Bere Regis double-deck FCG526 squeezes up to the grass verge in March 1956 to make way for the Hants & Dorset Bristol L5G saloon on which the photographer was riding. Just over three years later Hants & Dorset had the Poole road to itself.   DAVID PENNELS

6

IRONSIDE ASCENDANT

BILL IRONSIDE, ENSCONCED in the firm's Dorchester headquarters at no. 7 Bridport Road, lost no time to assert that he was the boss of what was still, on paper, a three-man partnership. Up until 1955 Reg Toop's name usually headed the list of partners. That year a passenger transport directory put Bill Ironside's name first. A year later *Passenger Transport* magazine named him as Managing Director.

The concern that ran the buses was still just Bere Regis & District Motor Services, with no 'Ltd' to its name. The other two partners may never have known that on 7 February 1952, W.J. Ironside registered company no. 504136, Bere Regis & District Motor Services Limited, at Companies House, with himself as sole director. In the event the limited company never took over the business and apparently never submitted any financial returns.

As a registered company Bere Regis & District would have been obliged to publish its annual accounts. Their absence cannot have helped the firm's bankers to keep track of how the business fared financially, or to work out how much each of its various activities contributed to revenue that was banked in different places. Ironside no doubt weighed the benefits and drawbacks of being a limited liability concern. He took the option that afforded greater privacy.

Later the main trading account moved from the National Westminster Bank in Wareham to the Midland Bank in Sherborne. Given the variety of activities conducted in the firm's name, one can only speculate as to whether there were other accounts with banks in Dorchester or Weymouth.

When Sylvia Gibbs, Percy Davis's daughter, worked in the office for a time, she

MTK328 waits at the Digby Road bus stop by Sherborne Abbey to return to Hazelbury Bryan. Like all 12 Bedford SBıs delivered in 1959/1960 it had a 41-seat Plaxton Consort Mark IV body.

COLIN CADDY

saw how things were run at the different depots. Whilst all the money was sent to Dorchester, it was impossible to identify how much any of the depots contributed to the profits. She suggested to her father that financial control might be tightened up. Whether he was too ill or just did not want to rock the boat, Percy took no action beyond perhaps mentioning his daughter's concerns to his partners. They made it clear to her that financial matters were none of her business.

At the end of the 1950s Bere Regis & District had just over 120 buses and coaches. Two types between them made up around half the total: Leyland Tigers with 33-35 seats, mostly of half-cab layout, and petrol-engined Bedford OBs, which normally seated 29. The latter were better suited to rural routes on which the driver collected the fares. In 1959 six diesel-engined Bedford SB coaches were delivered, the first of the type that the firm bought new (MPR705/6, MTK282/3 and MTK327/8). They had 41 seats, but as with the smaller OBs, the driver sat with the passengers and could collect fares.

Another innovation that year was the arrival of four 11-seat minibuses. They were intended mainly for private hire work carrying small parties like pub darts teams. They also proved useful as duplicates to regular buses. However, Bill Ironside and Ray Roper told *Bus and Coach*

The diesel-engined Bedford SB1s were put to all manner of duties, not least the weekend leave express services for sailors based at Portland. MTK327 is on its way to Gosport on 20 September 1964.   F.W. YORK

MPR706 passes Old Gaol Cottage in Cerne Abbas on its way to Sherborne. This was one of the first pair of Bedford SB1s bought new in 1959.
PSV CIRCLE, T.W.W. KNOWLES

Six coaches came with Herbert Butler's Milborne St Andrew operation in 1961. Plaxton-bodied Commer Q4 FTK496 did not stay long, passing straight to Flight Refuelling at Tarrant Rushton.   LES RONAN COLLECTION

that although a number of rural routes did not pay their way, there were none on which both outward and return journeys never exceeded 11 passengers. At first they were used mainly for work previously undertaken using bigger vehicles, but they were soon attracting business in their own right. *Bus and Coach* said 'The maximum publicity has been achieved by painting suitable wording on the vehicles, and when not in service the 11-seaters are displayed prominently outside the company's depots.'

Bere Regis & District took over another small competing operation in October 1961,

Waiting for passengers in Fire Station Yard in December 1961 HUO700 was still in Herbert Butler's cream livery, but it bore Bere Regis legal lettering. The Bedford OB, new in 1947 to Western National (no. 547), was already 12 years old when Butler acquired it.   DAVID PENNELS

that of Herbert Butler of Milborne St Andrew. He had contracts for a couple of works services, Sturminster Newton–Blandford Camp, and Milborne St Andrew–Bovington. For a couple of years in the early 1950s Butler had run a stage service between Dewlish and Dorchester which he acquired from B.L. Stone of Dewlish in 1951. Stone in turn had taken it over in 1948 from Lloyd Cutler, who had been running a motor bus service from Dewlish since 1924. Bere Regis inherited six coaches from Butler, three Bedfords and three Commers. There was a brief flirtation with the latter make: four second-hand Commer Avengers joined the fleet in 1962, which must have ensured a more certain supply of spare parts. The six Avengers

Left: Two Commer Avengers and a Q4 came from Herbert Butler in 1961. Manhire Chandler-bodied NLR618, parked at The Grove in Dorchester, was already eight years old, but it stayed with Bere Regis & District for five years.
                                   PM PHOTOGRAPHY

Right: Bere Regis & District went on a buying spree for 12-year-old Commer Avengers in March 1962 – four of them. JWY998, one of two with Plaxton bodies, came from a Huddersfield firm. There were regular market day excursions to Salisbury, where it waited for its passengers in the coach park in July 1963.
DAVID PENNELS

Lancashire Motor Traders supplied Commer Avenger REV682 in 1962. Its Whitson body seems in good condition as it nears the top of High East Street, Dorchester, but it only stayed for a year before going to a Shaftesbury firm of cleaning contractors.   A.J. DOUGLAS

Breathalysers, speed limiters and tachographs were all future technology. A couple more 51-seaters arrived in 1963, as well as what looked like the result of a successful Ironside shopping trip to Lancashire, nine second-hand Bedford SBs that had been new to that county's coaching firms.

Bere Regis & District's management structure was becoming more clearly defined by 1956. Ryan Carpenter wrote in the October edition of *Passenger Transport* that 'The nerve centre of the organisation is at Dorchester where Mr W.J. Ironside, the managing partner, has his office. Mr R.W. Toop is at the Bere Regis depot, while Mr P.W. Davis is normally at the Sturminster Newton office.' The firm was divided into two areas, Dorchester and Weymouth in the west, and Bere Regis and Poole in the east.

now in the fleet had bodies by five different coachbuilders.

In 1962 the partners bought their first 51-seat coach, an AEC Reliance with Duple Continental body (TFX597). Ray Applin described its first outing from Bere Regis, with Reg Toop aboard. Ted Steele, who was 29 at the time, was the driver. 'They had a brand new AEC Continental. Reg was full of this. This bus turned up, and it was its first trip out. It was a run to the brewery in Blandford, Hall & Woodhouse.

'Mr Roper, the General Manager, is responsible for the day-to-day running of the business and carries out any disciplinary action necessary, but each depot manager is

Reg said 'if any of you want to come on then you come on.' Well Ted had been in and I don't know how many he'd had but he'd certainly had three or four pints of bitter and about five or six stingos, which are little bottles of quite potent beer... Coming back, going down over Thornicombe, with Reg sat up front, Ted said: 'Look at that Reg. Eighty miles an hour. No trouble at all.' ....Reg, he didn't bat an eyelid.'

Bere Regis bought its first new AEC Reliance in 1962, with Duple Continental coachwork built at the former Burlingham factory in Blackpool. Posed a few years later by Radipole Lake, TFX597 was the coach that did 80 miles an hour "down over Thornicombe" on its first outing.   COLIN CADDY

responsible to Mr. Ironside.' Ray Roper's name first appeared as General Manager at about that time, but he had joined Bere Regis & District as soon as he was demobbed from the army after World War II. John Woodsford remembers Ironside asking him straight away to 'sort out the money.'

Along with Roper's name the 1956/57 passenger transport directory, The *Little Red Book*, named Maurice Crocker for the first time as Traffic Manager. He was responsible for licence applications to the Traffic Commissioner, whose *Notices and Proceedings* paradoxically continued until 1973 to cite the firm's address as 4 North Street, Bere Regis.

was General Manager once more, as well as Secretary.

Whatever their relations might have been with Bill Ironside in the 1950s and 1960s, Reg

850HTC, a 1959 SB3 that came via Lancashire Motor Traders, waits to leave for Dorchester at The Royal Oak Inn, Cerne Abbas. This was once a thriving market town but, like Bere Regis, the railway bypassed it. Nowadays it is better known for the figure of the Cerne Giant carved in the chalk of Giant Hill.
PETER IMPETT COLLECTION

JK9589, parked at Blandford depot, was one of the last Bedford OBs acquired. It only stayed from March to August 1962, and then passed to Dorchester County Council as an ambulance for wheelchair passengers.
DAVID PENNELS

In about 1962 Bill Ironside became General Manager, and Ray Roper took over as Secretary from Mr Baker, who left for a job at the Hyde sand and gravel pits, near Bere Regis. Ironside's move appears to have been just a temporary arrangement to give Roper time to settle into the new role, for by 1964 he

Toop was later to praise Roper and Crocker's 'years of devoted service'. In the future they were to play an important part in the story. Toop, working out of his native village, does not appear to have interfered a great deal in what was going on in Dorchester, but carried on drumming up business closer to home, sometimes in the convivial environment of the Drax Arms. However Dorchester engineers were given the task of servicing his black Wolseley saloon.

Percy Davis was already less active in the firm's affairs. His daughter said he was very ill with heart trouble between 1951 and 1954. Sylvia Gibbs told Norman Aish that her father resisted suggestions by his partners that they buy him out, even though he became largely a sleeping partner until he died in 1964.

Two of Bill Ironside's brothers, Charles and Arthur, had worked at Bere Regis since the 1930s. Like virtually everyone there, they turned their hands to whatever needed doing, whether out on the road driving a bus or getting their hands dirty in the garage. Both resourceful engineers, they were younger than Bill. Neither was called to arms in World War II, but the youngest Ironside brother, Leonard, who was 21 when war broke out, joined the army. He was killed in 1942 in the Egyptian desert, where he is buried in the British war cemetery at El-Alamein.

JP8050 came from J. Smith & Co of Wigan, which favoured full-front bodies by the local firm of Beccols. A 1949 Leyland PS2 Tiger, it waits for passengers to board in Castle Street, Salisbury, in 1964.   DAVID PENNELS

In 1949 Charles, then 39, took charge of the garage at Leigh Road, Wimborne, which came with the business of H.V. Fear. Three years later Arthur, who was a couple of years younger and previously lived at Wool, was put in charge at Blandford. Often known as Archie, he lived for the next 16 years above the office at 1 East Street, next to the garage, which back in the 1930s had been used by Wilts & Dorset. Arthur looked after the vehicle maintenance programme and was responsible for recovering broken down coaches, sometimes from far away places. His daughter Judith has happy memories of keeping him company as a little girl on journeys all over the country to deal with breakdowns. Sometimes they went as far afield as Birmingham. She said the Bedfords tended to suffer from injector pipes breaking.

Later Arthur moved to Wimborne where he handled maintenance and petrol pump service, while Fred Hann ran the office and tours bookings. Charles took charge of a tyre re-treading machine known as the Kentredder, which was first installed at Bere Regis and then transferred to what became the engineering

works that the firm established in Dorchester in 1964. This was on the Poundbury Industrial Estate, also known by the old name of the area as The Grove. During World War I this was the site of a prisoner-of-war camp, then used by the British army in World War II.

The Kentredder was developed by a company in Jersey, and was thus another Ironside connection with the Channel Islands. It was used to retread tyres for Norman House of Hilton and other commercial fleet operators, as well as the firm's own vehicles. One of the drivers, Ron Allen, used to work on this machine in between school runs. John Eyers, who worked in the engineering department, remembers how Charles Ironside fitted an old Leyland radiator fan to an electric motor to extract the dust buffed off old tyre treads from the remoulding workshop.

Commercial Motor wrote in 1964 that some of the retreads had done 27,000 miles without a single failure. However, John Woodsford related the sorry tale of EFX39, one of the Gurney Nutting-bodied Leyland Tigers. It set out on a weekend express to Leeds, with remoulds newly fitted to its rear wheels (never on the front). 'It only got as far as Blandford before a tyre burst with such force that it blew the mudguard off.'

The Kentredder was just one of the activities, other than running buses and coaches, in which Bere Regis & District engaged under Bill Ironside's leadership. Though there were no published figures to show which lines of business brought in the money, Ryan Carpenter wrote in Bus and Coach in 1966 that stage services lost up to a shilling (5p) a mile and works journeys were 'not exactly money spinners'. Norman Aish drew up a list of what he believed were the sources of revenue in 1970. He reckoned that private hire, including regular contracts such as providing school buses for Dorset County Council, accounted for something like 60 per cent of the takings. The other core activities, local buses, weekend leave express services, excursions and tours, all contributed too.

This reflected a pattern more typical of a small operator with less than 25 vehicles. A 1961 government report on rural bus services

Leyland PS2/3 Tiger LTE919 heads up High East Street, Dorchester. Already ten years old when Bere Regis and District bought it in 1960, it had a 33-seat body by Trans-United Coachcraft Ltd of Rochdale.   A.J. DOUGLAS

estimated that such operators typically drew about 31 per cent of their revenue from stage and express services, and 53 per cent from

contracts. For companies with 100 to 250 vehicles the typical pattern was 89 per cent stage and express and only four per cent from contracts. Excursions and tours accounted for 16 per cent for smaller concerns and seven per cent for bigger ones.

School contracts were consistently a big money spinner. Since the 1944 Education Act some small rural primary schools had been closed down, and new secondary schools had been built at Wareham, Blandford, Dorchester, Puddletown, Bovington, Sturminster Newton and Sherborne. All this meant that more children had to be conveyed greater distances. Part-timers were employed to drive many of the school buses, for which Bere Regis & District used what has been described as a separate fleet of more elderly vehicles.

Relations with the County Education Department came to a head in 1963. The ice and deep snow of an exceptionally severe winter had prevented many contract journeys from running and kept so many motorists at home that takings were down at the petrol stations in Dorchester, Blandford, Sherborne, Wimborne and Weymouth.

The following summer the firm gave the County Education Committee a month's notice that it intended to terminate its 44 school contracts, but would be willing to continue running them for £37,720 a year, an increase of nearly 30 per cent on the previous rate of £29,215. Councillor J.D. Rutland accused the firm of holding the County Council to ransom and said that 'If bus fares went up anything like this there would be a public outcry.' The committee authorised the Transport Officer to negotiate a temporary arrangement so that the service could continue from 1 July until March 1964. It also agreed to ask the Finance Committee for a supplementary estimate of £5,450, representing the extra cost over that period. A long term effect of this episode was that the County Council increasingly used its own vehicles for school transport.

An opportunity that might have been grasped with more enthusiasm came with the closure of the Somerset and Dorset railway line at the end of 1965. Bere Regis & District added a couple of journeys between Blandford and Sturminster Newton but Hants & Dorset and Somervale Coaches of Midsomer Norton shared the main subsidised bus services that were introduced to replace the trains. Geographically speaking, Bere Regis & District would have been well placed to run more of this operation, but, rightly perhaps, it did not see it as offering great reward. Indeed the replacement bus services were severely cut back within three years, as had happened elsewhere in similar circumstances;

One of the more extraordinary purchases was Daimler Freeline LRW377. A former demonstrator supplied by a Cheshire dealer in 1960, it had spent a few years with Samuel Ledgard of Leeds. It arrived in Dorset with its original two doors and 36 seats, but Bere Regis fitters panelled over the rear doorway and added six more seats.

OMNIBUS SOCIETY, ROY MARSHALL

generally the passenger traffic had disappeared long before the buses took over.

Besides buses and coaches, Bere Regis & District's other irons in the fire included taxis and self-drive hire, haulage and the sale of petrol, oil, spare parts and tyres, including the remoulds. Reg Toop already offered cars for hire in the early 1950s, when the BR&D timetable advertised: 'CARS FOR HIRE – R.W. TOOP, 4 North Street, Bere Regis 256,' the same telephone number as the bus business. It did not spell out whether the cars came with a driver or were offered for self-drive, not such a widespread business in those days.

Fifteen years later this business had expanded. Timetables published in the mid-1960s advertised self-drive car hire from £2.10s (£2.50) a day for a Renault Dauphine to £20 a week

HTJ36's previous owners, Silver Grey of Morecambe, had this Leyland PS1 Tiger rebodied by Harrington in 1952. Later on it worked on Bere Regis & District's weekend leave services. The label on the windscreen says "Gosport", but it is actually in Brighton. Two services were probably combined. SURFLEET

UFX567 was one of a pair of 1963 AEC Reliances with Plaxton Panorama bodies. It drove empty along West Street, Fareham, in February 1966. The destination display "TOUR" seems rather improbable. It is more likely it was passing through the Hampshire town for a weekend express or a private hire contract.   F.W. YORK

Coachwork by Alexander of Falkirk lent a Scottish touch, but Leyland Tiger Cub CU8625 actually came from Hall Bros of South Shields. It is passing through Salisbury in July 1961 on a weekend express to Leeds.

DAVID PENNELS

533JBU passed through Fareham with sailors aboard on the Portland-Brighton express in September 1964. It was one of a pair Leyland Leopards with Plaxton Panorama bodies delivered that year. When withdrawn in 1986 a newly acquired Volvo was given its Oldham registration mark.

F.W. YORK

15-year-old AEC Regal IV with the handsome Burlingham Seagull body (XMT52). However, a 19-seat Bedford (BTK2C) stayed for around ten years.

In the first half of the 1960s a number of local bus services were revised. Weekday journeys to Blandford from Milton Abbas and Winterborne Stickland were reorganised under a single licence. There were still 21 stage bus licences in 1964, including daily services from Dorchester to Sherborne and Yeovil. There were numerous licences for excursions and tours from towns and villages across Dorset, and express licences both for conveying civilians to military workshops and for weekend leave journeys by soldiers and sailors. To sustain all these activities, as well as school, works and private hire contracts, there was a fleet of 112 vehicles, described by the firm as 82 coaches and 30 single-deck buses

At the end of 1964 a series of changes resulted in journeys being withdrawn on certain days of the week. These affected the

for an Austin minibus. Also on offer were Hillman Minx, Vauxhall Victor and Ford Classic cars, which could all be hired at the Dorchester, Weymouth, Sherborne and Blandford depots.

Bere Regis & District used Rover and Vauxhall taxis, but also bought London taxis for use in Dorchester when faced with competition from another local firm. It had a contract with Dorchester Prison to transfer prisoners to London, Bristol and Dartmoor, and another with the Atomic Energy Authority to convey scientists from Winfrith to Heathrow. Besides people it carried special rods from Winfrith to Ruislip, Middlesex, and graphite rods to Risley, near Warrington. It also calibrated taxi meters for other owners.

Serious competition in Dorchester led to another acquisition in September 1967: W.S. Phillips' Dorchester Taxi Service Ltd, Dortax for short, had also built up a small fleet of coaches. The coaches were taken over and Walt Phillips subsequently drove for Bere Regis & District. Most of the coaches ran for less than a year with their new owner, including a

The relationship with Portland Dockyard meant there were social events there for Bere Regis & District's bosses. Bill Ironside stands with his hand on Percy Davis's shoulder. Primrose Ironside stands beside him.

IRONSIDE FAMILY

A Bedford SBG-Duple Vega, ex-Greenslades Tours of Exeter, enters Fire Station Yard. Waiting passengers would pay more attention to the "Dorchester-Sherborne" card in the window than to the destination blind. OFJ792 was one of two acquired in 1962 but it was scrapped three years later.   PSV CIRCLE, ROY MARSHALL

field to Percy Webb and Bere Regis & District. However ten services from Portland Dockyard continued throughout the 1960s. Two of these went to Leeds by different routes, and two to Manchester. The other destinations were Liverpool, Birmingham, Bristol, Chatham, Brighton and Gosport. When the Severn Bridge was opened in 1966 a new Portland-Swansea express was launched.

From Blandford there were coaches to Birmingham and Leeds, and from Lulworth and Bovington to Liverpool, Birmingham and London. Until the end of the 1960s there were also services to London from Dorchester Barracks and Piddlehinton Camp, and from West Moors, but these were both withdrawn in 1970.

routes between Dorchester and Bovington, Hurst, Little Bredy, Cerne Abbas and Buckland Newton, as well as Sturminster Newton-Yeovil, Shillingstone–Shaftesbury and Bere Regis–Blandford. A couple of these services were cut back to one day a week. In 1965 the Dorchester-East Knighton service was handed over to Percy Webb of East Chaldon, whose Dorset Queen Coaches had taken over the Saturday evening Winfrith-Weymouth journey in 1959.

The end of compulsory National Service in 1963 inevitably led to some fall-off in demand for weekend leave express services. Two years before this Sheasby's dropped out of the shared Lulworth Camp–London service, leaving the

While they were away from home the

Two Bedford SBs purchased in 1961 show how the livery was adapted to body style. UHN 887, which came from South Shields, had more dark brown than usual on the front of its Plaxton Venturer coachwork. Gurney Nutting-bodied FAN783 came from Herbert Butler of Milborne St Andrew.   A.J. DOUGLAS

weekend leave coaches were hired out to local independents in whatever part of the country they found themselves. One of these was Wainfleet Motor Services Ltd of Nuneaton, which

One of BR&D's earliest Bedford SBs turns into the Top o' Town garage at 7 Bridport Road. CKS265, with 1951-style 33-seat Duple Vega body, had eleven previous owners in Scotland and northwest England before coming to Dorset in 1965.

A.H. WALLER
COLLECTION

Dorset dialect poet William Barnes looks down from his pedestal outside Dorchester parish church as DJP566 heads down High East Street. Originally a petrol-engined SB3, it was fitted with a Bedford diesel unit when it arrived from Lancashire Motor Traders in 1961.

A.J. DOUGLAS

A couple of Spartan-looking Bedford SBOs came from R.W. Banfield of Beaminster in 1967. They began life with John Laing Construction Ltd. 99EME lasted a couple of years with Bere Regis, much longer than its twin, 101EME.

DORSET TRANSPORT
CIRCLE

Left: UFR123's Burlingham Seagull 60 coachwork could be regarded as one of the less popular styles which kept down the price when Bere Regis bought this six-year-old Bedford SB1 in 1966. It still kept going for more than 13 years.

COLIN CADDY

Below: Passing through Dorchester, OED11 shows off the lines of its Duple Vega body. Bere Regis & District bought this Bedford SBG in 1962 from a Warrington firm, and immediately replaced its petrol engine with a diesel unit.

CHRIS ASTON

Only four of the many Bere Regis Bedford SB types had Gurney Nutting bodies. LTG600, resting between duties in Sturminster Newton, was twelve years old when it came from Swansdown Coaches of Inkpen in 1964.

COLIN CADDY

used a Bere Regis coach to convey holidaymakers to the south coast on Saturday and take others back to the Midlands at the end of their stay in Torquay, Weymouth, Bournemouth, Southsea or Brighton. Wainfleet still hired Bere Regis coaches to supplement its own vehicles well into the 1970s. John Eyers, who started as an apprentice in 1971, said Dorchester fitters used to clean up

The damage caused when a lorry collided with the back of Bedford SB1 YWW549 challenged the body shop's ingenuity. It cut the chassis short and rebuilt the rear of the Harrington Crusader coachwork. This delicate operation left it with only 29 seats instead of 41.   PSV CIRCLE, G. SMITH

so they could drive holidaymakers home to Nuneaton, and ferry others back to holiday camps around Weymouth.

If they had a mind to do so long distance coach drivers could also seek out opportunities on the weekend trip away from Dorset. Colin Shepherd, who once drove local buses from Dorchester with his father as conductor, gained a school contract in Yorkshire and left Bere Regis & District to set up his own coach business in Leeds.

The daily express services for civilian workers at REME workshops in Bovington, Charminster and Lulworth continued to be a steady and reliable source of revenue. The places they served varied, but over time more than 40 licences were issued for REME workshop services, not all of them running concurrently.

The growth of private car ownership changed the nature of the excursions and tours business. Judith Lafferty, Arthur Ironside's daughter, said 'local' tours to places like Plymouth became less popular. However, when the regular three-yearly process of licence renewal came up in 1961, a large number of new destinations were added, for example 95 from Sherborne, 90 from Dorchester and 88 from Blandford. Not surprisingly British Rail and Associated Motorways, which wanted to protect its long-distance coach services, made representations to the licensing authorities, as did Hants & Dorset in respect of the tours from Blandford.

By the time Bere Regis & District ordered its own new Bedford SBs their Plaxton Consort coachwork was more elegant than the 1952 Venturer body on OTD635. The 37-seater turns off High East Street, Dorchester with "Sherborne" displayed on a card behind the windscreen.   A.J. DOUGLAS

Salisbury Cathedral provides an elegant backdrop to Bedford SBG WMB461. It was one of several coaches parked there on a private hire contract in June 1965. When it joined the fleet from Cheshire a couple of months earlier, the fitters at The Grove replaced its petrol engine with a diesel unit.

DAVID PENNELS

A proposal to add a new three-day tour from Wimborne to Blackpool was dropped this time round, but went ahead in 1965. Other new destinations for one-day excursions were added each time licences were renewed, and higher fares were often included in the process. In 1963 Bere Regis & District opted not to renew half a dozen E&T licences effectively inherited from small village concerns in the 1940s: Piddletrenthide, Winterborne Whitechurch, Litton Cheney, Winterbourne Abbas, Broadmayne and Owermoigne. Evidently demand for coach excursions from these villages had fallen too low to justify separate licences. Passengers might still be picked up by coaches starting from other places.

In the April 1966 *Bus and Coach* Ryan Carpenter reviewed the business under the title 'Second-hand coach solution in Dorset'. In the early 1960s thought had to be given to replacing the fleet of front-engined Leyland Tiger and AEC Regal coaches.

This had been built up over the previous ten years whilst good second-hand examples of these types came readily on to the market because luxury coach operators elsewhere were investing in the new underfloor-engined versions that carried more passengers.

Through the 1960s Bere Regis & District built up a sizeable fleet of Bedford SBs. Many of these had seen service elsewhere, but ten more new ones joined the fleet between 1960 and 1962, and three more came in 1965. By then the total fleet was around 90 vehicles, and a good half of them were SB types. Those ordered new all had bodies by Plaxton of Scarborough, but body makes on the older coaches included Duple, Burlingham, Harrington, Yeates and Gurney Nutting.

Carpenter said Bill Ironside was the architect of the firm's vehicle policy. The procedure was simple: all vehicles, whether

At the end of 1965 Bere Regis started to buy used Ford coaches from other parts of England. Most of them were 41-seaters like Burlingham-bodied UAW995, which waits in the Fire Station Yard to leave for Frampton. It was withdrawn in 1971 and ended its life as a racing car transporter.

PSV CIRCLE, J.C. WALKER

bought new or second-hand, were 'run into the ground.' How long they lasted depended on the state of the body. How rapidly vehicles were replaced was determined by how many were being scrapped and fluctuations in the number

Leyland Tiger Cub MUX796 waits at Dorchester to leave for Cerne Abbas. The nearside windscreen wiper is already saluting the Cerne Giant. Dating from 1956 and acquired four years later via Lancashire Motor Traders, it had the highly regarded Burlingham Seagull body.   DAVID PENNELS

£1,500. 'Making allowance for bulk purchase, perhaps a power unit in poor condition, an unpopular body styling or dark colour exterior paintwork, the price might be as low as, say, £1,200.'

'Vehicles are purchased several at a time and in this way a considerable saving in the initial cost can be made. No guarantee for running parts is sought and the Bere Regis livery of two shades of brown means that no account need be given to the exterior colour of the vehicle to be purchased.' The basic livery was a paler brown below the waist line and middle brown above it. The paler colour was known as 'tobacco' or 'bracken' depending on the paint supplier.

needed on the road. Bere Regis & District found that coaches between six and eight years old were best suited to its needs, typically costing up to

The twin-steer Bedford VAL14, with Leyland O400 diesel engine, proved popular with some operators in the 1960s, but Bere Regis & District was not a fan; it only ever owned two. CDK412C, with 52-seat Harrington Legionnaire II coachwork, is parked at The Grove. It came south from Manchester in 1968.   A.H. WALLER COLLECTION

Sometimes coaches were driven for a while in their previous owner's livery.

In the early 1960s a band of red paint around the windows was added to the two-tone brown. Three Bedford SB diesels delivered in 1961 (RJT671-673) may have been the first to carry it. Ray Applin suggested that Reg Toop introduced it to distinguish his Bere Regis-based vehicles from those at Dorchester. However, the change was applied sooner or later to the whole fleet. Dave White, who started his career with the firm in the body shop, said the colour used was signal red, except on newly delivered bodies from Plaxton, which used crimson.

Carpenter wrote that the firm was confident 'there will be no difficulty with certification when the 1959 vehicles purchased recently come up for Ministry inspection this month.' These were expected to last at least five years, with an annual depreciation factor of about £250. In addition withdrawn vehicles were often stripped for spares so they had some residual value. Retired coaches parked at the back of the depot in varying stages of disintegration were a common sight at Bere Regis premises.

By moving to lighter vehicles for run-of-the-mill work Bere Regis & District achieved considerable savings in both the initial and operating costs of second-hand units. 'Spares are often as much as 80 per cent cheaper and the replacement of new and reconditioned units is less time-consuming for the workshop staff.'

For a while the fleet of Bedfords was reinforced with Ford Thames Trader coaches. A model 570E demonstrator was briefly tried in 1961, but the firm only started buying this 41-seat type four years later when it became available second-hand, mostly from operators in Yorkshire and Lancashire. Several of these coaches had what one writer called the 'spectacularly unsuccessful' Burlingham Seagull 60 body, entirely different from

the body on Dortax's AEC. That same year Ford stopped production of the type and replaced it with the longer 676E; new regulations permitted coaches to be six feet longer, at 36 feet (11 metres). Bere Regis & District later had three of these 51-seaters.

The Ford was a little cheaper than its Bedford equivalent, but used slightly more diesel per mile. It had a more upright driving position. John Eyers said the Fords needed a lot of work before their annual Ministry of Transport (MOT) check-over, especially on the handbrake. They were prone to head gasket problems too.

At the beginning of the 1960s there were ten operating bases, at Dorchester, Bere Regis, Blandford, Hazelbury Bryan, Longham, Marnhull, Sherborne, Weymouth, Wimborne and Winterborne Stickland. The premises at Longham, which came with the Robertson business, were sold to Holloway Motors in 1961. By 1966 Dorchester had the largest allocation, 25 vehicles, whilst Wimborne had 17, Bere Regis 16, Blandford and Sherborne 10 apiece. Weymouth was a shadow of its former self with only eight, the same number as Sturminster Newton.

In 1964 Bere Regis & District moved into its new premises on the Poundbury Industrial Estate, also known as The Grove. This was just a stone's throw from the head office at 7 Bridport Road. It now provided workshop space which had five 60-foot bays with pits. There running parts could be completely overhauled, and reconditioned engines and gearboxes could be fitted. Covered accommodation was provided for

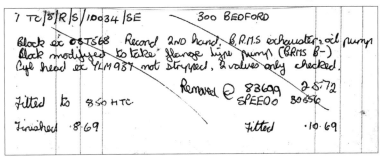

The running account of engine overhauls kept by the fitters at The Grove shows how engine parts were cannibalised from different Bedford SBs to keep others on the road. The engine block from OJT568 and the cylinder head from YLM 937 were put together so 850HTC kept working.

about half the vehicles allocated to Dorchester, and there were offices for the traffic and accounts departments in a building that had been a military hospital in World War I. Bodywork was still painted and checked over at Bere Regis.

In January 1969 the fleet consisted of 87 coaches. Of these 61 were Bedfords and 17 Fords. The fall in the total number of vehicles was compensated by the bigger seating capacity of the newer additions. Five AEC Reliances (TFX597, UFX567/8 and DBU487/8C), and a pair of Leyland Leopards (533/4JBU) were the only heavyweights, but their arrival between 1962 and 1965 allowed the firm to proclaim across the back cover of its timetable: 'Our large fleet now includes 51 seater air conditioned Super Luxury Coaches'. An Albion Victor (LMF86C) and a Commer coach (NPR383) made up the total, and there were also seven minibuses. The last of the half-cabs had long gone.

In the five years up to 1971 only three of the 50 vehicles that joined the fleet were new, a minibus and a pair of Bedford VAMs, the type that superseded the SB.

There were several avenues open to Bill Ironside when finance was too tight for comfort. Buying used coaches rather than new ones was one option. Selling off or renting properties was another, as was trying to squeeze more money from contracts with the Education Department. In 1961, the year the garage at Longham was sold, finances were also boosted by the lease of the Weymouth garage site to Pat McCausland. He and Bill Ironside formed a business partnership called Vogue Motors, which sold Renault cars from both the Radipole site and Bere Regis & District's Coldharbour premises in Sherborne.

Following some disagreement McCausland moved to a shed alongside the Weymouth garage. However, the firm needed to raise funds quickly in 1967, and sold the Weymouth garage, prominently sited beside the Dorchester road, to BMC dealers Channons. They were the first in a succession of seven motor firms to use the premises. John Woodsford left Bere Regis

& District so he could stay on in Weymouth to manage the car dealership. In the 21st century a Lidl supermarket took over the site.

To judge by the *Bus and Coach* article it seems clear that from the perspective of 1966 the future of the business lay with the Ironside family. 'The chief engineer, Mr A. Ironside, supervises the day-to-day running of the maintenance programme, but a very welcome addition to the engineering department's strength is Mr L.J. Ironside. B. Eng., elder son of Mr W.J. Ironside, who is currently at Dorchester depot at the start of a progression that will take him through the various departments of Bere Regis Motors.'

The Ironside name was still in the ascendant three years later. The small print of that annual *Little Red Book* no longer named Bill Ironside as a mere Managing Partner. He was now the 'Proprietor'. Ray Roper was still General Manager and Maurice Crocker Traffic Manager, but the Chief Engineer was now Bill's son Leonard John Ironside. Reg Toop did not feature in the small print at all. That might have been a mistake, and possibly not the printer's.

All this read like succession planning but, sadly for the Ironsides, the unforeseen can turn such plans awry.

MUY145 displays the wings motif on a trim Plaxton Venturer back end. In September 1962 the Bere Regis telephone number no longer features.

DAVID PENNELS

7
PARTNERS NO MORE

BILL IRONSIDE DIED suddenly on 27 March 1970, six years after Percy Davis. He was 64. Reg Toop, who was one year younger, was thus the sole surviving partner. The terms of the partnership agreement were unequivocal: whoever survived took possession of the business. But Reg had taken a back seat for some years and Leonard Ironside had already assumed a number of his father's activities. Had Bill outlived Toop, which some had seen as more probable, Leonard would have been well placed to step into his shoes as the proprietor.

But Ray Roper was still in place as General Manager and, whatever his motives may have been, he urged Reg Toop to take up his rights. Over the years Roper had effectively positioned himself at the top of the firm. Years earlier Maurice Crocker had been the more senior of the two. Those who knew Roper found that he preferred to manoeuvre himself into position, avoiding confrontation wherever possible.

Past experience had shown up legal loopholes in the 1937 Deed of Variation to the Partnership Agreement. It stipulated that the death of a partner did not dissolve the partnership, but after Percy Davis died in 1964 opinions differed as to how the Deed should be interpreted. His daughter Sylvia Gibbs, interviewed by Norman Aish thirteen years later, said her family and the firm each appointed their own valuer to determine the worth of the business, and the one acting on behalf of Bere Regis & District took no account of goodwill or the value of licences. The Deed provided for a pension of £15 a week to be paid to a partner's widow, and there was provision for any children should she die. It also said the partner's family could not withdraw their share of the business for 10 years.

If there was ill will between the Davis family and the two surviving partners in 1964, matters were much worse after Bill Ironside died suddenly in the night. In October 1970 the Probate Registry declared that no valid will of W.J. Ironside had been found. His widow Marjorie Louise Primrose Ironside was 'the only person now entitled to the estate of the said intestate,' whose gross value was found to be just £1,528 and

Duple-bodied Ford 7885UB emerging from under the old railway arch at Fareham, is on the road used by the Portland-Gosport express. Five years old when Bere Regis bought it in 1965, it stayed with the firm for twice that long.   F.W. YORK

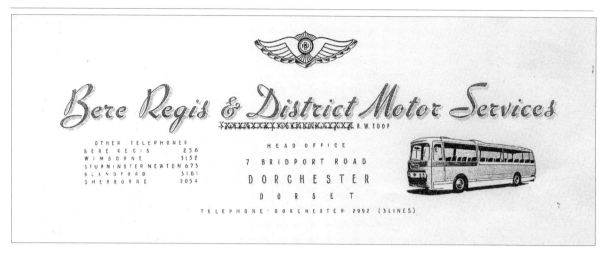

The letterhead bearing Bill Ironside's name was still in use in January 1971, but "PARTNERS – W.J. IRONSIDE (Managing)" was X-ed out, leaving just one name.

11 shillings. Some members of the Ironside family believed there had been a will in the office safe, but none was found. Primrose, who had married Bill in 1942, lived on for another 36 years at 5 Rothesay Road, Dorchester. In 2006 probate put the gross value of her estate at more than £250,000.

After Bill Ironside died the next edition of the *Little Red Book* left a blank space alongside the word 'Proprietor', but the following year R.W. Toop's name filled the gap. He had not followed the firm's day-to-day activities closely for some years, but had still called in at the Drax Arms to talk to his drivers. Ray Roper was still General Manager, and Maurice Crocker, who began his career with the firm working on wages and other office jobs, was Traffic Manager.

Leonard's name disappeared. In a long telephone conversation with Roger Grimley, a transport historian who followed the firm's activities over many years, Primrose Ironside said Leonard 'was told somewhat tersely that there was nothing for him in the business, and he was out.' He went to Saudi Arabia, where he managed the Saudi Electricity Authority's vehicle fleet, and then returned to Britain and worked for a time as Director of Transport for the Metropolitan Police.

In June 1972 Leonard and his brother, Bill junior, acquired the coaching activities of W.T. Davis & Sons Ltd of Sevenoaks when that

business decided to concentrate on vehicle sales. The Ironsides took over its express, excursions, and continental tours licences and a fleet of a dozen vehicles. After a transitional period they set up a limited company, Ironside Travel Ltd, which traded from 148 London Road, Sevenoaks. They based their vehicles at The Old Gravel Pit, Powdermill Lane, High Brooms, until the site was sold for housing development in 1978. They moved the garaging to Limepit Lane, Dunton Green. That year they also took over the fleet of Langton, Sevenoaks and set up an associated company, Economy Coach Hire Ltd, and ran a contract on behalf of EG Language School.

By the early 1980s their fleet had grown to twenty vehicles, including a couple of double-decks. They replaced most of what had been a mixed fleet of Bedford and other coaches, and all but two of their vehicles were AECs, which had been among the most reliable coaches at Bere Regis & District. Things became difficult: Ironside Travel Ltd ceased trading in November 1983, Ironside Economy Coaches Ltd in April 1984, and the brothers went their separate ways. When the Sevenoaks fleet was dispersed four of the 18 AECs found their way to Dorset, passing to the Stanbridge & Crichel Bus Co Ltd.

When Bill Ironside died in 1970, his brother Arthur, who had been Chief Engineer before Len was given the job, was still at Wimborne, living in a house provided by the

Two 1965 AEC Reliances with Plaxton Panorama bodies each gave well over 20 years' service. Thanks to Bill Ironside's relationship with Lancashire Motor Traders a number of new coaches came with Oldham registrations like DBU488C.

PSV CIRCLE, ROY MARSHALL

vehicles for a dozen years. The first two were AEC Reliances, followed by four Bedford YRQs and another pair of Reliances. RJT689K was a Bedford CFL 12-seater. It was at about that time that the firm moved its account to the Midland Bank in Sherborne.

There were now just 15 stage bus routes, many probably no longer profitable, if they ever had been. The vehicles used for these also did school and other contract work that contributed more substantially to the bottom line. Stage service timetables could be arranged so that they fitted between the demands of the contracts. Many stage services consisted of no more than a couple of journeys in each direction.

There was continuous retrenchment over the next two or three years. Several routes were cut back or completely abandoned, and in some places rival concerns replaced withdrawn facilities. When the Milton Abbas-Dorchester licence was surrendered in August 1970

firm. When the decision was taken to sell the Leigh Road garage, he had to leave. His daughter said Ray Roper was not prepared to find him alternative accommodation, so in order to make him eligible for social housing he was formally evicted from the property. His brother Charles went on running the tyre side of the business until he died in 1979.

Reg Toop still lived at 4 North Street in Bere Regis. At the beginning of 1971 he had a fleet of 90 vehicles. Well over half of them were Bedford coaches, many dating back to the 1950s. There were half a dozen more modern underfloor-engined AEC Reliance and Leyland Leopard coaches for long-distance or more prestigious work. The Leopards (533/4JBU) and two of the Reliances (DBU487/8C), as well as a handful of Bedfords (CBU51-53C and KBU782/3E) were all registered in Oldham, reflecting Bill Ironside's links with Lancashire Motor Traders. Between 1968 and 1971 no new coaches were bought. Could this have been a sign of financial constraint?

After Ironside died almost all new vehicles bore local registrations. Nine new coaches (RJT681-9K) were delivered between April and June 1972, the largest intake of new

For nearly five years Bere Regis bought no new vehicles, then all at once in 1972 there were nine, registered in sequence RJT681-689K. All but the last one were full size coaches. RJT689K, a Bedford CFL with 12-seat body by Deansgate, stayed on for a dozen years.

PSV CIRCLE, J.C. WALKER

Norman House's Mid-Dorset Coaches extended its Hilton-Dorchester route back to Milton Abbas to plug the gap. Bere Regis & District continued to run between Milton Abbas and Blandford.

In March 1970 the Dorchester-Frampton route was modified to serve a new housing estate in Charminster, but the two routes farther north to Sherborne, one via Cerne Abbas and the other up the Piddle Valley, were cut back in May 1971. The Cerne Valley route was split in two: Dorchester-Holnest and Sherborne-Bishop's Caundle-Glanville's Wootton. The Piddle Valley route was reduced to Dorchester-Duntish.

The Sturminster Newton-Yeovil service and all journeys to Shaftesbury were withdrawn. A new competitor in the shape of A.E. Faulkner's Marnhull Taxis filled in some of the gaps with two routes serving Sturminster Newton -- Shaftesbury on Thursdays and Hazelbury Bryan on Thursdays and Saturdays. There was more reorganisation in the Blackmore Vale in 1972, when the service from Dorchester to Sturminster Newton was cut short at Hazelbury Bryan, but there were still market journeys from Mappowder and Hazelbury Bryan to Sturminster.

Burlingham's Seagull Mark VII coachwork was one of the more bizarre styles that appeared towards the end of Bill Ironside's reign. VHO443 was one of three such nine-year-old Bedfords purchased in 1968. It only lasted until 1971.

A.H. WALLER COLLECTION

The 1968 Transport Act let councils subsidise rural bus services in order to keep them running. Dorset County Council began to do so in 1970/71, paying out £19,000 that financial year. The 1972 Local Government Act gave local authorities a much greater role in transport matters. Most years Dorset's revenue support to bus services increased, reaching £59,000 in 1974/75. A year later town services were included as well and the total subsidy reached £100,000, topping half a million pounds the next year. By 1978/79 it was £590,000.

An item in an Omnibus Society newsletter observed: 'As bus usage continued to decline subsidies became increasingly important for bus operators. With funding came influence, and one result was that County Councils could be more regarded as the customers than passengers were.'

Dorset CC decided whether to support a bus service by comparing the cost of running it with the fares that were taken. It was usually prepared to subsidise a route if

Three 52-seat Ford 676Es, all with Duple Marauder coachwork, were added to the fleet in 1967. ADY72B came from an operator in Aspatria, Cumberland, and stayed with Bere Regis until 1973.

BRIAN BOTLEY

it met more than 40 percent of its costs. On the ground of local needs a few services which failed to meet this criterion were found to be special cases. One such was the route between Sherborne and Holwell, which had been part of the now truncated services to the Blackmore Vale.

District councils, as well as county authorities, could subsidise bus services if they saw a benefit to local inhabitants. When Bere Regis & District proposed to revise its service between Okeford Fitzpaine and Blandford, the town council agreed to support it to the tune of £147 a year, believing that it would help pensioners living at the top of the town. Of the two Rural District Councils in the area Sturminster Newton also agreed to support it, but Blandford RDC refused to do so.

The weekend leave services were still important even without National Servicemen. There was a long drawn-out exchange with Southdown Motor Services, which took exception to sailors buying single tickets to travel on Bere Regis coaches from Brighton to Portland; based on normal military express operations the need for such a facility should have been quite obvious. Maurice Crocker wrote to his opposite number at Southdown House, E.G. Dravers, in January 1971: 'the only single passengers we wish to carry are those who wish to return to the Naval Base at Portland late on a Sunday night and for whom you can offer no alternative facilities'.

Crocker requested a prompt response: 'We shall be pleased if you can favour us with a reply by return of post as we are being pressed by the Traffic Commissioners who wish to finalize this application. It is now nearly five months since you promised over the telephone to give the matter consideration and inform us of the outcome.'

The services from Portland Dockyard were slightly reduced in 1970: henceforth only one route went to Leeds and one to Manchester. The services to Birmingham, Liverpool, Chatham, Gosport and Brighton continued. The fares steadily rose, but still offered good value compared to rail travel from Weymouth. A return ticket from Portland to Liverpool cost

Two brand new Bedford VAM14s were delivered in March 1967. KBU782E, the first of the pair, posed for publicity shots in Dorchester, showing off its gleaming 45-seat Plaxton Panorama coachwork. The VAM14 was powered by a Leyland O400 engine.   IRONSIDE FAMILY

£2.95 after fares rose in 1971. It went up again in 1972 and three years later it cost £4.35. In 1977 it was £7.70. Operating costs were rising, and from 1976 these services would not run unless at least 20 passengers wanted to travel, twice the previous minimum.

The construction of motorways meant that coaches could reach their destinations faster. In 1973 the Traffic Commissioner gave Bere Regis & District blanket permission to run its express services along these new highways as they became available.

While Ray Roper and Maurice Crocker carried on managing the firm's affairs in Dorchester, Reg Toop himself was in poor health. By the late summer of 1973 he was seriously ill. He drew up his will, which was signed and witnessed on 31 August. The document set out his intention to register Bere Regis & District as a limited company. He died less than a month later, on 20 September, before this could be achieved. There was no indication that he was aware that Bill Ironside had actually registered company no. 504136 in 1952.

The will said that if Bere Regis & District Motor Services 'shall have been formed into a limited company formed by me for that purpose prior to my decease' Ray Roper and Maurice Crocker were each to be apportioned some of his shares in it. In 'recognition of their many years of devoted service in my employment' Roper's holding of ordinary shares in the company was to be brought up to 30 per cent and Crocker's to 10 per cent.

The wording of the will was to prove significant over the next few years. It said: 'I appoint my wife Evelyn Gladys Toop and Raymond Ernest John Roper of 6 Bridport Road Dorchester in the said County (who and the survivor of them and any new additional or substituted trustee or trustees of this my Will are hereinafter referred to as 'My Trustees') to be the executors and trustees of this my Will.'

He directed that so long as Roper remained General Manager and Crocker Traffic Manger they 'shall be paid by way of additional salary such respective sums as will ensure that their respective salaries for each year are equal in the case of the said Ernest John Roper to three-tenths and in the case of the said Maurice Crocker to one-tenth of the net annual profits for the said business for that year.'

Should they form the business into a limited company after his death he directed that Roper should receive 30 per cent of the ordinary shares, and Maurice Crocker ten per cent. Mrs Toop was to have a life interest in the remaining

60 per cent. On her death this was to pass to their daughter Sandra Hewitt.

The will continued: 'Upon the death of the said Sandra Maureen Hewitt I direct that my Trustees shall hold my residuary estate as to both capital and income upon trust for the child or children of the said Sandra Maureen Hewitt who survive both me and her and attain the age of Eighteen years...'

Sandra's son Simon Jeremy Hewitt, a one-year-old baby at the time, would be 18 in 1990.

The will listed seven premises that belonged to the business. Three of them were in Dorchester -- 7 Bridport Road, Poundbury East Camp, and 34 Cornwall Road. The others were at Leigh Road in Wimborne, Coldharbour in Sherborne, 1 East Street in Blandford, and West Street, Bere Regis. The Cornwall Road house stands opposite 7 Bridport Road, and provided flats for two senior members of staff. Probate put the gross value of Reg Toop's estate at £194,355.

The owners of the business were now legally described as 'Executors of R.W. Toop deceased'. They took over a fleet of 84 vehicles, of which 61 were Bedfords. There were ten big 51-seaters, eight AEC Reliances and a pair of Leyland Leopards. The remainder comprised eight Fords, an Albion Victor, and four minibuses.

ENGINE OVERHAUL RECORD		SHEET No c 148
ENGINE No. 10.\52\3\H.\195057	TYPE	220 BEDFORD
DATE IN 5.3.72	EX VEHICLE	BTK 2C
SPEEDO REMOVED 21486	DATE REMOVED	10.3.72
FITTED 05916	FITTED	7.5.71
TOTAL MILEAGE 15570	TOTAL INSTALLED PERIOD	
WHY REMOVED Boiled to a standstill		

From the 1970s the engineers at The Grove kept meticulous records of engine overhauls. Ex-Dortax Bedford 19-seater BTK2C developed a faulty thermostat. The fitters had to surface the engine block and the cylinder head and they found cracks in all the exhaust valve seats.

Bere Regis & District had already sold or scrapped most of its Bedford OB-Duple Vista coaches when KDD989 came with W.T. Elliott's Sturminster Marshall operation in 1965, so this already elderly vehicle retired after little more than a year.

COLIN CADDY

By 1959, when Lancashire Motor Traders supplied this AEC Regal with 33-seat Burlingham coachwork, Bere Regis & District already had several underfloor-engined coaches that could carry more than 40 passengers.

COLIN CADDY

Twelve-year-old Commer Avenger REV682 came from Lancashire Motor Traders in 1962. Its Whitson body looks in good condition, but it only stayed for a year before being sold to a firm of cleaning contractors in Shaftesbury.

PHOTOBUS

Contrasting body styles on a pair of Bedford SBs huddled up close in the snow at The Grove: 4761AC, with Duple Super Vega body, came from a North Shields firm in 1965. It was nearly a year older than Plaxton-bodied OJT567, new to Bere Regis & District in 1960.

JOHN CUMMING

On West Street, Blandford, Bedford SB POT508G waits by the Three Choughs Inn, the very hostelry where Bere Regis carrier Reuben Day used to put up his horses on market days a hundred years before.

JOHN CUMMING

LMF86C was on a market-day excursion to Salisbury in 1973. The only Albion Victor VT21L that BR&D ever owned, it gave 15 years' service, but once had to be towed back from Sheffield with a broken camshaft. It had 41-seat Duple Northern Firefly coachwork.   DAVID PENNELS

On a sweltering summer's day in 1973 the Milton Abbas school bus drops off its charges at Lane End, Milborne St Andrew. Bedford SB YLM937's second passenger window looks very clean, but in fact it had slipped below the waistline when the children opened the windows for more air.   LES RONAN

POT507G, one of a pair of two-year-old Bedford SB5-Plaxtons acquired in 1971, nestled into what served as the garage at Cerne Abbas.

JOHN CUMMING

Two Bedford SB-Plaxtons on a school run come down the hill from Plush into Piddletrenthide. BFP235C was already nearly 13 years old when it arrived in Dorset in 1977. OBA776, acquired via Lancashire Motor Traders in 1963, worked for Bere Regis for more than 20 years.

KEITH NEWTON

On hire to National Express, JFX235N pulled into Cheltenham Coach Station in June 1975. It was one of four Bedford YRTs with Plaxton Elite coachwork new in May that year. They all transferred to Dorchester Coachways in 1994, but by then they had bus seats.

CHRIS ASTON

The cattle look on as KAO839E climbs a hill near Little Bredy on the twice-weekly service to Swyre in the summer of 1983. This Bedford VAM14 was two years old when it came south from Manchester, and it stayed with Bere Regis another 23 years.

KEITH NEWTON

Eight years or so after Reg Toop sank his last pint at the Drax Arms, Bedford YRT-Plaxton JFX235N works the Fridays-only Bere Regis-Wimborne journey. This was introduced in 1981 after Hants & Dorset cut back its services in the area.

KEITH NEWTON

After the garage at Bere Regis was demolished to make way for new homes, two coaches were still kept at the site. The roof of the old Methodist Chapel, once flanked by bus sheds, is still visible behind OPR386, one of half a dozen Volvo B58 coaches bought from Smiths of Wigan in 1986.

JOHN CUMMING

The school bus negotiates a sharp turn by the Tolpuddle Martyrs' Tree in May 1989. HJP485V was one of the Volvos that came from Smiths Tours of Wigan in 1987.

LES RONAN

In the mist near Aberdeen Wimborne driver Brian Napper stands alongside the Leyland Tiger demonstrator that he drove for the 1984 holiday tour season: A198RUR.

BRIAN NAPPER

Bedford YRT LVS442P matched the window frames of the Blandford office when it stopped en route from Yeovil to Bournemouth in the mid-1980s. It was one of a couple of Bedford YRTs with Plaxton Supreme coachwork that came from Armchair coaches of Brentford in 1977.

JOHN CUMMING

GNV981N passes through Okeford Fitzpaine on the 112 Thursday Hilton-Blandford working, wrongly showing the route number for Milton Abbas-Dorchester, the other service taken over from Mid-Dorset Coaches in 1987.
DORSET PASSENGER TRANSPORT

Bere Regis goes Continental: Volvo-Duple A599 LJT rests among other holiday coaches in the Netherlands.
BRIAN NAPPER

Bere Regis goes Transatlantic: Brian Napper drives Leyland Leopard JFX521V over Clachan Bridge, also known as "Atlantic Bridge" because it links the Scottish mainland with the island of Seil, the other side of a narrow Atlantic seawater channel.
BRIAN NAPPER

A Scottish ferryman watches closely as Malcolm House drives his coach off the Rothesay ferry in case it should scrape the slipway. E220GCG was one of five Volvo B10Ms with Hungarian-built Ikarus 336 bodies delivered in 1988.
MALCOLM HOUSE

Still wearing its National Bus Company logo, former United Counties Bedford YRQ RBD167M emerges from the mist at Mappowder. John Cumming had just seen his mother aboard so she could judge whether enough passengers used it to justify their Blandford Bus Company putting in a rival tender for the service. They did.

JOHN CUMMING

Bedford YRQ GNV981N climbs Dewlish Hill on a frosty November morning in 1987. on the 0945 Cheselbourne-Dorchester run, which was transferred from Mid-Dorset Coaches a couple of months earlier.

LES RONAN

In the early spring of 1990 RLJ186R wends its way from Winterborne Houghton down to Winterborne Stickland. This 1977 Plaxton Supreme-bodied YRT was one of the three Bedfords that Sandra Wylie retained in 1994.   KEITH NEWTON

After 1986 Dorset County Council published its own bus timetables. Four years later there was a big decline in the Bere Regis offering, but the cover featured one of its coaches stopping in Piddlehinton on its way south from Duntish. Bedford YRT HHE546N was inherited from Elliott & Potter.

DORSET PASSENGER TRANSPORT

For a short while in the mid-1990s Dorchester Coachways still ran buses painted red and brown, but they reached parts that Bere Regis & District never did. A287LNF, one of a pair of 1984 Ford Transits, turned up in rural Batcombe.
JOHN CUMMING

Where the Ironside business began: First Dorset Transit's Dennis Dart T826AFX waits by Winfrith Newburgh Church on 15 May 2000. Loading was so quiet that the driver could nip out and photograph his bus.
LES RONAN

"You have been warned": Sherborne drivers take note.
JOHN CUMMING

The agent's "For Sale" sign adorns the garage wall at 7 Bridport Road in 1993. The miniature coach, still on its shelf, can just be seen through the gap between the petrol pumps.
JOHN EYERS

Heathrow. When bad weather delayed their plane for 24 hours, Roper told the drivers to park eight of the coaches and all return to Dorset for the night in the other one. He was not going to pay them overnight meal allowances, for 'he didn't like bills' as another driver observed. They drove back from the airport without stopping even to change drivers or use wayside facilities. If the driver was tired another one slid behind the wheel as the coach sped westwards. Anyone who was desperate made use of an access trap in the gangway.

Like most of the fitters, Dave White, who worked for the firm for 24 years, was driving buses before very long. At first Roper barred him from driving on tours, saying 'You look a bit young behind the wheel.' However, not long after that Dave was assigned to tours work and remarked 'but you said I looked too young'. 'I think you look old enough now,' Roper replied. Later on he was trusted to drive on continental tours.

Besides the daily school runs, Bere Regis often had private hire contracts to convey large numbers of children across the country. Percy Parsons lived next door to the Ropers; his daughter Jeanette Davenport said that Mrs Doris Roper used to organise exchange visits with French teenagers, and the firm ran coach trips for them. It also ferried college students from Exeter to London, with a change of drivers in Dorchester. That job sometimes needed ten to a dozen coaches.

Ray Applin remembered a convoy of around 30 coaches taking Dorset schoolchildren to Dover to catch the ferry to France. On the way there they had to book in at the Little Chef on the Hog's Back, near Guildford, no more than two or three coaches at a time, so they left Dorset in relays. On that sort of run there were a couple of spare coaches in case of problems, and the fitters stowed the tools they might need in the boot.

But a driver on his own had to use his initiative to fix problems. The lights failed one night on Applin's coach as he headed back from Dover with a party of Spanish children.

One of the Shropshire-registered Bedford YRQs drove a party of schoolchildren to the Great Steam Working at Stourpaine Bushes in 1974. Children were let in free on the first day of the event.   DAVID PENNELS

In 1979, to mark 50 years since Reg Toop started his bus service, the miniature Commer-Harrington coach was repainted and set up on a wooden shelf on the office wall at 7 Bridport Road, and so became a Dorchester landmark.

PM PHOTOGRAPHY

He pulled in at Guildford and called Ray Roper, who had a man out to him within 15 minutes to solder a loose alternator wire. Some of the Bedfords had a habit of throwing a fan blade. On his way to fetch some sailors' children from a school somewhere beyond Chelmsford 'I'd just got on to the North Circular, when bang: one of the fan blades had gone right through the radiator.' He snapped the opposite blade off in order to balance the fan, got two five-gallon cans of water from a garage so he could keep topping up the radiator, and made it to Chelmsford and back to Dorset.

On 29 October 1979 the firm celebrated its golden jubilee. To mark 50 years since Reg Toop struck out on his own the miniature coach which had been used to promote tours up until 1972, was given a new lease of life. Its engine was removed, its roof was fixed and it was set upon its plinth on the office wall at 7 Bridport Road.

8

NEW REGULATIONS CHALLENGE MANAGEMENT

THE CONSERVATIVE VICTORY in the 1979 General Election heralded big changes for the country, including the bus industry. The new Prime Minister, Margaret Thatcher, was all for competition and private enterprise, so the Tories aimed their fire at the nationalised and municipal bus operators. The changes challenged all the independent bus concerns as well. If they were to flourish they had to understand and grasp the new opportunities.

Ray Roper was long accustomed to the set of regulations that Reg Toop had found so irksome half a century earlier. Now the task was to re-think constructively. School and works contracts, a new express service, holiday tours and the sale of assets all helped to keep the business afloat in the 1980s. Then, in 1988 a single contract gave Bere Regis & District a far healthier cash flow than it had been accustomed to. Sadly it no longer had Bill Ironside's

Around 1980 Bere Regis Coaches started using Setright Speed ticket machines that printed the fare, date etc. They came from other operators who had converted to more modern systems, such as Western Welsh and Manchester City Transport.

entrepreneurial flair to invest the new found wealth in laying a sure foundation for future prosperity.

Bere Regis Coaches, as the firm now styled itself, was just as affected by the challenges of the 1980s as were its big competitors that were about to be privatised. Two Transport Acts transformed the legal framework, first for express services and tours, and later for local buses. The two nationalised neighbours, Western National and Hants & Dorset, were broken up into smaller units. These planned their business in a manner quite different from the publicly-owned giants from which they had sprung. At the same time new small nimble competitors sought to take advantage of what was now on offer.

The 1980s also saw two important figures in the Bere Regis setup leave the scene, and for the first time a man with long experience of working in big bus companies was to exert his influence on the firm's activities.

The 1980 Transport Act freed operators from the need to apply to the traffic commissioners for a licence to run an express service with more than 30 miles between stops. Nor were licences required for excursions and tours. Since the 1930 Road Traffic Act every operator had to have a road service licence issued by the commissioners. Now anyone who applied could obtain such a licence unless the commissioners were satisfied that to issue it would be against the public interest, thus shifting the burden of proof from the applicant to the objector.

Neither Ray Roper nor Maurice Crocker seized the opportunity at that moment to launch a new express service between Dorset and London. When Bere Regis Coaches did so several years later it was an immediate success. But other changes, affecting local bus services, were to take place first.

Bere Regis made small-scale incursions into Weymouth in 1981. One was a local service between Weymouth and a couple of camp sites, at Sea Barn Farm and Bigwell

Taking over of Elliott & Potter of Sturminster Marshall in 1982 brought in a number of school contracts and nine Bedford coaches. Three of these were VAS-type 29-seaters. Duple-bodied HXG306F was new to a Teesside firm in 1968 and spent ten years in Scotland before it came to Dorset.
COLIN CADDY

Farm, out to the west of Chickerell. There was also a Thursdays-only link from the village of Crossways, which stood on the site of RAF Warmwell, whose fighters had flown to the defence of Portland naval base in the 1940s.

This was small beer compared to a service that went to a local competitor the next year. The Western National Omnibus Co Ltd, which had absorbed Southern National O.C. Ltd in 1969, ceded its Dorchester town services to Barry's Coaches Ltd (Interbus) of Weymouth. If this involved any undertaking by Barry's not to compete elsewhere it would have run counter to the spirit of the new legislation. However, Bere Regis perceived that such a deal had been struck under its very nose. It had sought two licences for Dorchester town services, but withdrew its applications, only to return to the fray at the end of the 1980s. Barry's Coaches' town service lasted just over five years. It was abandoned in October 1987 in the face of competition from the resurrected Southern National Ltd, which was spun off from Western National in 1983.

In May 1982 Bere Regis Coaches took over W.T. Elliott & F.C. Potter, of Sturminster Marshall, bringing in additional school contracts in east Dorset. The deal included nine Bedford coaches of various types; the oldest dated from

1962 and lasted another five years. This gave Ray Roper the opportunity to sell off the garage and petrol station on the busy Leigh Road and the Wimborne operation moved to Elliott & Potter's old premises at the Stone Lane Industrial Estate on the northern outskirts of the town.

An eastward extension beyond Wimborne had passed with little notice four years earlier when Bere Regis & District applied for the E&T licences of a small coach proprietor, E.R. Bailey of Ringwood. Tours from this Hampshire town proved popular and Ringwood was to play a significant role in the firm's activities in the years ahead.

In October 1982 Maurice Crocker died. A man of such girth that they had to take out a window so they could remove his body from his house, he had become a familiar figure in his office at The Grove. He had been Traffic Manager for around 30 years, and Roper needed to find someone with a good track record to take his place. He hired Henry Frier, who started with Southdown in 1952 and had years of experience with big bus companies. At Southdown he had worked on road service licensing, fares and legislation. In those days this was one of a number of large bus companies in the British Electric Traction (BET) group, which resisted nationalisation under the postwar Labour government. BET saw things differently in 1969, and its bus companies were nationalised. Southdown thus became part of the National Bus Company, along with Bere Regis & District's neighbours, Western National, Hants & Dorset and Wilts & Dorset; the last two merged under the Hants & Dorset name in 1972.

The NBC sought to move people between the former BET companies and those that had long been in public ownership. This expanded the job opportunities for Frier, who moved to Bournemouth to work for Hants & Dorset. When the Conservatives won power once more in 1979 and set about breaking up the NBC, fragmenting big companies into smaller units, Frier saw the writing on the wall. Bus companies were now easier to sell off to the private sector. Frier left Hants & Dorset just a month before it was divided in five. He was already familiar with Bere Regis & District's operations and on 1 March 1983 he became its Traffic Manager.

In Peter Roberts' *Bere Regis & District – The story of their bus services* Henry recalls that he 'had a thoroughly enjoyable career and gained much from NBC training courses, and experience in financial controls and the development of 'Operational Costing'.' He was destined to have an interesting career at Bere Regis & District. It must have been a bit of a roller-coaster ride but Henry is far too polite a man even to hint that this might reflect the Chinese curse: 'May you live in interesting times.'

Frier said Crocker had been a knowledgeable man, good at his job, and

'untouchable'. However, he found that despite Ray Roper's undoubted managerial skill, 'sorting out the money' was not his greatest strength. He was good at managing operations, finding drivers at short notice to fulfil commitments made, and he knew which job each one of them was working on.

'Ray Roper liked to control everything,' Frier commented. 'In many ways he was very secretive.' After Reg Toop died he progressively sold off the firm's assets in order to make ends meet. The books were checked by an accountant in Hove, well away from local eyes that might be tempted to pry.

Frier said Roper had no idea of operational costings. He did not want bus service revenue to be checked as 'the county makes up the difference', a reference to school contracts and subsidies. Ray Applin's experience bore this out. Roper occasionally asked him to drive a local bus service, which he was ready to do, but he did not want to handle fare collection. 'Oh, you go on and do the job. Don't worry about taking the money and we won't worry about it,' Roper told him.

On a typical day he appeared at The Grove at about half past nine in the morning,

The old military hospital at The Grove was for many years the headquarters of Bere Regis Coaches. Much of the outside paintwork still wore the firm's distinctive brown more than a decade after it had vacated the premises.   LES RONAN

his secretary Helen Christopher recalls. First he would talk to people in the downstairs offices, then went upstairs to his own office at around 10 o'clock. After dealing with the post, all of which he went through himself, he wrote out the next day's Orders, listing each driver's duties. These were then telephoned to Sherborne, Blandford and Wimborne, with each name called out together with the list of duties. Blandford covered the Hazelbury Bryan outstation, and Henry Frier dropped off the Bere Regis duties on his way home to Poole. Apart from a couple of staff who handled the day-to-day accounts, Helen said Roper did all the accounts himself and dealt with the banks.

She said the internal communications system at The Grove was antiquated; Roper used a buzzer to call people to his office. 'You could tell what sort of mood he was in by how long he kept his finger on the buzzer.' Helen started at The Grove as a 16-year-old junior, and worked as Henry Frier's secretary, then as the General Manager's secretary. 'I really enjoyed the time I spent there. Everybody made me feel welcome. Everybody was friendly,' she said.

In the early 1980s Bere Regis Coaches covered more school bus contracts for Dorset than any other operator. At that time not all coaches had seat belts, but one of the Bedford SBs (SAK32) was fitted with them; Dougie Woodward used to drive it to take disabled children from Dorchester to a special school in Bridport.

Barry Thirlwall said the county Education Department realised at that time that the commercial market

could fulfil much of the work and gradually reduced its own school transport fleet. However, from 1987 local authorities were required to give more weight to questions of safety when assessing whether a child was entitled to free school transport. This meant that more transport had to be provided. By the early 1990s 9,257 pupils went to school by hired-in transport, while the Education Department's bus fleet had halved and conveyed just 950 school children.

A condition of the DCC contract was that the buses should have doors controlled by the driver. Indeed the new regulations insisted on power-operated doors for service buses, Bere Regis Coaches dug in its heels because of the age of its fleet and the rural nature of its operations. The Traffic Commissioners apparently relented. In a typically practical approach to innovation, one driver's solution was to attach a dog lead to the door so he could open it.

Henry Frier believes Roper failed to grasp the implications for Bere Regis Coaches of the 1980 and 1985 Transport Acts. The second one ended the 56-year-old licensing system and introduced a completely new regulatory

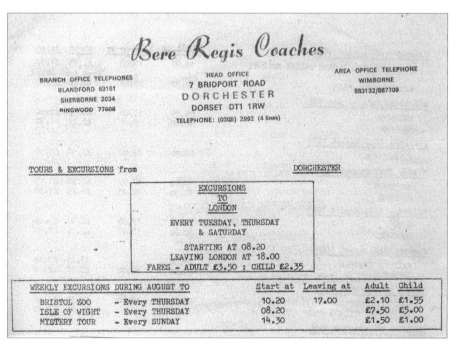

The August 1981 Tours programme highlighted the three-days-a-week excursions to London. The addition of a Ringwood telephone number followed the takeover of ER Bailey's E&T licences from the Hampshire town.

environment from October 1986. Bus operators had either to register their stage services as commercial operations, or to tender for local authority subsidised routes where the service was deemed to be socially necessary but not commercially viable. The lowest bidder usually won the tender, but at the risk of unreliable operation or indeed financial failure.

When Frier joined Bere Regis Coaches there were already thrice-weekly excursions to London, on Tuesdays, Thursdays and Saturdays. Some passengers bought 'single' tickets for successive excursions, so that they could spend more time in town and come home a couple of days later. This suggested there was a market for an express service from the Weymouth/Portland area in place of these excursions. On 2 June 1983, just three months after Frier became Traffic Manager, the express service was launched.

The London terminus was opposite the Old Vic Theatre in Waterloo, and the coach called at Wimborne and Ringwood on the way. At first it ran on the same three days of the week, but within two months it was running daily. Agents were appointed to sell tickets in Dorset towns and villages along the route; Henry Frier said this contributed to the success of the London express. For one summer, in 1990, there was also a Portland-Dorchester-Bristol express.

As the London service developed feeders from other parts of Dorset linked up with the London coach at Ringwood. If there were too many passengers for one coach, one of the feeder coaches went on to London too. If necessary a company car could be pressed into service. Wimborne depot had a seven-seat Peugeot 504 saloon (DWA787V), painted in Bere Regis colours, usually driven by Ray Dunningham. He once had to chase the coach all the way to Richmond when a doctor who was supposed to be aboard was left behind.

In time the London service was licensed as a stage carriage operation, which meant it could benefit from fuel tax rebate. It picked up quite a few passengers at Fleet, which was also served by a fast rail service to Waterloo, so it was no surprise that British Rail tried to oppose it. However, the matter never reached the Traffic Court. In a telephone call from Dorchester it was pointed out that the railway had raised no such objection when two NBC concerns – Southdown and Hants & Dorset – had launched a competitive limited stop bus service between Southampton and Portsmouth. Henry Frier could of course remember this episode from his days in Bournemouth.

Austin minibus EFX678D came with the Dortax business in 1967. In the 1980s it was painted grey and used to drop off packages for TNT around Dorchester. The international parcels service had despatched them on the previous day's express coach from London.   JOHN CUMMING

As a sideline the evening coach from London brought packages back to Dorset on behalf of the TNT parcel delivery service. Sporting a grey livery and the legend 'DESPATCH POST TNT Nationwide next day delivery – Guaranteed', an elderly Austin minibus (EFX678D) then dropped them off around Dorchester and nearby villages the following day.

Legally speaking, when Reg Toop died, the firm became 'Executors of R.W. Toop, deceased.' Before the 1980 Transport Act no-one questioned this. But under the new dispensation the Traffic Commissioner for the South Eastern Area, R.S. Thornton, ruled that the act made no provision

A surprise purchase in 1980 was a Bristol LHS6L with Plaxton 33-seat body. Bristol chassis had not long been available to privately-owned operators, but once the restriction was lifted the LHS proved popular as a smaller-capacity coach. LLJ605W is parked at The Grove.

JOHN CUMMING

her, and paid for her petrol. As a 40th birthday present she was given Ray Roper's Porsche, and he bought a new one for himself.

Towards the end of 1983 the firm was seriously in need of funds, so Roper sold the garage at Coldharbour, Sherborne. Unlike Arthur Ironside, who was declared homeless at Wimborne, local manager Jack Toop was found new accommodation.

Jack was not related to Reg Toop, but Roper treated him with great respect. He had worked for the firm since the 1930s, and was living in a flat on the premises at Coldharbour. Every Friday he used to drive down to Dorchester to deal with wages and the Sherborne drivers' detail, and also banking matters, for by this time the firm's bank account was held at a Sherborne branch.

On Wednesdays Jack Toop used to go off to play golf, whilst his wife was at Dorchester market. She was said to be a formidable lady, who once took a lad who worked in the garage to task for the heinous offence of 'Sherborne doing

for licences to be granted to executors. No such objection had been raised in the Western Area, where the majority of the licence applications were heard, but services that ran further afield needed what were called 'backing licences' from each traffic area. Roper and Mrs Toop consulted lawyers and decided in 1982 to turn the business into a trust, so that licences would be granted to 'Trustees of R.W. Toop, deceased.'

On 5 July 1983 Ethel Toop died. Probate valued her estate at almost £64,000. She had appointed Ray Roper as one of her executors and trustees. But the fellow-trusteeship of Reg Toop's estate now passed to his daughter Sandra, who had remarried and was named in Mrs Toop's will as Sandra Maureen Simonds. She was the principal beneficiary under her mother's will.

Sandra's trusteeship may not have had much impact on the business in the short term, but became much more significant as her son's 18th birthday approached and after she remarried once more. All the same, Frier said, Roper 'had to keep her fairly sweet.' The firm maintained a car for

There were always coaches parked outside the Tachograph Centre at The Grove. Plaxton Panorama-bodied CBU52C was one of three Bedford SB5s delivered in 1965, the last of the type bought new by BR&D. This one lasted 21 years, but identical CBU53C survived nearly 27.

A.H. WALLER COLLECTION

something for a Blandford coach.' The visiting Blandford driver had asked the young man to clean the inside of his coach because a passenger had been sick.

The fleet was formally transferred from Executors to Trustees in the spring of 1985. It consisted of 84 buses and coaches, exactly the same total as the Executors inherited from Reg Toop in 1973. Now there were 65 Bedfords, but the Luton factory that had turned out this marque since 1931 was to cease production of passenger chassis by the end of 1986. Sooner or later Bere Regis would have to choose another make; its first two Volvo B10Ms (A599/600LJT) arrived in April 1984 and the Swedish manufacturer, which had established its U.K. presence in 1967, won the future business. The rest of the Trustees' fleet consisted of nine Leylands, four AEC Reliances, two Bristol LHS6Ls, and a couple of Ford Transit minibuses. Apart from some of the Bedfords and five of the Leylands, all of these had been bought new; the Bristols, one of which has been preserved (CLJ413Y), were an unusual choice for an independent operator.

Unrest among the drivers provoked Ray Roper into writing a strongly worded letter to 'Dear Staff' on 29 April 1985. It started: 'During the past week three drivers have approached me by telephone regarding the harassment that has been applied to persuade them to join a trade union.' Another driver, who had long been a union member, had handed in his resignation 'because of the very bad atmosphere that has been created.'

At that time Roper, like Ironside before him, was adamant that he would not formally recognise a trade union. Anyone on the staff was free to join a union, but they would be treated exactly the same way as non-members. He continued:

Bedford SB1 OBA776 turns into the Cornhill before leaving Dorchester for Cerne Abbas and Holnest. New in 1959, it came to Dorset after four years with a Salford company. It soldiered on with Bere Regis Coaches well into the mid-1980s.

PM PHOTOGRAPHY

Bere Regis having been in business for the past 56 years without any closed shop trade union agreement must be allowed to continue in the same manner in the very difficult years ahead . . .

I have noticed a small element of bad feeling and trouble making within this depot at Dorchester during the past month and I must therefore request those responsible to cease doing so forthwith and instead concentrate their energies in keeping this firm in business. It would appear to me that what is happening at the moment is greatly assisting our past competitors to move into this area and so jeopardise our business and of course your own jobs here. I must warn you that should a staff member at any time do anything which would endanger the livelihood of other employees or damage this firm, I shall not hesitate to place the matter in the hands of my legal advisors for their necessary action against the person, or persons, concerned.

This particular period of run-up to the proposed new Transport Bill for deregulation is a most serious one for all large business people, and thus your 100% support will be required to take us through this period and we hope into better times. After all, Bere Regis Coaches was left in trust by the late Mr Toop so that everyone

The letterhead used in the mid-1980s.

could have a job for as long as they required one, in appreciation of their hard work in building up the business in the early years, so let us continue to work in harmony as we have in previous years, for the benefit of all.

Henry Frier found the firm had more administrative staff than it needed, and the drivers became restless. He said Roper controlled the drivers well but their pay was 'somewhat depressed,' so they were keen to do a great deal of overtime. Roper was aware that they were able to enhance their hours worked for the weekly timesheets, but 'as long as you did what you were told you were fairly safe.' John Eyers said the firm paid overtime at time and one eighth or time and a quarter.

Roper used to hammer out pay and conditions with the drivers each year at an independent operators meeting in the Western Area. 'Between pay and perks the drivers did OK,' Henry Frier said. However they became increasingly unsettled and there was a strike on the day of the Chelsea Flower Show. This hit school contract work and excursions to the show and elsewhere.

ACAS, the government's Advisory, Conciliation and Arbitration Service, became involved and the Transport & General Workers' Union was then recognised. The ensuing settlement cost the firm money, including fringe benefits, such as lunch allowances, which were negotiated. Henry Frier said Ray Roper called on him to deal with difficult issues, like sacking employees. 'We won one tribunal and lost another,' he added.

Under Roper's management Bere Regis Coaches regularly recruited apprentices for its engineering workshops at The Grove, where Jerry Jackson was Chief Engineer from the mid-1970s. Bus operators were required to pay a levy to the Road Transport Industry Training Board, but they could gain exemption from it by training their employees up to a certain standard. Bere Regis Coaches' training programme was of high enough quality to achieve this. By this time bodywork repairs were also carried out at The Grove, the Kentredder was still in business and there was also a grease shop.

For some years Percy Parsons was responsible for training the apprentices. Dave White said there were 20 of them when he joined in 1976. Percy also opened up at The Grove every morning, checked the oil and water in all the 30 vehicles that were due to go out on the road, and fed the feral cats that kept down the workshop mice. On a cold winter's morning a fog of exhaust fumes shrouded the coach park as he started up the coaches to warm up their engines. His daughter Jeanette said he always wore brown overalls with a length of wire or string round his waist. When he drove a bus his spectacles were usually perched on top of his head.

Percy Parsons worked for Bere Regis & District for 37 years. He rose to be Assistant Chief Engineer and set up and managed the Tachograph Centre at the Grove.

JEANETTE DAVENPORT

Since the majority of the fleet was more than three years old, many of the coaches had to pass the annual MOT test. A facility to conduct these tests was set up at The Grove to deal with Bere Regis's own coaches as well as generating revenue from other concerns that brought their vehicles in for their MOT.

Under the 1980 Transport Act the speed and times of travel of commercial vehicles had to be monitored by tachograph, so a centre for maintaining these devices was also established alongside the works. For the appropriate fee this facility was made available to all operators of public transport or goods vehicles in western Dorset. Mick Mescus took over as Assistant Chief Engineer and Percy Parsons set up and ran the tachograph centre until he retired in 1987, when Mike Hussey took over the job.

A driver's working day was supposed to be no longer than 11 hours, with a break of at least 30 minutes after five and a half hours on the road, and at least 11 hours rest time between working shifts. A Wimborne driver recalled later that if they overran the limit they

VXE278G fills the autumn morning air with a cloud of exhaust in front of the Tachograph Centre. When it came to Dorset in 1981 this rear-engined Leyland Panther had three previous owners. It was already 12 years old, but its 51-seat Plaxton coachwork stood up to another nine years' work.　　　　　　　　　　　　　　　　　BRIAN BOTLEY

REBUILT UNIT.		26	SHEET No. A
FITTED TO _RJT 683 K_	DATE FITTED	_MAY 1978_	
SPEEDO _27184_	FITTED BY	_J EYRES_	
DATE STARTED. _____			

OVERHAUL DETAILS.

ENGINE REBUILT WITH CRANK FROM SFX233N

Removed 14-11-78.

Broken Crank - Block

The engineers still used parts from one coach to put another one back on the road. RJT683K and SFX233N were both Bedfords YRQs.

would just report that the tachograph was out of order.

Engineering and bodyshop work was also carried out for Dorset County Council, whose premises were next door, the West Dorset National Health Service Trust, and a variety of commercial customers. These included Dorchester Timber and the Bridport depot of builders' merchants Travis Perkins, but not their Dorchester one. The lorries of ECC Quarries, which regularly drove from Warmwell to Frome, in Somerset, used to call in on the way to have their brakes adjusted.

Among the ancillary vehicles kept at The Grove were a heavy-duty breakdown and recovery lorry and a couple of Land Rovers. For several years Bere Regis & District advertised a 24-hour recovery service to other firms. One winter, when deep snow blocked many roads, the Land Rovers were also pressed into service for an unusual customer: the Dorset Police borrowed them so they could reach parts of the county where the deep snow proved too much for their own cars.

Every fitter was trained to drive buses. Dave White, who worked in the bodyshop, was told to start driving when he passed his test at the age of 24. Ray Roper evidently kept an eye on the workshop, but the fitters were adept at avoiding trouble. When Roper's Daimler Sovereign came in for respraying, the foam

cushioning in the back seat caught fire. A fitter went down to Dorchester market to buy new foam to replace it. Who should see him there but the boss himself, who asked what he was doing there, but the real purpose of the trip to market was not divulged.

Another time a freshly painted coach demolished a low wall as it backed out of the paint shop. Soon after it was driven back into the paint shop for repair, Roper appeared. He saw that someone had knocked over 'my wall' and wanted to look at the coach. A quick-thinking painter warned him not to go alongside the offending coach, because the paint was still wet.

For a time there was no telephone in the workshop. If a coach broke down and needed to be rescued, the driver phoned the office on Bridport Road, and the petrol pump attendant drove down to The Grove to tell the engineers. Some problems, however, turned out to be trivial: John Baring, who drove the Hurst bus, complained that its drive shaft 'chinged'. The fitters believed this was because he used to engage too high a gear, but they attached a jubilee clip and it 'chinged' no more.

Clearly reflecting on the business as a whole and not just the mechanical side of it, Henry Frier observed rather elegantly that the engineers 'kept the wheels on'.

Most of the fleet was ageing. Between 1982 and 1984 nine Bedford YRQ saloons were acquired. They had 45-seat Willowbrook bodies with driver-controlled doors, but they had seen ten years' service with the United Counties Omnibus Co. Ltd of Northampton. They were unheated, so the Dorchester drivers recycled old heaters from disused coaches still parked around the yard, and fitted them near the driving position. Passengers still felt the cold, but the drivers were quite content in their shirt sleeves. These Bedfords were good for the kind of stage operation on which they were used. They were easy to maintain and gave good mileage to the gallon.

Feeder services for the London express fanned out across territory never served by Bere Regis Coaches' ordinary bus services. Ex-United Counties Bedford YRQ GNV981N waits at Charmouth in August 1986 to take London passengers as far as Dorchester.   KEITH NEWTON

The first time a Bere Regis coach travelled abroad was in 1983, on private hire. Three years later the firm entered the continental holiday business, offering tours to Austria, the Rhine Valley and the Dutch bulb fields. By now it had been running two- and three-day tours within Britain for ten years or more. It made good use of its network of agents around Dorset to promote the holidays.

Among those who drove the continental tours were Brian Napper, who was based at Wimborne, Dave White, and Malcolm House, who had moved from Hazelbury Bryan to Dorchester in 1962. In his time House had driven Portland leave expresses to Birmingham and Liverpool. He drove to County Kerry a couple of times, to the Normandy Beaches, and took a party from Blandford on a visit to farms in the Netherlands. The drivers entered into the spirit of things: at their own expense they had jackets made with the legend 'Bere Regis Coaches Holiday Tours'.

In the mid-1980s a couple of Leyland Tiger demonstrator coaches were loaned by the manufacturers for use on extended tours to Scotland and elsewhere. The continental holidays market called for smarter coaches than the existing fleet could muster, so eight more Volvos were acquired in 1986. Two were new B10Ms that bore 'cherished' Dorset registration

Television may have taken traffic away from the buses for well over 20 years, but popular TV programmes like "Last of the Summer Wine" could still be a draw for the tours side of the business.

The holiday tours business demanded smart new coaches. Two brand new Volvo B10Ms arrived in 1986, each taking the registration mark of a retired Bere Regis coach (with no year letter). UFX567, which had a 55-seat Duple body, stayed on briefly after Sandra Toop took over in 1993.

PM PHOTOGRAPHY

Before putting them on the road Bere Regis Coaches reregistered the half dozen seven-year-old Volvo B58s that came from Smiths Tours of Wigan in 1986. No doubt Ray Roper hoped the passengers who rode to London on 4506UB (ex-BTB684T) would not detect its age.

PM PHOTOGRAPHY

Eleven Volvo B58s joined the fleet from Smiths Tours of Wigan in 1987. Two of them were reregistered so their age was not obvious. Blandford driver Tony White stands beside UXF850 (formerly HJP490V), branded for the flagship "Bere Regis Holidays".

JOHN CUMMING

Bere Regis bought eight brand-new Volvo B10M 57-seaters in 1988. E222GCG was one of five with Hungarian-built Ikarus 336 bodies, a new departure for the firm.

OMNIBUS SOCIETY COLLECTION

numbers recycled from withdrawn Bere Regis vehicles (OJT568 and UFX567). The other half dozen were 1979 Volvo B58s, which came from Smiths Tours of Wigan. All six were reregistered before entering service, most of them taking numbers donated by retired Bere Regis coaches.

Another 11 B58 coaches, dating from 1980, came from Smiths in 1987. Like the previous six they had Duple bodies. They usually bore the fleet name 'Bere Regis Holidays'. A couple of them were given old registration numbers with no year letter (UXF850 and UFX330), which hid their true age from anyone not in the know. The other nine kept their original Warrington registrations (HJP479-85/7/8V). These coaches also ran to London on the express service.

In 1988 Ray Roper took delivery of eight brand new 57-seat Volvo B10Ms (E217-224ECG) under a lease-purchase arrangement with Kirkby Bus & Coach, of Anston near Sheffield. Plaxton bodied the first three, and the other five bore Hungarian-built Ikarus 336 coachwork – a first for Bere Regis Coaches. In due course Roper had to decide whether to purchase them outright. He opted to continue the lease. Leasing costs were high, and without a solid business plan this led to problems.

Towards the end of the 1980s Roper appointed a Tours Manager, Steve Ring. He was taken on as a pump attendant at 7 Bridport Road, but one day the boss told him he would like him to join the office staff down at The Grove. After this rapid promotion Henry Frier said that before long he became Roper's right-hand man.

A few routes were modified in the years running up to the big changes that came with the 1985 Transport Act. In August 1983 the Dorchester-Bovington service, which in those days only ran on Wednesdays and Saturdays, was extended to follow a circular route round the camp. The next year Bere Regis Coaches went to Yeovil once more, but only on Thursdays, with a service from there to Bournemouth.

Before Deregulation Day, 25 October 1986, bus operators could register the services they intended to run on a commercial basis, without financial support. Bere Regis Coaches registered 21. Ten of these were school or college journeys, two of which were cancelled before D-day. Another six ran at most one day a week, including Yeovil-Bournemouth. There were three limited-stop journeys that linked in with the London express service: Portland-Poulner, Blandford-Poulner and Bridport-Dorchester.

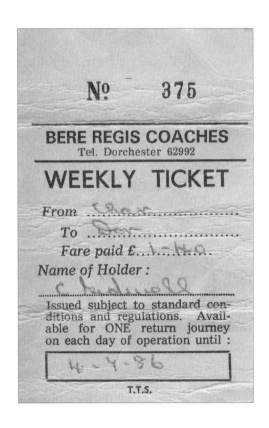

Weekly tickets were available where there was a daily bus service, like the road between Dorchester and Charminster.

The only other registered services that ran more than one day a week were Sturminster Newton-Weymouth, which ran on three days a week in summer only, and Bovington Camp-Dorchester.

The Bovington service was combined with Dorchester-Moreton and increased for a while from market days only to six days a week.

Thereafter its timetable was frequently revised. The County Council had now started to give numbers to bus services; after a year or so it allocated no less than seven different numbers to variations of the Bovington route. In the process Bere Regis took over the Dorchester-Wool-Bovington service of Rosemary Hodder's Dorset Queen Coaches. (Her father, Percy Webb, had died in 1976). For a couple of years Southern National Ltd (part of what had been Western National between 1969 and 1983) ran the Saturday journeys, but Bere Regis took them back in 1990.

Henry Frier said Ray Roper failed to spot other potential operators who vied for services that were put out to tender: 'If he had put in sensible prices for Blandford-Sturminster Newton he would have got it.' Instead it went to Oakfield Coaches of Blandford. Ray Roper put out a notice to customers saying that 'following the Government's Bill of Bus Service deregulation Bere Regis have been forced to cease operation of the above service.'

His wording left little doubt that he felt Bere Regis Coaches had been victimised. 'I can assure you this has not come about voluntarily, but due to the fact that following the new system of tendering for bus services, the Dorset County Council have awarded the above bus services to another operator in this area. Thus after forty years of continuous service to the villages between Sturminster Newton and Blandford, quite apart from others in those Towns and beyond, we feel sad that the day is drawing near when we have to say goodbye for a while at least.' The usual driver on the route, Chris Ryalls, who had worked for the firm for many years, would be deployed on other routes and school contracts. He 'would wish me to add his thanks and appreciation for the way in which you have accepted him over the years.'

Roper urged passengers to contact the County Council's transportation and engineering department if the replacement bus service 'is not up to our standard.'

The Dorchester-Sherborne service was also lost. It went to A. Tucker's Air Camelot, of Wincanton, Somerset, along with the local route between Sherborne and Holwell. However, the County Council took the contract away from Air Camelot the following summer and offered Bere Regis Coaches a temporary contract to run its old service once more. Ray Roper turned it down, saying his vehicles were needed to meet the demands of the coaching season.

For a while the County Council ran its own Dorchester–Sherborne Saturday service, and in 1988 the route passed to a rival concern, Pearce, Darch & Willcox (Comfy-Lux), of Cattistock; Glen Willcox had once been a Bere Regis driver (see chapter 4). That year John Cumming set up another competing business, the Blandford Bus Company.

Two Ford R1014 45-seaters came with the House family's Mid-Dorset Coaches in 1987 -- the last operator that Bere Regis took over. Plaxton-bodied OWO703M almost hides Mid-Dorset's other Ford, JWC525N.

BRIAN BOTLEY

Local operations in the Blackmore Vale were severely reduced, leaving little more than school journeys. R.J. Cuff of Piddletrenthide took over Gillingham-Sturminster Newton during the school holidays, and Bere Regis withdrew completely from this route in 1990, leaving it to Ray Cuff and Wake's Services (Sparkford) Ltd.

Mervyn House used to drive Mid-Dorset's Ford-Duple JWC525N to Dorchester before his family's long-established bus service passed to Bere Regis Coaches. It was then painted brown and red and used to launch the Dorchester "Town Shopper" service in 1989.   JOHN CUMMING

However, the Thursday service from Yeovil to Bournemouth continued, calling at Sherborne, Marnhull, Sturminster Newton, Blandford and Poole, as well as other villages along the river Stour. This survived until August 1991. During school terms the firm also had a Mondays-only circular working between Sturminster Newton and Shillingstone,

In September 1987 Bere Regis Coaches took over Mid-Dorset Coaches' Thursday service from Hilton to Blandford, which served villages along the southern rim of Blackmore Vale, but not for long. Over the next three years the route was worked in turn by Adams Bros (Victory Tours), of Sixpenny Handley, Bere Regis Coaches again, Lewis Coaches, Stalbridge, and then John Cumming's Blandford Bus.

The House family, of Hilton, who owned Mid-Dorset Coaches, had been in business for 60 years, but it was decided to sell up after Norman House had a heart attack. His brother Mervyn told Norman Aish that they offered the business to Bere Regis & District because the firm had been so helpful to them around the end of World War II. However, some years earlier Norman House told Aish that if he saw Ray Roper walking along the street in Dorchester sometimes he would stop to talk, and at other times he totally ignored him.

This was the last time Bere Regis Coaches took over another bus concern. It included the Houses' long-established Dorchester service, which started at Milton Abbas and ran via Hilton, Cheselbourne and Puddletown four days a week. The following year Bere Regis added Hilton-Dorchester journeys on two more days a week, but in November 1989 Southern National took over most of the journeys, leaving Bere Regis with a school run and shopping trips. Bere Regis handed out a typewritten timetable with the message: 'PLEASE SUPPORT THIS BERE REGIS ROUTE, otherwise more journeys will be withdrawn. USE IT – OR LOSE IT.' Lose it they did; the service was withdrawn in April 1990.

In 1987 two Thursday market services to Blandford were combined in a series of roundabout journeys, starting in Bere Regis and calling at Milton Abbas, Winterborne Stickland and villages between. It was withdrawn in April 1990 after John Cumming registered a commercial service covering the same area. He

0998

	RETURN	
	FARE	
	1/-	

This Ticket is available only for date as punched, and must be shown on demand.

Avery, Printer, Troytown

Before they moved on to machine-issued tickets Mid-Dorset Coaches had theirs printed at Troytown, near Puddletown.

combined it with parts of his Melcombe Bingham-Blandford route and continued to work it in one form or another until Damory Coaches of Blandford took it over from him in 1994. (This was a new subsidiary of the privatised Wilts & Dorset Bus Co. Ltd).

West of Dorchester Bere Regis fared ill on Deregulation Day. The Wednesday and Friday journeys to Swyre passed to Barry's Coaches. But Bere Regis regained the route a year later, and in April 1988 extended it to Bridport. However, Barry's took it back once more in November 1989 and withdrew the Bridport-Swyre section.

Bridport was still not entirely abandoned: Bere Regis Coaches launched a weekly journey from there to Bournemouth in November 1988. This ran on Thursdays from April to December, with a feeder for passengers from Portland and Weymouth who wanted to join the coach at Dorchester.

By this time funds were running low again. The Blandford depot at no. 1 East Street was sold to a housing association, but was leased back until work on the new homes began. Meanwhile Bere Regis Coaches, seeking to stem the tide of local competition, objected when John Cumming sought a subsidy for his Blandford Bus Company from the Council for Small Industries in Rural Areas (CoSIRA). The Wilts & Dorset Bus Company and Adams' Victory Tours also objected. Cumming wrote to Nicholas Baker, then MP for North Dorset, to seek his support, and in the end the Rural Development Commission, CoSIRA's new incarnation, agreed to his subsidy.

Leyland Leopard EHJ76T, working the London express service in about 1983, passes a waiting Hampshire Bus on Winchester Broadway. The coach had only been with Bere Regis a few months. Plaxton rebodied it in 1979 but the chassis dated from 1968.   A.H. WALLER COLLECTION

In the summer of 1988 BP set about drilling for oil on the western shore of Poole Harbour. For a time this dramatically turned round Bere Regis Coaches' fortunes. The firm won its most lucrative contract ever, to convey construction workers to Wytch Farm, near Wareham, which was to become the largest onshore oilfield in Western Europe. At its height the contract, which began in August 1988, was worth £25,000 a week.

Bere Regis Coaches actually had money on deposit. Transport was required round the clock seven days a week. Fifteen coaches were kept busy every day, conveying workers between the holiday camp where they were housed at Osmington and the drilling site by Poole Bay. There were journeys to and from bed and breakfast accommodation in Christchurch as well, and trips to Heathrow and even Glasgow.

Many of the workers had come off North Sea rigs to drill in Dorset, so a holiday camp near Weymouth was a big change for them. Ray Applin, who drove one of the coaches, said they were picked up at Osmington at six o'clock in the morning. 'Mr Roper paid us sort of extra... It put our wages up. I know we were doing more hours, early in the morning and whatever. But that was seven days a week. We did all right out of it.'

When the contract ended in June 1991 Henry Frier said the money had 'vanished'. Ray Roper told him he had better find another contract. A new contract was signed with BP, to provide transport for oil workers travelling home to Glasgow at the weekend, but that only ran until the end of December that year.

BP's Wytch Farm development, on the shore of Poole Harbour. The contract to convey workers there did wonders for Bere Regis Coaches' earnings in the late 1980s.   © BP plc

9
END OF THE INHERITANCE

A T THE END of the 1980s Bere Regis Coaches were still ready to fight the big local rival, Southern National, which had been running its Dorchester Shuttle minibus since April 1987. This had been criticised for not providing enough luggage space. Bere Regis Coaches launched its own 'Town Shopper

Publicity announcing the Town Shopper Service, January 1989.

Service using real buses' on 9 January 1989. Henry Frier told *Bus Business*: 'We are the local operator and we have the resources to operate the town service.'

Barely a month after the hourly service began, using a Ford 45-seater (JWC525N), the Town Shopper was already covering its marginal costs. Six times a day it left Trinity Street on the first of three circular trips out to the edge of town and back: west to Poundbury, east to Fordington and Came View, and south to Castle Park and Victoria Park. The first journey of the day started at 9.30 in the morning, but the service proved such a success that on 23 April 1990 another four journeys were added, starting at 8.05. If you were minded to take a tour of the town you could stay aboard the bus, which was inherited from Mid-Dorset Coaches, for the whole hour at the flat fare of 28 pence.

Henry Frier said that if Bere Regis Coaches wanted to continue running stage bus services it had to look at new developments. It had lost three contracted County Council services the previous autumn, two to Southern National which had put in a block tender for a large number of routes, and the other to Wilts & Dorset.

Dorset County Council's April 1990 timetable listed 20 stage bus routes operated by Bere Regis Coaches. Within a month of the timetable being

Five Plaxton Supreme-bodied Bedford YMTs bought new in 1977 were still going strong in 1991. In May that year SFX784R, working the Duntish service, picks up passengers at the stop by the Dorset County Museum.

BARRY THIRLWALL

The Dorchester town service and the express service to London still flourished. So did the holiday tours. In April 1990 a new express service from Portland to Bristol was announced, running every Tuesday and Saturday until December that year, via Weymouth, Dorchester, Yeovil and Bath. The Weymouth to Bristol return fare was £6.

Bere Regis Coaches took the fight to the heart of Wilts & Dorset Bus Co. territory too, by winning the Poole Park & Ride contract in 1991. Henry Frier put in a lower bid than 'The Wilts', as insiders call it, much to the larger company's annoyance. This was a summer Sunday service for which a Volvo coach shuttled between car parking in central Poole and the seashore at Sandbanks, where there was very little space to park a car. However the

issued a number of the market services had been withdrawn so the firm's local bus network was whittled down. According to *Bus and Coach Management* Bere Regis blamed this on 'cowboy operators which had sprung up after deregulation, increasing diesel costs and falling passenger numbers, which had caused some routes to become unprofitable.'

The Bovington Camp–Dorchester and Pulham/Duntish–Dorchester routes remained. For these Bere Regis Coaches had bid for subsidies of £5,500 and £13,000 respectively. The highest bidders had sought £30,000 and £14,477. Bovington-Dorchester now followed five varied routes at different times, so that small villages between the two places retained some service. At the same time Southern National gained the Milton Abbas-Dorchester service, and Lewis Coaches of Stalbridge took over Marnhull-Dorchester and Hilton–Blandford.

H443JLJ was the last vehicle delivered new to Bere Regis Coaches, in August 1990. Lettered for both the London Express service and for Bere Regis Holidays, this 57-seat Volvo B10M-Plaxton did not stay long. In October 1993 it passed to Worth's Travel of Enstone, Oxfordshire.

PM PHOTOGRAPHY

service was not a great success and the Borough of Poole did not put it out to tender a second year.

For Bere Regis drivers the contract with Slattery's of Tralee for the London-Ireland express service could prove quite an adventure. The police once stopped a coach to check for explosives. There were none. Volvo A600LJT rests at home between journeys in 1993. 　　　LES RONAN

cold, but Dave White brought along a spanner with which to turn on the hot water. At first one or two of the coaches ran on the London-Holyhead leg, leaving Victoria Coach Station at around seven o'clock in the evening, and travelling via Luton, Coventry and Birmingham. After a short break on Anglesey they returned by the same route with passengers off the ferry from Dun Laoghaire, many of them enlivened by the refreshment they had taken on the ferry. Four Bere Regis drivers were assigned to London-Holyhead, working five days on and five days off. Dave White shared the driving with Mick O'Brien, as the hours were too long for a single driver. Slattery's also had a coach on the route, and other Slattery's vehicles covered the Dun Laoghaire-Tralee leg.

Experience gained from running the London express served Bere Regis Coaches well when it won a contract in the early 1990s to provide coaches for the UK leg of an express service between Ireland and London launched by Slattery's of Tralee. This family business had started out as greengrocers with just one shop in Tralee, near Killarney. It developed into a travel agency and small-scale coach hire business. CIE, the Irish national transport board, used to hire Slattery's coaches for its Dublin-London service, a joint operation with the UK's National Express. Air fares were still high, and Slattery's decided they would do better to start their own routes between Ireland and London. Some used the Dun Laoghaire to Holyhead ferry and others Rosslare to Fishguard.

In time, to support the contract, Bere Regis kept up to four coaches at Victoria, in a yard near London Transport's Gillingham Street garage. There was bed and breakfast accommodation for its drivers nearby. Keith Poyser, who became the firm's lead driver, said the showers only ran

Parked at the back of the offices at The Grove, Volvo A600LJT named four local offices prominently across its rear panelling. 　　　COLIN CADDY

Later Bere Regis Coaches ran a second overnight route from Victoria Coach Station to Waterford via Fishguard, or subsequently Pembroke Dock. Coach and driver would board the ferry. An Irish company's driver took over the wheel at Waterford for the onward journey to Cork, Killarney and Tralee. Poyser said the

British police stopped one of the coaches on the motorway on its way back to London to check for bomb-making equipment. None was found but after that the drivers were very careful. The contract continued until Slattery's sold their routes to CIE and they became the main Irish routes of Eurolines. While it lasted the drivers ensured that their Traffic Manager was supplied with Gilbey's gin.

C734TJF was one of a pair of Volvo B10Ms that came from a Merseyside concern in 1991. It was the last vehicle to join the fleet before Bere Regis Coaches split apart. By then the coach had already been sold to a Scottish firm.

COLIN CADDY

Back in Dorset school and other contracts still contributed a share of the revenue. Before long services up and down the Piddle valley, most of them supported by the County Council, were shared four ways between Southern National, Lewis of Stalbridge, Wakes of Sparkford, and Bere Regis Coaches. The weekly workings from Yeovil and Bridport to Bournemouth continued, as did the summer journeys from the Blackmore Vale to Weymouth. However, by 1993 the Yeovil and Blackmore Vale services had ceased.

So long as Ray Roper was in charge the workshops at The Grove continued what outside customers found to be an efficient maintenance service for their vehicles. These included the DCC school bus operation, and a few other local bus firms. John Cumming praised the work of Bere Regis engineers who, in the few hours between its morning and afternoon Puddletown school runs, replaced a faulty gearbox in a Blandford Bus Company Leyland Leopard.

However, the age of the Bere Regis fleet meant that maintenance costs were higher than they would have been for newer vehicles, and the firm often held on to elderly vehicles that had become surplus to the needs of the operation.

As Roper set about slimming down the business, he sold off properties and reduced the size of the fleet. In September 1991 five Volvo B58 coaches with Duple Dominant II bodies were advertised for sale in *Bus and Coach Week* at £15,000 apiece, after the main Wytch Farm contract came to an end in June that year. At the time eight still remained of the 11 Volvos that came from Smiths Tours in 1987, and it appears that none were actually sold then, except for one that burned out and went for scrap. However, in January 1992 the firm invoiced the Bromyard dealer Wacton Trading for the sale of 14 vehicles – 10 Bedfords, two Fords, an AEC and a Volvo.

Sandra Simonds, Ray Roper's fellow trustee since the death of Mrs Toop, inevitably had her own views on his stewardship of the business that her son was due to inherit in 1993 under her father's will. In October 1991 she married Alex Wylie and urged Roper to give her new husband a job in the firm. Henry Frier told Roper: 'You realise you won't be able to sack Alex Wylie'.

Nevertheless Wylie, who had been in the army at Bovington, was given a job. Frier remarked that he had no experience of the bus business, but was very keen on the firm's contract to convey enthusiasts to Poole Speedway. By the end of 1992 Alex Wylie realised that the

Ray Roper relaxing by the yacht harbour at St Jean Cap Ferrat while visiting his son in France.
JEANETTE DAVENPORT COLLECTION

firm's finances were in a parlous state, so he sought advice to preserve Sandra and Simon's inheritance.

Frier said Roper, who marked his 70th birthday in 1989, had wanted his son to follow in his footsteps, but that was not to be. Nigel Roper fell for one of the French exchange students. They married and went to live in France. The prospect of returning to Dorset to run buses may not have appealed to him, but Nigel still had a house in Dorchester and came over once a year. His father went to the south of France at Christmas time to see his son and two grandsons.

Wylie took the opportunity of Roper's absence to set in train what turned out to be his downfall. On his return from France on 6 January 1993 he found a note in his letter

box, telling him to hand over his keys to Henry Frier at the Top O' Town booking office. That very day there was an emergency meeting at the firm's Weymouth solicitors, Cousins Coombe and Mustoe.

Bere Regis Coaches was rapidly running out of money and saleable assets, and Ray Roper agreed to give up control. Sandra Wylie took over and an emergency plan of action was decided upon. Henry Frier said he had a meeting on behalf of Roper with Sandra in the Drax Arms at Bere Regis. When asked to sign a document for a further sale of assets he remarked: 'You do realise what you are doing, don't you?'

Alex Wylie assumed the position of General Manager and appointed Frier to be Transport Manager and Assistant General Manager. In the months that followed Frier said he worked out a proper form of costings and monthly takings. Wylie wanted hire purchase payments left out of the accounts presented to the bank, which would make them look healthier. These included payments for a car that the firm had bought for Simon Hewitt, who took his new stepfather's surname.

Helen Christopher, who was on maternity leave at the time, was offered a new job on her return, which she said would have meant

How the legal name on the side of Bere Regis coaches changed: R.E.J. Roper on 31 January, S. & S. Wylie on 10 March 1993.
LES RONAN

Bere Regis Coaches only needed one bus to run the Dorchester Town service made up of three circular routes each covered once an hour. In the early 1990s ex-United Counties Bedford YRQ GRP922N replaced the Ford that had launched the service in 1989.

PM PHOTOGRAPHY

covering for all the other secretaries, including those in other depots, without being given the resources to do so. After being told she could take it or leave it, she left, took the firm to a tribunal and won her case. It took the bailiffs more than six months to recover the money to pay her, she added.

Sandra Wylie worked in the office, but Steve Ring, who had been appointed Operations Manager by 1992, looked after day-to-day activities.

Alex Wylie offered sponsorship for the 1993 season of the Poole Pirates' speedway champion and captain: that year Craig Boyce was photographed with the legend 'Bere Regis Coaches' emblazoned on his leathers. John Eyers remembers a party of Bere Regis employees being taken to the speedway and lavishly entertained in the VIP lounge.

Keith Poyser said he was present when the sponsorship offer of £10,000 was made at the Sun Inn in Poole. However, Boyce, who went on to captain the Australian National Speedway team during its 'English' season, later told Poyser no money reached him.

Money evidently remained tight for the firm. In some distress Ray Roper told Poyser he had received a bill for £7,000 to pay the lease on the office that the Wylies had taken in Blandford.

John Cumming, who had started the Blandford Bus Company in 1988, believes the writing was already on the wall when Alex Wylie took over. The loss of bus services when they went out to tender under deregulation in 1986, particularly to Oakfield Travel and Air Camelot, the loss of Blandford area school contracts to Oakfield in 1989, the end of the Wytch Farm contract and the subsequent failure to slim down the operation fast enough, in terms both of property and of coaches, all contributed to the decline of the business.

To improve the financial position Wylie decided that the Top O' Town petrol station and booking office at 7 Bridport Road had to be sold off. This gave the impression that the business was in difficulties, so word of the decision sparked the interest of rival concerns around Dorchester. Henry Frier answered a phone call from the Cawlett group and a meeting in Weymouth was arranged with its Southern National subsidiary. Other possible buyers of the business included the Wilts & Dorset Bus Company Ltd and Bournemouth Transport

Bere Regis Coaches headed the list of sponsors of the Poole Pirates' top speedway rider Craig Boyce in their 17 October 1993 programme.

Ltd (Yellow Buses). There was also a meeting with Nick Adams of Victory Tours of Sixpenny Handley, a family business that dated from 1921 and continued until it closed down in 2005.

Bournemouth Transport expressed interest; it had set money aside to develop the coaching side of its business. Frier believes it would have offered the Wylies an exceptionally good deal, but they did not wish to entertain it.

Cawlett Ltd was created in March 1988 by senior managers of North Devon Ltd and Southern National Ltd, who had jointly acquired these two former National Bus Company concerns. In the early 1990s they took over Pearce, Darch & Willcox (Comfy Lux) who had moved their centre of operations to Martock, and another small Somerset concern, Taylors of Tintinhull. There was good geographical logic in the group adding Bere Regis Coaches to its portfolio, but they walked away from a meeting when told the Wylies wanted a million pounds for the business.

Andrew Bryce, Wilts & Dorset's Operations Director at the time, said his company was approached at one time or another: 'by all of the more significant Dorset and Wiltshire rural bus and coach operators seeking expressions of interest in being acquired by us. When the Wylies decided to try to achieve a sale of Bere Regis, the directors of Wilts & Dorset were invited to visit the Dorchester premises and to look over the business, which we duly did. It was very clear to us just how much the business had suffered from under-capitalisation and lack of investment.'

The Dorchester operations filled a gap between Cawlett's two main bases in Weymouth and Yeovil, so that seemed to Wilts & Dorset the most obvious purchaser. Bryce continued: 'In the end we decided not to make an offer for the whole business, but we advised the Wylies that if they were unable to achieve a complete sale, Damory Coaches might be interested in acquiring the Wimborne based operations only.'

Damory was Wilts & Dorset's own arm's-length rural bus business in Blandford, which it had taken over from Vic Kimber in May 1993. In November that year Damory absorbed the network of routes formerly served by Oakfield Travel, Blandford, and the Stanbridge & Crichel Bus Co Ltd. These two concerns, eastern neighbours of Bere Regis Coaches, had belonged for just 11 months to Guildford & West Surrey Buses. Damory also bought out a small operator in Belchalwell, G.K. Stoneman. Then, in January 1994, it acquired John Cumming's Blandford Bus Company.

Bryce's account illustrates the febrile atmosphere in the bus industry in the early 1990s, as the first flush of post-deregulation enthusiasm bumped up against hard economics. Opportunities were still around, but it was a cut-throat market. Bryce said, 'from Wilts & Dorset's viewpoint undoubtedly the immediate post-deregulation experience in both Poole and Salisbury of intensive competition for our core businesses from former National Bus Company colleagues influenced our future strategy. Having successfully fought off these early challenges to our independent existence, we considered how best to protect ourselves against any future such incursions.

'While Damory Coaches was primarily a coach and school contract operator, it was a well run business which had run happily alongside Wilts & Dorset's entirely bus-service-based business in Blandford. The primary initial purpose in expressing an interest in acquiring Damory ourselves was a defensive one, but it also gave us an opportunity to test a developing strategy of creating a cordon sanitaire around our core bus operations. We recognised that in the rural areas surrounding our main operations a lower cost basis was necessary and this was better achieved through separate arm's length subsidiary company operations than through the main Wilts & Dorset business.'

Wilts & Dorset consolidated the former Oakfield and Stanbridge & Crichel operations with Damory Coaches, but it rapidly decided to

Some of the 1988 Volvos returned to their leasing company near Sheffield in 1993. E218 and 219ECG made it under their own steam, but another one had to be towed by the Bedford TM1000 recovery vehicle (B917UBM). They paused on their journey up the M1 at Woodall services.   JOHN CUMMING

pass on the tendered services from Dorchester to Sherborne and Yeovil, which Guildford & West Surrey had set about obtaining. Wilts & Dorset made its move and purchased Damory in 1993 when word reached it that the Surrey firm was approaching Vic Kimber as well. Taking over his business would have given the Surrey concern a stronger basis from which to challenge Wilts & Dorset from the west.

Over the next few years Damory grew rapidly and at one point had a fleet of nearly 40 vehicles, substantially outgrowing the main Wilts & Dorset depot in Blandford and developing a local bus network stretching over much of former Bere Regis territory. (The westward expansion of Damory Coaches in 2011 is another story).

In the early 1990s consolidating what it had already gained was the higher priority for Wilts & Dorset. As far as Bere Regis Coaches' beleaguered management was concerned sale to that company was not an option. The task of restarting negotiations with Cawlett fell to Henry Frier. He found that the three board members of Cawlett, Garry Charles, group managing and finance director, Graham Roberts, engineering director, and Andrew

Vernon, commercial director, were always 'very gentlemanly and knowledgeable'.

In the end Cawlett took over the main part of the Bere Regis business, centred on Dorchester, on 17 March 1994, and renamed it West Dorset Coaches Ltd, trading as Dorchester Coachways.

Bere Regis Coaches had vacated the premises at 7 Bridport Road in February 1994. They were sold to West Dorset District Council to provide a much needed coach and car park. The firm's head office moved down the hill to the old military hospital at The Grove, near the garage and workshops. More than 15 years later the building's gutters and window frames still preserved their Bere Regis-brown paint.

Probably the last timetable issued by 'Bere Regis Coaches, 7 Bridport Road, Dorchester' was for a weekly Portland-Poole-Bournemouth service, via Weymouth and Dorchester. It was to start on 3 March 1994 and run every Thursday until 15 December that year, leaving Portland at 9.30. It reached Bournemouth just over two hours later, and set off on the return journey at five o'clock. The adult return fare was £4.75 from all points; there were no stops between Dorchester and Poole.

After 17 March the Wylies retained the Bere Regis & District legal name and a handful of coaches which they kept at Stone Lane, Wimborne. They ran the rump of the business from an office in Blandford, on the corner of Salisbury Street and The Plocks. Because tours from Ringwood were popular they had another office there, in the shopping arcade at Meeting House Lane.

Sandra Wylie sent round a circular 'To All Staff', telling them:

> As you are no doubt aware there is to be a change regarding the structure of Bere Regis Coaches.
>
> In brief due to the inherited problems we undertook to attempt to resolve at this time last year the past twelve months have been difficult and although the situation has not deteriorated, life under the present format would continue to be difficult.
>
> We have, therefore, made after considerable negotiation what we consider to be a prudent decision.
>
> The Dorchester operation is to be passed to another operator who will inherit current operations, contracts etc. including Staff.
>
> Bere Regis Coaches will re-locate to Blandford offices with Wimborne as the Depot. We shall take with us nine vehicles and all Contracts, Private Hire, Excursions, Holidays for the area East of Bere Regis Village.
>
> We would of course wish to retain ten drivers plus one engineer who would be totally responsible for day to day maintenance, vehicle records etc.
>
> Although we cannot take everyone we would like to (this has to be negotiated with the company who will be taking over in Dorchester) we will endeavour to retain those people who wish to transfer with us.
>
> Please indicate to Mr A. Wylie at your earliest convenience whether or not you would like to transfer.
>
> Thanking you for your loyal and undivided support over the past 12 months.
>
> S.M. Wylie

In the late 1980s Bere Regis Coaches offered vehicle recovery to all comers. On one occasion it got more than it bargained for: the recovered lorry shunted the Bedford TM1000 into the ditch.   JOHN EYERS

The Wylies kept five of the Volvo coaches (UFX567, HJP483V, E217GCG, E220GCG and G432SNN) and three Bedfords (RLJ186-188R, with which they ran school contracts in East Dorset, as well as private hire and holiday tours. Later in 1994 they added a 19-seat Mercedes-Benz (C86AHW). Sandra Wylie also retained the miniature coach that had adorned the office at 7 Bridport Road.

Alex Wylie issued an ambitious programme of one-day tours for the 1994 season. They were set out in a 12-page brochure with a bright red cover that told a little of the

Hiring coaches to other operators was always a handy way to boost flagging revenue. When it was not needed for a holiday tour 1988 Volvo-Ikarus E220GCG did a turn on a Green Line Associated service.
PM PHOTOGRAPHY

firm's history and contained a message to passengers. Wylie said Bere Regis Coaches had always strived to serve the people of Dorset, and it would continue to do so.

He added: 'You will no doubt have heard a multitude of rumours concerning Bere Regis Coaches. I would like to put the record straight. It is true we have reduced the size of our fleet and operational area. We have also disposed of all diverse commitments, such as petrol sales and engineering contract work. This decision was made to enable us to concentrate purely

on coach transport in the area that has always shown loyalty to Bere Regis Coaches through good times and bad.'

The brochure listed a different tour every day during the height of the summer holidays, with some quite enterprising destinations. They went as far afield as Cornwall, the Vale of Evesham, a hop farm in Kent, and the set of Granada TV's Coronation Street. For the rest of the season several coach trips were offered every week. These went to places like Portsmouth for the D-Day 50th anniversary celebrations or Gardener's World Live at the Birmingham National Exhibition Centre. One trip even included an underground tour of a South Wales coal mine.

Holiday tours lasting a week or more continued too. A couple from Bryanston who had long been loyal Bere Regis customers, Bill and Margaret Sherwood, remember going on a ten-day tour of Ireland in September 1995, which proved to be the firm's very last holiday tour. Bill said the coach was painted white. It must have been one of a pair of Volvos acquired that year that never sported the brown livery. 'It rattled a bit,' he added.

The two Volvos (E581/6UHS) bore the name 'Bere Regis Coaches' across the front, whilst the legend at the back read: 'Bere Regis Coaches, Blandford'. On a nearside panel the legal name of the firm was given as 'Bere Regis & District Motor Services, S & S Wylie, Trustees'.

School contracts, which had been such a mainstay of the business in bygone years, became more problematical. Barry Thirlwall, who negotiated them for the County Council, said the Wylies seemed keen to preserve a smaller scale Bere Regis operation and they held on to a handful of school contracts. 'This was not a happy period, with Bere Regis just a shadow of its former self.' Vehicles failed to turn up, leaving children stranded all morning. 'Although DCC tried to be supportive the quality of operation of the remaining school contracts unfortunately left much to be desired.' Thirlwall concluded: 'The final collapse was perhaps inevitable but also sad... I think they just gave up.'

The Wylies obtained a pair of Plaxton-bodied Volvos E581 and E585UHS, formerly with Parks of Hamilton, just months before they decided to wind up Bere Regis Coaches. One of them ran the last holiday tour, to Ireland, in the summer of 1995. On 3 August that year E581UHS was parked at Lodmoor Car Park in Weymouth.

LES RONAN

Peter Impett, who at the time was Public Transport Development Officer at County Hall in Dorchester, said the Wylies decided that new safety requirements and driving regulations demanded expenditure that were beyond their means, and Bere Regis Coaches was quietly put to sleep on Saturday 30 September 1995.

On its very last journey, on Friday 29th, it conveyed Bournemouth University nursing students to Odstock, where they took up four- or five-month placements at Salisbury District Hospital.

Roger Grimley, who followed Bere Regis & District's fortunes for the best part of 50 years, believes the deaths of Ironside and Toop 'robbed the firm of initiatives.' In 1996 Impett wrote an unpublished history of the firm, whose activities he had observed ever since riding on its coaches on school trips. He has generously given us permission to reproduce here his monograph's last chapter: 'Epitaph for Independence – The Company's Place'.

Bere Regis & District Motor Services gave valuable service to the County for over sixty years. It was *an important part of its culture and even its folklore. It spread its wings with troop contracts and eventually with inclusive tour holidays but its very extensive services network was almost totally confined to Dorset. Its forays 'abroad' brought the village of Bere Regis to a much wider public than would normally have been expected to have heard of the village. That wider public would have been struck by the elegant but unusual company livery applied to slightly dated vehicles which seemed to be maintained to high mechanical standards.*

In the 1960s and 1970s the Company seemed to be omnipresent on the public transport scene in rural parts of the County. Certainly in the period between 1935 and 1960 the Company built itself into a major force in the industry by its acquisitive activities. It did not appear to be acquisitive for the sake of being aggressive. In many cases it suited both parties to consolidate the provision of public transport services. The circumstances of history also helped the process with wartime acquisitions occurring often of necessity. The federal structure of the Company put it in a strong position at this time and it was able to take advantage of any opportunities that arose in the market. It was also operating, as most companies were, from a protected position. The industry was regulated in such a way that there was little or no competition. This apparent monopoly to a greater extent worked in the community's favour and fares were relatively cheap. The Company does not seem to have exploited its monopoly position and that was very much a product of life and times in a rural area. The Company appeared to prosper as a result of intuitive business decisions and by taking opportunities that presented themselves, so why and how did things go wrong to the extent that the Company ceased effectively to exist in 1995?

The argument advanced in earlier chapters [of Impett's monograph] suggests that while officers of the Company were very adept at making intuitive business decisions, they were much less able to take the longer term financial view of business that was required. Business methodology became more sophisticated and required a full analysis of investment. A range of new regulations came into force which imposed new costs on the Company. The customer was also seeking new standards of comfort which could not be met by the ageing fleet that the Company had accumulated. Effectively the Company was asked to make a rapid change of gear without the benefit of a detailed business plan. That change of gear needed to be applied to a large fleet operating a wide range of tasks. The Company did not reduce its commitment to any particular area of work except where it was forced to. This occurred particularly in the field of scheduled services and school contracts where the tendering procedure led to the Company losing routes they had often held for over fifty years. Those losses were often to operators who were unstable and sometimes disappeared in the middle of contracts. That in turn generated instability for the Company itself.

Lacking a comprehensive business plan the Company was set back by the deaths of Ironside and Toop within two years of each other. Ray Roper carried on the business on behalf of the Executors and then the Trust but perhaps the death of two of the principals robbed the Company of the intuitive spark which made it successful. However, it must be said that many of the innovative activities introduced by the Company occurred in the 1980s. It has also to be said that the 1980s offered both the opportunity to be innovative but also forced companies to become innovative to survive. The innovation had to be consistently successful and economically sound at one and the same time. The Company seemed capable of competing and capable of setting up new initiatives but it seemed unable to come to terms with the loss of its core business. Perhaps it could be argued that if the legislative goal posts had not been changed in the 1980s then Bere Regis & District Motor Services might still be in business. Alternatively if the Company had identified its strengths and restructured accordingly, then it might also have survived. Perhaps it found it difficult to shake off a notion of service to the community which it felt required it to satisfy all of that community's needs for transport.

Although Dorchester Coachways actively promote themselves as Bere Regis – Dorchester Coachways and outstation vehicles at Bere Regis, and in November 1996 there are still vehicles wearing the chocolate brown and red trim of the Company, sixty years of service have come to an end. The tradition of independent bus companies has gone, to be replaced by the corporate business unit often divorced from the community in which it trades.

PETER IMPETT

10
Epilogue ~ The Cawlett Years

BY THE TIME Cawlett took over the Dorchester operations of Bere Regis Coaches in March 1994 the turmoil in the bus industry touched off by deregulation was simmering down. The Conservatives had set about ending what they saw as restrictive practices by breaking up large groupings of bus companies. A host of small operations sprang up, taking advantage of more relaxed rules about who was fit to run a bus service. Some seriously underestimated what it took to keep them going, and became early targets for bigger concerns to swallow up.

The five years that Cawlett ran Dorchester Coachways came at a time when new large groupings were steadily consolidating their hold on the industry, much as other big groups had done before the 1980s. One difference was that now they bore trendy names like First Bus,

Go Ahead! and Stagecoach in place of such staid titles as British Electric Traction or The Tilling Group. By and large the big individual bus companies stayed around and became part of one or other of the new big groups, with some shuffling of names and centres of operation.

Cawlett inherited a fleet of 28 vehicles in Dorchester, most of them Volvo or Bedford coaches, but there was a Bedford bus for the Dorchester town service and a trio of Ford Transits. In addition to the premises at The Grove, West Dorset Coaches had outstations at Bere Regis (in a car park on the site of Reg Toop's old garage), Bovington, Hazelbury Bryan, Sherborne and Hurn.

Some Dorchester Coachways vehicles still wore the two-tone brown and red livery well into 1995, and even appeared in this guise on bus routes in West Dorset that Bere Regis & District itself had never served. Keith Poyser said that on at least a couple of occasions the Shell company tried to impound such coaches for unpaid bills when they called at service stations to refuel; it had to be explained that despite the livery they no longer belonged to Bere Regis Coaches.

The last bus to run in regular service in these colours was almost certainly the Wylies' 19-seat Mercedes. It passed to Levers Coaches, a Wilts & Dorset subsidiary, who used it on

Probably the only vehicle still at work in Bere Regis colours after 2000 was Mercedes Benz-Reeve Burgess 19-seater C86AHW. By then Wilts & Dorset subsidiary Lever's Coaches was the owner. After it was withdrawn it joined other retired vehicles awaiting their fate at Sutton Mandeville.
A.H. WALLER COLLECTION

West Dorset Coaches had a varied collection of Bedford YMTs. Some were ex-Bere Regis, but Wadham Stringer-bodied TKM108X came from Kent in 1996. It could seat 60 passengers, not in great comfort.　　BARRY THIRLWALL

right opposite the garage and workshops which were now the heart of Dorchester Coachways operations.

Henry Frier, who became Manager of West Dorset, and subsequently Business Development Manager, said contract and private hire each brought in about 30 per cent of its revenue. Express and stage services, which centred on Dorchester, accounted for roughly 20 per cent, as did excursions and tours. The Slattery's contract continued for the present and there were still contracts with the military for troop movements from Bovington and Blandford Camp to Catterick.

school contracts in south west Wiltshire. There it remained in its Bere Regis colours until it was withdrawn in 2002. Another Bere Regis coach, Bristol LHS CLJ413Y, which had been withdrawn in 1987, returned to its original colours after John Hembry of Sturminster Newton bought it so he could ensure it was preserved. Sandra Wylie kept the miniature coach at her home until 1997, when it joined a collection of such little vehicles in the Midlands.

Cawlett Group operations were organised in three divisions: Red Bus, in Barnstaple, Southern National Somerset in Taunton and Southern National Dorset, centred on Weymouth. Besides absorbing the bulk of the Bere Regis Coaches operations, it consolidated its hold on the Weymouth area by taking over Smith's of Portland Ltd, to which the London express service was transferred in 1998.

Between them Cawlett's Southern National division and the Wilts & Dorset Bus Co, through its Damory Coaches subsidiary, provided the majority of rural Dorset's bus services through much of the 1990s. Watching from his Wilts & Dorset perspective, Andrew

R503NPR, one of the eight Mercedes-Benz Varios delivered to Dorset Transit in 1998.　　BARRY THIRLWALL

A number of the Dorchester-based school contracts, which Southern National did not want to take up, passed to Bluebird Coaches of Chickerell Road, Weymouth. They kept the coaches they used on these contracts at the Dorset County Council garage at The Grove,

Bryce felt that Cawlett did not find it easy to turn its acquisition of Bere Regis Coaches into a successful business.

However, Cawlett's ownership of West Dorset Coaches proved to be a boon when fierce competition on Southern National's Weymouth-

Portland service led to that company being penalised. It had battled with the minibuses of local independent Weybus for three years. Passengers were offered bargain fares, lines of buses were bunched together, and timings were erratic. There were reports that Southern National and Weybus blocked one another's vehicles at bus stops, in the same way as competing buses had done in the 1920s, before the 1930 Road Traffic Act put a stop to such dangerous activities.

The Traffic Commissioners weighed in with an inquiry in March 1994, just as they had when they confronted Reg Toop in 1933. Cawlett's Southern National was banned from the Portland route for a year. Potentially this was a heavy blow because the route accounted for about 35 per cent of the revenue at its Weymouth operation. Southern National's Weymouth-Wyke Regis service was suspended too.

Cawlett, in its West Dorset guise, acted fast: Graham Roberts, the engineering director, rang Henry Frier at about 5.30 one evening and asked him to prepare a timetable for Dorchester-Weymouth-Portland in time for a board meeting at nine o'clock the next morning. Henry describes how he sat at home, and, with a tot of whisky to keep him going, drew up the requested timetable. Dorchester Coachways and its bus operating arm, Dorset Transit, were to run a joint service over the route every 20 minutes. Reg Toop would surely have relished the thought of his old firm's offspring outflanking the regulators, and of a company called Southern National being penalised.

Weybus still ran between Dorchester and Weymouth but this ceased after another Traffic Commissioner's inquiry. It was banned from the Portland route as well, and then had its licence revoked altogether.

Much to Henry Frier's relief the new timetable for the Portland service worked perfectly when it began on 1 April 1994. Thenceforth Weymouth-Portland became the focus of Cawlett's stage bus activities in this part of Dorset. A new timetable introduced in April 1997 provided a frequent service along the main road between Southwell and the King's Statue in Weymouth and a bus every half hour between Weymouth and Wyke Regis.

A year later Mark Williams, Dorset Transit's Manager, told the media that passenger numbers on this route had risen steadily over the past two and a half years 'thanks to dedicated route branding and excellent driving staff.' He said this success justified the investment of almost £400,000 in eight new Mercedes-Benz Vario buses which arrived in March 1998, (R501-508NPR). They had 27-seat Plaxton Beaver 2 bodies.

At that time West Dorset Coaches Ltd, still the legal name of the company, kept 17 minibuses and a pair of larger vehicles at Edward Street, Weymouth. The Grove Estate in Dorchester still had the biggest allocation, with

The Dorchester-Bovington service was given a press launch at Colliton Park in March 1999. Standing in front of a Dorset Transit low-floor Dennis Dart are, from the left, Michael White of Dorset County Council, Gil Streets, Chairman of the DCC Transport Committee, with David Beaman and Henry Frier representing the company, on the right. Keith Poyser is at the wheel.

LES RONAN

A few Bere Regis vehicles stayed around long enough to appear in the Cawlett-era white, grey and orange colours. 1984 Volvo B10M-Duple A600LJT, bearing the Southern National name, is parked alongside a Dorset Transit Leyland National at Weymouth.   JOHN CUMMING

In March 1999 four low-floor Dennis Darts with 39-seat Plaxton bus bodies were delivered for use on a Lulworth-Bovington-Wool-Dorchester service. It was run from Dorchester garage and was supported by both Dorset County Council and the Rural Development Council. Henry Frier said that for the first time it provided an hourly bus between Bovington and Dorchester and generated a lot of traffic. It ran to and from Lulworth less frequently. Evidently not every journey was well patronised: part-time driver Les Ronan recalled: 'I spent many a happy hour driving empty Darts around. It was a good try but ultimately doomed to failure.'

51 vehicles, including most of the 23 Volvos and Bedfords inherited from Bere Regis Coaches. Other vehicles were still outstationed at the same five sites as in 1994.

Some of Bere Regis Coaches' Volvos stayed on in Dorchester for several years, but West Dorset Coaches reregistered them. E224GCG became TJI3138 in 1995: a Northern Irish plate, like this one from Omagh, did not betray the vehicle's age. However it still worked from The Grove.   JOHN EYERS

On 8 April, barely a month after the Lulworth service began, Cawlett sold out to the much bigger First Bus Group for £10.6 million. Two years later, the last link with Bere Regis Coaches was severed: First Bus closed the Dorchester garage in April 2001. One of the Darts was used for the very last duty from there, conveying drivers and office staff back to their homes after a farewell get-together at the Borough Arms pub. Perhaps under protest, it refused to start until the driver gave the battery a break by turning off the lights

First Bus transferred the management of routes and staff to Weymouth. Just five weeks later, on 13 May 2001, Ray Roper, who had run Bere Regis Coaches for almost 20 years, died at the age of 81.

In April 2003 First Bus reorganised its West Country operations once more: the Weymouth and Bridport areas were joined on to First Hampshire in Southampton, thus turning it into First Hampshire & Dorset. (The well-remembered Hants & Dorset name would have tripped more lightly off the tongue, but it was not available. It is the legal name by which back in the 1990s Wilts & Dorset had rather smartly registered Damory Coaches to prevent a potential competitor making use of it).

First ran the London express under the Dorset Transit name, but decided to dispense with the agents who since the 1980s had sold tickets for the service in towns and villages along the route. Henry Frier believes its subsequent decline was a direct result of this decision. In November 2003 First withdrew the London service. Two days later, at the request of Dorset County Council, Bluebird Coaches of Weymouth started a new London express service.

This revived the enterprise shown by Bere Regis Coaches 20 years before, but the familiar brown buses, loved by some but often longer-lived than most bus companies would tolerate, had left for ever the picturesque villages and winding lanes of Dorset.

Appendix A
Bere Regis carriers, from horse to motor 1830-1920[1]

Horsedrawn carriers, from 1830

1830	William Taper[2]	Dorchester *Sat* Poole *Thu*	By 1842 also Poole *Mon* Not listed 1867
By 1846	Robert Shaddock[2]	Dorchester *Wed & Sat* Poole *Mon & Thu*	Not listed 1867
By 1851	Reuben Day[2]		Died by 1867
By 1851	Robert Poore[2]		Not listed 1867
By 1867	Selina Day (Mrs),	Dorchester *Wed & Sat 0800* Poole *Mon & Thu 0800* Blandford *Tue & Fri 0800*	Reuben Day's widow. By 1871 Blandford *Fri only*, Wareham *Tue*. Still listed 1889
By 1871	William Purchase	Dorchester *Sat*	Not listed 1889
By 1889	Charlton Toms	Dorchester *Wed & Sat*	Continued until at least 1915, not listed 1920
Post 1889	Charles Day	As Selina Day	Son of Reuben and Selina Day. Continued until at least 1898, ceased by 1903
1903	Henry House	Dorchester *Wed & Sat* Poole *Mon 0800* Blandford *Fri 0800*	By 1907: added Poole *Thu*, Blandford ceased. No longer listed 1911
1903	Robert Gregory	Dorchester *Wed & Sat*	No longer listed 1907
1911	Frederick Roper[3]	Dorchester *Wed & Sat* Poole *Mon & Thu 0830* Blandford *Fri 0830*	G. Vacher took over in 1915
1911	Ernest Roper[3]	Dorchester *Wed & Sat*	Ceased 1915
1911	William & Frank Hoare	Wareham *Mon, Thu & Sat 0900*	Extant 1915. No longer listed 1920
1915	George Vacher	Dorchester *Wed & Sat* Blandford *Fri 0830*	Motorised 1918

1. The carriers' names are derived principally from editions of Kelly's *Directory* for the years cited. Family relationships are confirmed by census records.
2. In 1851 William Taper, Robert Shaddock, Reuben Day and Robert Poore between them ran to Dorchester, Blandford, Poole and Wareham.
3. The 1915 edition of Kelly's *Directory* still listed Frederick and Ernest Roper, as well as William and Frank Hoare. However, according to records at The Keep Military Museum in Dorchester the two Ropers and their younger brother Percy all joined the army that year. George Vacher, who at the time of the 1911 census was a carrier at Hilton, took over from Frederick Roper.

Motor bus/carriers, post World War I

1918	George Vacher	Dorchester *Wed & Sat 1000* Poole *Mon & Fri 1000*	By 1923: added Blandford *Fri 1000*
1920	Harry Farr	Wareham *Thu & Sat 0900*	By 1923: added Blandford *Fri 0900*

APPENDIX B
BERE REGIS BUS SERVICES IN 1930 AND 1938

George Vacher (Bere Regis Motor Service)
Routes taken over by Hants & Dorset Motor Services Ltd, 1930

Dorchester–Bere Regis–Poole, *daily*

Bere Regis–Winterborne Kingston–Poole, *Tuesday*

Bere Regis–Bloxworth–Poole–Bournemouth, *Friday*

Bere Regis–Cold Harbour–Wareham Market, *Tuesday*

Bere Regis–Bloxworth–Wareham Market, *Saturday*

Bere Regis–Almer–Wimborne, *Tuesday*

Bere Regis–Dorchester Market, *Wednesday*

Bere Regis–Almer–Blandford Forum, *Thursday*

Bere Regis & District Motor Services (RW Toop, WJ Ironside & PW Davis) stage services, December 1938

Bere Regis–Poole via Bloxworth and Morden, *Monday–Saturday*, (ex-Davis)

Bere Regis–Poole via Winterborne Zelstone, Morden, *Friday to Monday*, (ex-Toop)

Bere Regis–Wimborne via Bloxworth and Morden, *Tuesday*, (ex-Toop/Davis)

Bere Regis–Wimborne via Winterborne Zelstone and Almer, *Tuesday*, (ex-Toop)

Bere Regis–Wareham via Bere Heath, *Thursday*, (ex-Toop)

Bloxworth–Wareham via Morden, *Thursday*, (ex-Davis)

Bere Regis–Puddletown–Dorchester, *Wednesday and Saturday*, (ex-Toop/Davis)

Winterborne Zelstone–Bere Regis–Puddletown–Dorchester, *Wednesday*, (ex-Toop)

Winfrith–Dorchester via Owermoigne and Broadmayne, *Wednesday and Saturday*, (ex-Ironside 1930)

Winfrith–Weymouth via Owermoigne and Osmington, *Friday and Saturday*, (ex-Ironside 1930)

Winfrith–Wareham via Wool, *Thursday*, (ex-Ironside 1930)

APPENDIX C
BERE REGIS & DISTRICT MOTOR SERVICES:
OPERATORS TAKEN OVER, ABSORBED OR REPLACED

1930	Frederick James Ironside, Winfrith	RW Toop took over three stage services: Winfrith–Dorchester, Winfrith–Weymouth and Winfrith–Wareham
1936	Israel Davis & Son, Bloxworth	Reginald Toop, Percy Davis, son of Israel, and William Ironside (son of Frederick James) form partnership, with Davis contributing two Chevrolets and three stage services: Poole–Dorchester, Morden–Wimborne, and Bloxworth–Wareham.
1940	William John Laws, Briantspuddle	BR&D acquired Briantspuddle–Dorchester service and a Dennis 14-seater.
1941	Edwin Russell, Broadmayne	BR&D acquired a Guy coach and West Knighton–Dorchester service, which absorbed AJ Bishop's Broadmayne–Dorchester in 1937. Russell's suspended E&T and West Knighton–Weymouth licences were revived post-WWII.
	Cyril Edward Jeanes, Dorchester	Henley–Piddle Valley–Dorchester service acquired, plus a Thornycroft coach.
1942	Henry Hawker, Piddletrenthide	Piddletrenthide–Dorchester service acquired. Suspended E&T licence revived post-WWII.
	Frank Whitty & Son, Dorchester	Garage at 7 Bridport Road, two Bedford buses and Dorchester–Frampton service acquired. (Frampton service ex-RL Platt 1939, ex-Bertie Cox 1937).
	Frank Thorne, Cerne Abbas	Cerne Abbas–Dorchester service (dating from 1913) taken over, with a REO and a Dennis. Suspended E&T and Cerne Abbas–Weymouth licences revived post-WWII.
	Edgar Markey, Winterbourne Steepleton	Winterbourne Abbas–Dorchester service acquired
	Lewis Sprackling (Ivory Coaches), Winterborne Stickland	Milton Abbas–Dorchester and Milton Abbas–Blandford services acquired, with three Leyland Cubs and a Morris coach. Milton Abbas and Winterborne Stickland E&Ts revived post-WWII. (In 1930 Sprackling took over the Milton Abbas Motors of TK Bower, who succeeded Robert Lovell in about 1927. In 1933 Sprackling took over the Winterborne Stickland–Blandford service that EH Lyne, Tarrant Rushton, had acquired a year earlier from RJ Vacher of Winterborne Stickland).
1943	Jack Orchard & Herbert E Butler, Milborne St Andrew	J Orchard, Winterborne Whitechurch 1932, in partnership with HE Butler 1941. Business ceased but not taken over. BR&D acquired a Bedford coach, and subsequently replaced E&T licences post-WWII.
	George J Caundle, Puddletown	Dorchester service abandoned, replaced by BR&D, which also revived Puddletown E&Ts post-WWII. Two coaches acquired: Albion and Chevrolet.
1944	Emma Lugg (Girl Pat Service), Hazelbury Bryan	Business acquired. Gilbert Lugg took over from Edwin Drake in 1919. BR&D gained stage services from Hazelbury Bryan to Dorchester, Sherborne, Yeovil and Sturminster Newton, E&Ts and two vehicles, a Chevrolet and a REO.
1945	Charles Fripp, Okeford Fitzpaine	Okeford Fitzpaine–Blandford and Ibberton–Sturminster Newton services taken over, along with a Morris and a Bedford bus.
	George Churchill, Puncknowle	Puncknowle–Bridport service dating from the 1920s taken over, plus an elderly Ford bus.
	Alfred J Pitcher, Litton Cheney	BR&D took over Litton Cheney–Dorchester service, motorised since 1911, with Morris bus.

1946	Ernest John Bale, Owermoigne	Hurst–Dorchester, E&Ts and a Morris bus acquired upon Bale's retirement after 21 years
	Betsy Hannah Coombes & Sons, Hazelbury Bryan	Bus and coach operations acquired. Started by William J Coombes in 1926, succeeded by his widow in 1928. BR&D took over bus services to Dorchester, Sherborne, Yeovil and Sturminster Newton, plus E&Ts and a Bedford coach.
1947	James E Pickett, Buckland Newton	BR&D took over services to Dorchester and Sherborne, E&Ts and a Bedford bus. Pickett started services in early 1920s.
	Vic C Little, Marnhull	BR&D took over services from Marnhull to Dorchester and Sturminster Newton, E&Ts and a Commer bus. Little acquired the business from his boss, Albert Trim, who retired in 1945.
1948	Sidney G Harmer, Milton Abbas	BR&D took over bus services to Dorchester and Blandford, E&Ts and a Dennis Ace bus
1949	HV Fear (Wimborne Queen), Wimborne	Ex-William Fear 1920s–1947. BR&D took over Leigh Road garage, E&Ts and six coaches
1952	G Robertson (Longham) Ltd), t/a Rambler Coaches, Longham	Garage, contract and E&T business acquired, along with eight coaches, including three Dennis Lancets and a pair of Commers. Business dated from 1918.
1954	EA Seager (Enterprise Garage), Sherborne	JB & EA Seager pre-1927: BR&D took over Coldharbour Garage, E&Ts, three Gilfords and a pair of Bedford coaches.
1955	AJ Macklin (Antelope Tours), Sherborne	E&Ts acquired, along with three Bedford coaches
1961	Herbert E Butler, Milborne St Andrew	Business acquired. (Butler took over BL Stone, Dewlish 1951, ex-Lloyd GC Cutler 1948)
1965	WT Elliott, Elliott's Garage Ltd, Sturminster Marshall	WT Elliott sold business and two coaches to BR&D and went into partnership with FC Potter. (See Elliott & Potter, 1982)
1967	Dorchester Taxi Service Ltd (Dortax)	CV, WS & CJ Phillips' taxi and coaching business acquired, including five coaches
1978	ER Bailey, Ringwood, Hampshire	C Bailey 1939-1970s. BR&D took over E&Ts and one Bedford coach.
1982	WT Elliott & FC Potter, Wimborne	Partnership formed 1965 at Stanbridge, later moved to Wimborne. BR&D took over E&Ts, school contracts, nine Bedfords and premises at Stone Lane Industrial Estate
1987	NAW, HM & MD House (Mid-Dorset Coaches), Hilton	Sixty-year-old family business taken over when Norman House retired: bus services from Hilton to Dorchester and Blandford, plus two Fords and a pair of Bedford coaches

APPENDIX D
BERE REGIS & DISTRICT MOTOR SERVICES: LOCAL BUS SERVICES 1949-1970

This table summarises the services listed in the 1949 timetable, when the firm had its most extensive network of bus routes, and shows what became of them by 1970, the year that Bill Ironside died, leaving Reg Toop once more as the sole proprietor. Detailed changes in the intervening years are omitted, but the number of journeys had been reduced on virtually all routes, and many villages had a bus on fewer and fewer days of the week.

1949		1970	
1	Bere Regis–Poole, *Daily*	–	To Hants & Dorset 1959
1A	Bere Regis–Dorchester, *Daily*	–	To Hants & Dorset 1959
2	Bere Regis–Poole via Winterborne Kingston, *Fri-Mon*	–	To Hants & Dorset 1959
3	Winterborne Zelstone–Dorchester, *Wed & Sat*	–	To Hants & Dorset 1959
4	Dorchester–Sherborne via Cerne Abbas, *Daily*	1	*Daily*
5	Dorchester–Yeovil via Piddle Valley, *Daily*	2	*Mon-Sat*
6	Dorchester–Stur. Newton via Piddle Valley, *Daily*	3	*Mon-Sat*
7	Dorchester–Henley via Piddle Valley, *Wed & Sat*	–	Withdrawn 1955
8	Dorchester–Sherborne via Pulham & Holwell, *Thu*	–	Withdrawn 1957
9	Dorchester–Bridport, *Tue, Wed, Fri, Sat*	–	Withdrawn 1967, partly covered by 6
10	Dorchester–Little Bredy/Compton Valence, *Mon-Sat*	6	Dorchester–Litton Cheney *Wed, Fri, Sat*
11	Dorchester–Frampton, *Mon, Tue, Wed, Fri, Sat*	4	*Tue, Wed, Fri, Sat*
12	Dorchester–East Knighton, *Mon-Sat*	5	To Dorset Queen 1965
13	Dorchester–Bovington Camp, *Tue, Wed, Fri, Sat, Sun*	8	*Wed & Sat*
14	Dorchester–Hurst, *Tue, Wed, Fri, Sat, Sun*	9	*Wed, Fri, Sat*
15	Dorchester–Winterbourne Came, *Wed & Sat*	10	*Wed & Sat*
16	Okeford Fitzpaine–Blandford, *Daily*	13	*Mon-Fri*, Woolland–Blandford *Sat*
17	Woolland–Shaftesbury, *Daily*	14	*Mon, Thu*
18	Sturminster Newton–Yeovil, *Daily*	15	*Mon-Sat*
19	Stur. Newton–Bishop's Caundle, *Mon, Tue, Fri, Sat*	–	Withdrawn 1958
20	Winterborne Kingston–Wimborne, *Tue*	–	Withdrawn 1952
21	Bere Regis–Wareham via Hyde, *Thu & Sat*	–	Withdrawn 1964
22	Bere Regis–Wareham via Bloxworth, *Thu*	–	Withdrawn 1952
23	Kingston–Hazelbury Bryan–Dorchester, *Wed & Sat*	–	Withdrawn 1957
24	Winfrith–Wareham, *Thu*	–	Withdrawn 1952
25	Winfrith–Weymouth, *Sat*	–	To Dorset Queen 1959
26	Winterborne Whitechurch–Dorchester, *Daily*	–	Merged with 12, 1961
27	W'borne Whitechurch–Blandford, *Tue, Thu, Sat, Sun*	–	Merged with 12, 1961
28	Puddletown–Dorchester, *Mon-Sat*	–	Merged with 1A, 1951
29	Piddlehinton–Dorchester, *Daily*	–	Withdrawn 1970
30	Marnhull–Stur. Newton via Hinton St Mary, *Mon*	17	Sturminster–Marnhull or Todber, *Daily*
31	Marnhull–Dorchester via Plush, *Wed & Sat*	16	Mappowder–Hazelbury Bryan, *Daily* Mappowder–Dorchester, *Wed & Sat*
32	Milton Abbas–Blandford, *Daily*	–	Withdrawn 1970
33	Hurst–Moreton–Wareham, *Thu*	–	Withdrawn 1952
34	Buckland Newton–Weymouth, summer only, *Fri*	–	Replaced 1955: Blackmore Vale express
35	Bloxworth–Blandford, *Tue, Thu, Sat*	20	Bere Regis–Blandford, *Thu*
		19	Sherborne–Lillington, *Tue & Thu*, started 1959.

APPENDIX E
DEREGULATION, 1986

Bere Regis services listed in July 1985 timetable, 16 months before deregulation

1	Dorchester–Sherborne via Cerne Abbas, *Monday–Saturday*
2	Dorchester–Hazelbury Bryan, *Wednesday*
3	Mappowder–Sturminster Newton, *Monday*
4	Woolland–Blandford, *Monday–Saturday*
5	Gillingham–Sturminster Newton, *Monday*
6	Bere Regis–Blandford, *Thursday*
7	Holwell–Sherborne via Bishop's Caundle, *Monday–Friday*
8	Woolland– Sturminster Newton, *Monday*
9	Marnhull–Dorchester via Sturminster Newton, *Wednesday & Saturday*
10	Swyre/Little Bredy–Dorchester, *Wednesday & Friday*
11	Dorchester–Duntish–(Pulham) , *Monday–Saturday*
12	Winterborne Houghton–Blandford, *Thursday*
13	Hurst–Dorchester, *Wednesday, Friday & Saturday*
15	Dorchester–Bovington, *Wednesday & Saturday*

In preparation for Deregulation on 26 October 1986, operators registered services that they intended to run commercially. Bere Regis Coaches registered 21. Ten of these were essentially school or college services. The other 11 are listed below. Dorset County Council put other services out to tender; the lowest bidder generally won. After 1986 services saw frequent changes as the County Council became increasingly active in determining where they were needed.

1	Bovington–Dorchester/Charminster, *Monday–Saturday*
2	Gillingham–Sturminster Newton, *Monday*, school terms only
6	Bere Regis Blandford, *Thursday*
8	Sturminster Newton–Belchalwell, *Monday*, school terms only
9	Marnhull–Dorchester, *Wednesday*
12	Winterborne Stickland–Blandford, *Thursday*
17	Sturminster Newton–Weymouth, summer, *Monday, Wednesday & Friday*
X1	Portland–Poulner, *Daily* feeder to London service
X2	Yeovil–Bournemouth, *Thursday*
X3	Blandford–Poulner, *Daily* feeder to London service
X4	Bridport–Dorchester, *Thursday & Saturday* feeder to London service

APPENDIX F
DEPOT ALLOCATIONS, 1966 AND 1981

Source: PSV Circle news sheets

1966	Bere Regis	16	Sherborne	10	Weymouth	8
	Blandford	10	Sturminster Newton	8	Wimborne	17
	Dorchester	25				

1981	DORCHESTER	39	2 AEC, 30 Bedford, 3 Ford, 3 Leyland, 1 Austin minibus
	Sub-depot		
	Bere Regis	7	1 AEC, 6 Bedford
	Outstations		
	Bridport	2	2 Bedford
	Cerne Abbas	1	1 Bedford
	Marnhull	1	1 Bedford
	Weymouth	1	1 Bedford
	BLANDFORD	13	1 Albion, 10 Bedford, 1 Bristol, 1 Ford
	Sub-depot		
	Hazelbury Bryan	4	4 Bedford
	Outstations		
	Poole	1	1 Leyland
	Shaftesbury	1	1 Bedford
	SHERBORNE	12	11 Bedford, 1 Leyland
	WIMBORNE	9	1 AEC, 6 Bedford, 2 Leyland
	Outstations		
	Bournemouth	1	1 Bedford
	Bransgore	1	1 AEC
	Christchurch	1	1 Bedford
	Fordingbridge	1	1 Bedford

APPENDIX G
COMPARATIVE FARE SCALES 1980

Adult single fares, March 1980. Independents' fare scales varied between routes, and were only loosely based on mileage. *(Source: Dorset Structure Plan – Public Transport, 1980).*

	Minimum fare	2 miles	5 miles	10 miles	20 miles
INDEPENDENTS					
Bere Regis Coaches	7–8p	9–13p	15–21p	21–28p	28–41p
Pearce, Darch & Willcox, Cattistock	10p	10–14p	25–29p	41p	79p
Adams Bros, Sixpenny Handley	–	15–26p	30–33p	40–44p	–
NATIONAL BUS COMPANY					
Hants & Dorset (rural services)	10p	30p	50p	70p	90p
Western National	5p	27p	48p	67p	88p

Bibliography & Further Reading

Books, and Reports by public bodies

Crawley, R.J., and Simpson, F.D.: *The Years Between 1909 1969 – Vol. 3 The Story from 1929*, Calton Promotions, Exeter, 1990

Grimley, Roger: *Along the Dusty Road, Motor Buses and Carriers from Dorchester, Parts I to IV*, Roger Grimley, Kingsbridge, Devon, 2008-2009

Hibbs, John: *The History of British Bus Services*, David & Charles, Newton Abbot, 1968

Hibbs, John: *The Dangers of Bus Re-regulation*, The Institute of Economic Affairs, London, 2005

Jackson, B.L.: *Isle of Portland Railways, volume 3, Railway, Associated and Other Bus Services*, The Oakwood Press, Usk, 2000

Lambert, Alan: *Hants & Sussex*, B.M. Lambert, Emsworth, 1983

Morris, Colin: *Hants & Dorset – a history*, DTS, Croydon, 1996

Morris, Colin, and Waller, Andrew: *The definitive history of Wilts & Dorset Motor Services Ltd, 1915-1972*, The Hobnob Press, East Knoyle, Wilts, 2006

Pitfield, F.P.: *The Book of Bere Regis*, The Dorset Publishing Company, Milborne Port, 1978

Pitfield, John and Legg, Rodney: *Bere Regis – Past and Present, Hardy's Kingsbere*, Halsgrove, Tiverton, 2006

Roberts, C.G. and Jackson, B.L.: *Trams and Buses of Poole*, The Oakwood Press, Usk, 2001

Roberts, Peter: *Bere Regis & District*, The Countrybus Dorset Series, Quarrington, Lincs, 2008

Stanier, Peter: *Dorset in the Age of Steam, A History and Archaeology of Dorset Industry c1750-1950*, Dorset Books, Tiverton, 2002

Report of the Committee on Rural Bus Services, HMSO, 1961

Dorset Structure Plan – Public Transport 1980, Dorset County Council

Journals and magazines

Anon: 'Bere Regis Operator's Licence Suspended,' *Dorset County Chronicle and Somersetshire Gazette*, 5 October 1933

Aish, Norman.: 'Bere Regis & District Motor Services, one of the largest independents,' in *Buses Special*, 1976

Aish, Norman,: 'School transport: spotlight on Dorset' in *Buses*, April 1982

Aldridge, J.M.: '11-Seaters Supplement a 120-Vehicle Fleet, A Dorset Operator's Experiment,' in *Bus & Coach*, February 1959

Carpenter, Ryan C.: 'Rural Operation in Dorset', in *Passenger Transport*, 17 October 1956

Carpenter, Ryan C.: 'Independents have served Mid-Dorset well,' in *The Omnibus Magazine*, March 1959

Carpenter, Ryan C.: Second-hand Coach Solution in Dorset' in *Bus & Coach*, April 1966

Carter, Christopher: 'When Cawlett decided to call it a Day,' in *Buses*, October 2009

Delaney, Peter: 'Bere Regis. This is a story that could fill many pages, indeed it's a book waiting to be written' in *WHOTT's News*, November 2007

Frier, Henry: 'The History of a Dorset-London Express Service – in Tickets', in *Journal of the Transport Ticket Society,'* May 2004

Guttridge, Roger: 'Small is beautiful,' in *Blackmore Vale Magazine*, 15 September 2006

Guttridge, Roger: 'When Goldflake went to London,' in *Blackmore Vale Magazine*, 22 December 2006

Hale, Peter: 'Was MAP the Start of the Modern Bus Service?' in *Provincial Historical Research Group newsletter*, The Omnibus Society, November 2010

Hobbs, John: 'Cawlett Holdings,' in *Buses*, August 1994

Maund, T.Bruce (but unsigned): 'Growth of Independent Bus Operator, Bere Regis & District Motor Services', in *Modern Transport*, 22 June and 6 July 1946

Moses, F.K.: 'Enterprise in Dorset,' in *The Commercial Motor*, 10 January 1964

Wilding, A.J.P.: 'Kentredder Explained.' in *The Commercial Motor*, 10 January 1964

INDEX

Percy Davis's "Rosie".

IRONSIDE FAMILY

Early days at the Top O' Town depot, Dorchester. The dog keeps watch while Johnnie Bowring relaxes by the tyre store. EAC79 was a Mulliner-bodied Bedford OWB that started out as a colliery bus near Coventry, then worked in Derby for a while before heading south in 1947.

IRONSIDE FAMILY

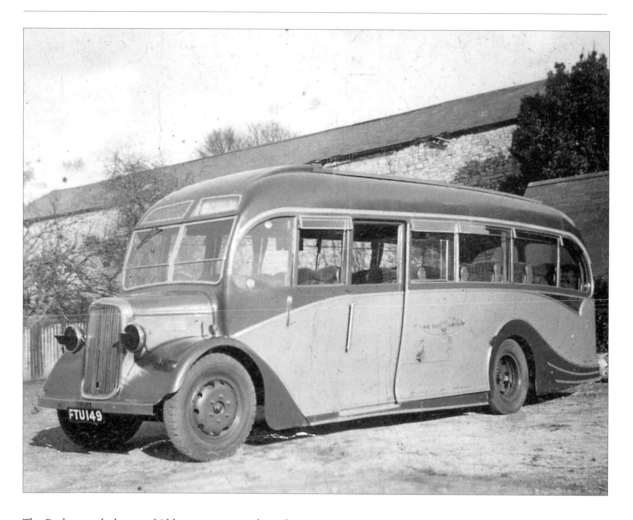

The Dodge coach that was hidden away to stop the military commandeering it still had its headlamp masks when it was brought out of the shadows.

IRONSIDE FAMILY

BJT894, new in May 1946, posed before the Keep in Dorchester. It was one of the 12 Bedford-Duple Vista coaches delivered that year. They were the firm's first ever brand new coaches.

IRONSIDE FAMILY

Aerial view of the premises at The Grove, Dorchester. The headquarters were in the brick building at the bottom of the image. Ray Roper worked upstairs at the end farther from the camera. Below his office were the stores. Maurice Crocker's office was just to the left of the porch. There were two flats for staff members at the end near the camera.

In the big workshop behind the building there were four pits to give the fitters access to the chassis of the coaches. The Bedford coach behind the workshop is still in its previous owner's livery, which dates the picture to 1973. The old

wooden barrack hut to the left of the picture, with the Bedford TK truck parked in front of it, housed the staff rest room. The covered parking area between the hut and the trees was later to house the tachograph centre.

The body shop was out of the picture, up the hill off to the right. On the right of the photo four County Council school buses are parked outside their garage.

JP6686 was the first of many coaches that came from Smiths of Wigan. A 1948 AEC Regal with 33-seat Beccols coachwork, it was on the Bovington service in August 1958, but at weekends it could sometimes be found on the Chatham express.
DAVID PENNELS